Labor Relations in
a Public Service Industry

Kenneth M. Jennings, Jr.
Jay A. Smith, Jr.
Earle C. Traynham, Jr.

The Praeger Special Studies program, through a selective worldwide distribution network, makes available to the academic, government, and business communities significant and timely research in U.S. and international economic, social, and political issues.

Labor Relations in a Public Service Industry

Unions, Management, and the Public Interest in Mass Transit

Praeger Publishers   New York   London

Library of Congress Cataloging in Publication Data

Jennings, Kenneth M
    Labor relations in a public service industry.

    (Praeger special studies in U.S. economic, social,
and political issues)
    Bibliography: p.
    1. Trade-unions—Transport workers. 2. Industrial
relations—United States. I. Smith, Jay A., joint author.
II. Traynham, Earle C., joint author. III. Title.
HD6515. T7J46   331.89'041'38050973   77-13717
ISBN 0-03-040866-0

This research was funded by a contract with the Office of
University Research of the U.S. Department of Transportation and the U.S. Government assumes no liability for
the contents or use thereof.

PRAEGER SPECIAL STUDIES
200 Park Avenue, New York, N.Y., 10017, U.S.A.

Published in the United States of America in 1978
by Praeger Publishers,
A Division of Holt, Rinehart and Winston, CBS, Inc.

89   038   987654321

© 1978 by Praeger Publishers

Printed in the United States of America

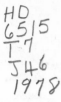

Collective bargaining in the public sector is often subjected to the following paradoxes: (1) it is viewed as being dynamic even though many public unions are still attempting to receive certain working conditions obtained 40 years ago by their private sector counterparts; (2) many of the job classifications in the private and public sectors have identical content, yet the essentiality of the work performed is generally viewed in entirely different terms by public officials and by taxpayers; and (3) private sector impasse resolution techniques, that is, the strike, are rarely sanctioned in the public sector; however, public unions' bargaining power is typically viewed as being greater than in the private sector. These paradoxes reflect the growing concern over collective bargaining in the public sector, a subject we analyze from the perspective of the mass transit industry. This industry is of particular significance as it:

1. represents an unusual combination of traditional private enterprise and increased monitoring by the local, state, and federal governments.
2. has a service that has received a great deal of public attention in terms of its essentiality and impact upon the public interest.
3. has labor costs representing 50–85 percent of total annual operating costs.

We maintain that informed policy decisions regarding collective bargaining in mass transit can only be made on the basis of a systematic analysis of the collective bargaining output, the labor agreements, and the attitudes and observations of the affected labor and management practitioners. Consequently, we used three approaches in our research. First, an in-depth review of the literature, including trade publications and academic journals, furnished key questions to guide our research. Our rather extensive footnotes and accompanying bibliography will furnish the readers with appropriate follow-up information. Second, the authors interviewed scores of management and union officials at 20 mass transit properties. These interviews were somewhat structured; however, extensive question design and length of interview sessions permitted the practitioner to bring rich detail and insight into labor-management issues. Finally, the authors developed and applied a detailed contract analysis guide of 249 variables to 37 mass transit labor agreements.

Using these approaches, we examine potential problem areas in labor-management relations, identify areas of mutual agreement, determine union and managerial perceptions of management rights, and assess current issues in collective bargaining. Specific topics include the collective bargaining process (Chapter 2); institutional and administrative issues (Chapters 3 and 5); economic issues (Chapter 4); impasse resolution techniques (Chapter 6); role of the unions in technological change, the public interest and collective bargaining, unions and minorities, and employee protection provisions (Chapter 7).

This book will merge the interests of practitioners and academicians concerned with public sector labor relations regardless of the particular public service involved, as the described dimensions of the collective bargaining process (strategies, issues, and outcome) and cited sources apply to all sectors of public bargaining. Consequently, the book will appeal to all public sector union and management officials, as well as to individuals involved in local, state, regional, and federal transportation agencies. This is particularly true for those locations not presently engaged in union-management relationships, as the detailed contract analysis guide will furnish the readers with a realistic indication of what a typical union seeks and obtains. Academicians interested in public sector collective bargaining will find the mass transit industry to be a rather unique case study—as previously mentioned, this industry does not neatly fit into public or private sector categories; instead, as indicated throughout the book, it combines elements of both. Therefore, this book will be useful as a supplemental or primary text in classes concerned with urban transportation, transportation policy, public sector bargaining, collective bargaining, and labor relations.

Our major objective is to promote informed and meaningful interchange among union and management practitioners and the academic community. Our initial discussions with these individuals have been fruitful; however, we encourage the reader to suggest issues and ways in which this interchange can be made more effective.

ACKNOWLEDGMENTS

A great many people, representing different organizations and interests, assisted in the research undertaking for the project. Without their assistance and spirit of cooperation, a difficult assignment would have been almost impossible; yet, individuals from organized labor, management, public officials, the academic community, and governmental agencies gave freely of their time, assisted in clearing up the area of difficulty, and provided a basis for better understanding of labor-management relationships in urban mass transit.

We are indebted to Mr. Dan V. Maroney, Jr., Mr. Walter J. Bierwagon, and Mr. Earle W. Putnam of the Amalgamated Transit Union; Mr. B. R. Stokes and Mr. John B. Schnell of the American Public Transit Association; Dr. Frank W. Davis, Jr. of the University of Tennessee; and Dr. Stan Rosen of the University of Illinois - Chicago Circle for their assistance and support. We also wish to thank Mr. Larry F. Yud, special assistant for mass transit, U.S. Department of Labor, who provided us with an overview of Section 13(c); and Dr. Paul Gerhart of the University of Illinois, for the use of his labor agreement analysis guide, which was modified for this research.

Special recognition must go to Dr. Marion W. Forrester, the project monitor representing the Office of University Research. Dr. Forrester's understanding of the problems of labor-management relationships and the need for independent research provided direction and enthusiasm for the project. Also, her replacements as technical representatives for the project, Dr. Frank E. Enty and Mr. Keith Prouty, have added greatly to the success of this project.

Our greatest debt is to the individual respondents—union officers, committees, and members, and management officials—who answered many questions and provided much insight into labor-management relationships for the transit industry in the Southeast. Without their cooperation and patience, this research would not have been possible. These individuals provided us with answers to difficult questions with an openness and concern that contributed greatly to our understanding of the environment in which bargaining takes place.

Both the graduate and undergraduate students who participated in the research provided invaluable assistance, and we are particularly indebted to Mr. Hank Hennessey. For the long, trying, and difficult task of typing the manuscript of this research, we are indebted to Ms. Gloria Bell, Ms. Ruth Hackenson and Ms. Catherine Nix.

We also wish to thank our wives, who suffered through many months that entailed much time away from our families in completing this research. With their support, this project has been successfully completed.

CONTENTS

LIST OF TABLES AND FIGURES

Labor Relations in
a Public Service Industry

The urban transit industry is characterized by a high degree of unionization, moderate levels of skill, and great dependence of the public on continuity of service. Every metropolitan area in the United States is confronted by a transportation problem that seems destined to become more aggravated in the years ahead. Continuing economic growth and the certainty of further transport innovation and change in methods of operations threaten to widen the gap between present systems of transit and satisfactory levels of service. The spread of private automobile ownership, reducing the demand for transit, has made operations unprofitable in many areas, subjecting collective bargaining to more constraints than in industries where increased labor costs can be offset by productivity gains or possibly rising service demand. The resulting shift from private to public ownership, in an effort to provide services vital to the public, in turn has placed employees under legislation applicable to public employees. In many instances, this shift has denied the right to strike and limited, to varying degrees, the scope of collective bargaining. Yet, strikes, illegal as they may be, have occurred with significant impact on the public.

The organizational ownership in the transit industry has undergone a dramatic change, and while only approximately 35 percent of the industry systems are publicly owned, these transit systems account for approximately 90 percent of total revenue passengers and employ about 85 percent of all workers. This change has taken place in the last ten years and whether efforts to revive urban mass transit will be successful is still in doubt; however, any successful attempt must recognize the problems and issues regarding labor-management relations in the transit industry. While suffering a decline in passengers, the mass transit industry has been experiencing a steady increase

1

in costs of operation. All systems have had to meet sizable wage increases in the inflationary period of the past ten years; for example, during this period, the cost of transit labor has increased over 100 percent in many cities, with the bill for labor ranging from 50 to 85 percent of total annual operating costs. Increased fringe costs have been added to overall expenses, as well as expenditures for new equipment and sharply increased fuel costs. If mass transit is to be revitalized, one critical factor will be viable labor-management relations that can insure stability and maintain financial integrity for the transit systems.

Noting the particular importance of transit labor, the 1974 National Transportation Report stated:

> Labor costs constitute a substantial portion of the cost to operate public transportation systems, particularly bus systems. As the financial condition of the transit industry has worsened, there has been a growing concern about the relationship of labor compensation and pro- ductivity to the transit industry's financial and operating performance. Transit management has argued that the financial condition of transit systems has deteriorated partly because labor costs have increased more rapidly than other costs and more important, faster than revenue. Moreover, management claims labor productivity has decreased. Transit labor, on the other hand, argues that its compensation has not increased at a rate greater than the cost of living, annual earnings per employee are not out of line with respect to other transportation workers, and transit labor productivity has not decreased.
>
> When one examines the data . . . it becomes clear why so much confusion exists regarding this issue. Management's argument that labor cost is rising faster than other costs appears correct, although not in dra- matic terms. For the period 1962-72, labor costs increased 65.8 percent, whereas total costs increased 63.0 percent. Payroll as a percent of total expenses increased from 67.2 percent in 1962 to 68.4 percent in 1972. Labor cost also increased faster than revenues, but this is mainly because patronage declined 22.8 per- cent during the period.[1]

The report also commented that management argues concerning productivity decreases seem valid as does labor's contention that employees' annual earnings are not out of line with respect to other transportation workers. While the report suggests several alternatives to the dilemma facing the transit industry, the important fact is that significant attention is being paid to the issues and process of labor-management relations.[2] Although there is disagreement as to the exact role that government should play in the transit industry, the simple fact is that the prevailing federal legislation does provide funding and direction for transit systems in the public sector. The realization of a need to develop an understanding of the collective bargaining climate is an important first step. Secondly, a fuller understanding of the specifics of the labor agreement is needed. Finally, a knowledge of the concept of public interest and its relationship to the resolution of labor-management problems is vital. The fact that labor-management relations policies have not been formalized by federal agencies providing funding assistance for urban mass transit results in de facto policy making. Again, it must be stressed that organized labor is a critical element in the successful revitalization of urban mass transit and the urban areas of the United States. Lack of comprehension on the part of policymakers and participants of the collective bargaining process will provide less than optimum solutions, resulting in both loss of efficiency and effectiveness.

It must be recognized that even when urban transit facilities were almost everywhere privately owned and operated, the public interest was heavily involved in the industry. A public body granted the charter to use the streets, the rates charged were and still are regulated, and portions of the public that could not afford private transport depended upon the services provided by transit. Nor could union and management be allowed to fight out their differences in a strike of long duration, except in a smaller community where the service was of secondary importance. In a metropolitan area, the losses borne by the immediate contending parties and the losses of wages to workers and of operating income to management were far less than the loss of the public in money terms, as well as in time and convenience. A strike of transit workers is apt to bring quick intervention by public officials, whether the facilities are publicly or privately owned and whether or not there is legislation that authorizes intervention.

Unions and mass transit are interrelated and it is the researchers' contention that an understanding of mass transit prospects and problems cannot be adequately approached without first considering the role played by organized labor and management. Similarly, it can be contended that any management or governmental policy decision affecting mass transit, whether it deals with technological changes, revenue funding, expansion of operations, and so on, should include a consideration of union behavior and objectives.

With the shift from private to public ownership of transit systems and the resulting changes in the status of employees and their bargaining rights, an understanding of the environment in which negotiations take place is mandatory. Employees, who previously enjoyed the right to organize and bargain collectively under the National Labor Relations Act, are now public employees and, where public authorities accepted the unions that they found in takeovers of transit systems, continue to negotiate; however, in many instances, the statutes under which the private companies were acquired are not clear, or state legislation prevents the continuation of rights that the unions sought to protect, including wage levels and fringes. With the infusion of federal funds, and resulting protections offered by Section 13(c) of the Urban Mass Transportation Act of 1964, and the arrangements with contract management service firms, the continuation of collective bargaining has been accomplished in the Southeast. However, there have been costs for each of the resulting takeovers. The question of diminishing management rights in the scope of collective bargaining presents a bitter battle for some localities, as every union contract, including Section 13(c) agreements, is seen by some public officials and management representatives as a limit on management freedom to run the operation. Likewise, the efforts to diminish the rights of collective bargaining and employee protection are viewed by organized labor as an attempt to restrict the opportunity for a worker to earn a "fair day's wage." It must be pointed out to the reader that regardless of the funding, marketing efforts, and other managerial prerogatives, the collective bargaining arrangement is paramount and affects every aspect of transit, particularly the quality of service and the cost of providing transport to the community. Public policy in the urban mass transit area must seek simultaneously to assure fair treatment for employees and continued adequate service to the public at a reasonable cost. It seems unlikely that transit employees will subsidize transit operations, whether privately or publicly owned, by working at rates and conditions less than their view of market conditions.

DIMENSIONS OF LABOR-MANAGEMENT
RELATIONS IN MASS TRANSIT: AN OVERVIEW

One of the most significant dimensions of labor-management relations in mass transit is collective bargaining, which is often concerned with preserving the respective strengths and functions of the union and management organizations. While many times it is difficult to determine the underlying forces and their specific impacts in the bargaining process, the provisions of the labor agreement generally reflect the more important and lasting features of the collective bargaining relationship. The labor agreement represents that unique set of conditions under which services will be performed.

Few attempts have been made to understand the patterns of similarity among agreements and the deviations from those patterns. Several surveys have provided information concerning the extent of union membership, percentage of workers organized by certain unions, and the legal requirements of particular states, but no one study has attempted to relate all of the factors in the environment and provide some understanding of the extent and importance of union influence on the terms of the labor agreement and the overall nature of collective bargaining for mass transit in a specific region of the country. Through an examination of labor agreements and in-depth field interviews, this research attempts to bring an understanding to the environment of mass transit in which collective bargaining takes place. The outcome should assist in estimating the roles of unions and managements in collective bargaining while allowing for indications as to how those roles may change or be changed.

Paul Gerhart notes that the scope of bargaining refers to the range of issues included in negotiations and includes more than just a listing of issues on which the union has had some influence.[3] The amount of influence wielded by a union on a given issue may range from token involvement to complete domination, and without some knowledge of the amount of influence, the discussion of a particular issue within the scope of bargaining reveals little useful information. Through the use of in-depth, on-site interviews of both management and union officials, this research was able to better identify the amount of specific union influence on each issue, revealed through the application of a 249-variable list to all labor agreements in the Southeast on a provision-by-provision basis. Therefore, the scope of bargaining applicable for this research involves a listing of issues present in the labor contracts, an indication of union involvement and a measure of how the issue is resolved in the agreement.

While the scope of bargaining can be defined as the end result of the bargaining process, the definition of collective bargaining is not universal. The bargaining process is considered by some as simply the negotiation of the written agreement; however, it is more frequently defined to include both the negotiation and administration of the labor contract. For the purposes of this study, the second and broader view of the bargaining process will be utilized, recognizing that the written agreement may reflect a scope of bargaining considerably more narrow than the actual set of issues upon which there has been joint decision making by the union and management. As several authorities note, there may be a discrepancy between the formal scope of bargaining and the real scope, with the source of difference being alternative channels of influence available to the parties.[4] These alternative channels include the informal contact between union and management during adminstration of the contract;

a degree of formality in certain issues that may be found in "side agreements," generally referred to as "company policy" by respondents at a few transit properties; and discussions with leaders of political units, such as transit coordinators.

Margaret Chandler notes that in our property-conscious society, collective bargaining issues frequently are phrased in terms of a second dimension, namely, the rights of the respective parties; these rights are the hidden dimension underlying all labor-management decisions. [5] The fact that labor-management questions are structured as rights issues provides an important starting point for understanding behavior in this field. It is the perceived protection of rights that, in many instances, has caused unions to move into particular subject areas; and in some instances, labor has refused to specify the reserved rights of management on the grounds that such specification might limit their own ability to adequately represent their members' rights. There appears to be a common opinion amongst transit union officials that any managerial decisions or authority threatening the security of transit workers must be included in the scope of bargaining. As Gerhart notes, components of economic security include wages; personnel policies that involve the employees' rights in the matters of job security; and enlargement of the area of control of the employee in his own affairs, such as the scale and schedule of operations. [6] Any issue that might conceivably have an impact on one of these components is a candidate for the union's list of negotiable issues, although there may be a difference in the degree of emphasis placed upon specific items by either the local unit or the international office of the union.

PURPOSE OF THE RESEARCH

This research was designed to provide an insight that would lead to an understanding of collective bargaining and the labor-management processes in the transit industry for a nine-state southeastern area. The study examined the extent of collective bargaining, its effects, and specific conditions of the environment to determine the nature of the negotiation process as well as the attitudes of union and management officials. The scope of the research was purposely broad because of the nature of the problems and the fact that the relatively meager amount of academic and practitioner attention devoted to the subject has generated few insights into the many dimensions of the issues. The boundaries of the research were brought into perspective by examination of relevant theory and by a series of key questions regarding significant issues. One of the project's goals was to ascertain from involved participants which variables they regard as significantly affecting labor-management relationships. The dimensions of the study were broadly structured through the following key questions. First: What are the degree and dimensions of union involvement in management's decision-making process? Issues such as hiring practices, policies on training and apprenticeships, work-sharing and layoff systems, promotion policies, work scheduling, technological change, disciplinary policies and procedures, employee protection provisions, wage structures, and negotiation of labor agreements were examined. Second: How do management and union officials define the "public interest?" The public interest concepts were made operational through statements of issues and conditions in employment of minorities, efficient service, reasonable wages, collective bargaining practices, and fare levels. The study examined the assessment of roles by each party to the agreement in specific terms and value assignment. Third: What is the degree of cooperation or conflict found in labor-management relations? Fourth: What roles do management and union officials envision for government(s) in the collective bargaining relationships? Fifth: What factors appear to facilitate or inhibit the labor-management relationship? This dimension was studied through an examination of ownership, unionization of work force, length of bargaining relationships, extent of appropriate labor legislation, size of population, and size of operations.

RESEARCH METHODOLOGY

The data reported in this research were derived from several sources. First, an extensive review of related literature was undertaken (see the Bibliography). In spite of the significance of labor-management relationships in the transit industry, the literature of collective bargaining contained few transit-specific items and the transit literature contained few references about the nature of labor agreements and the attitudes that shape the collective bargaining environment. One notable exception was a dissertation and several resulting articles by Darold T. Barnum. Second, the research design called for obtaining all labor agreements from transit systems that had negotiated contracts and formally recognized a local bargaining unit. The study area was defined as a nine-state southeastern area, including Louisiana, Mississippi, Tennessee, Kentucky, North Carolina, Alabama, Georgia, South Carolina, and Florida. Additional legal and side agreements were requested, as well as any Section 13(c) agreements that had been negotiated. These contracts were analyzed on a provision-by-provision basis to determine the degree of union involvement in decision making concerning contract

terms. The data obtained from the contract analysis of individual
items were cross-categorized with several independent variables to
explain possible variations among transit systems. The collection
of labor agreements was accomplished prior to starting the on-site
visits in order to understand the unique issues and problems for
each of the individual properties.

The third source of data was information gained from the
administration of an extensive interview guide at 20 sites selected
as representative of all transit properties in the study area. This
in-depth analysis provided knowledge of the relationships among the
variables considered in the study and allowed for a more complete
identification and understanding of the scope of the bargaining issues
as well as the bargaining climate in the transit industry. A note of
caution to the reader: the research does not contend that the values
derived from the administration of either the interview guide or the
provision-by-provision analysis of labor agreements accurately
describes any other section of the United States. The attempt was
to develop a technique for understanding and analyzing the
collective bargaining environment and relationships in mass transit,
and to report, based upon that research design, the findings concerning
labor-management relationships in the Southeast. While it would be
improper to impute the findings in the Southeast to any other section
of the country, the researchers do feel that the research instruments
and techniques developed and utilized in this project have applicability
not only to transit operations in other sections of the country, but to
other transportation modes as well. Additional data concerning
operations, including route schedules, company policy manuals, and
management service firms' contracts, were obtained and provided
a further basis for understanding the climate of collective bargaining
in the Southeast.

A final source of data was provided by two conferences held
in 1976, entitled "Unions, Management Rights, and the Public Interest
in Mass Transit." These conferences, jointly sponsored by the
Program of University Research of the U.S. Department of Transportation and the University of North Florida, brought together union
officers, management representatives, and government officials from
transit systems throughout the United States. The exchanges in these
meetings provided current positions on collective bargaining issues
in the United States and the proceedings of the conferences have been
integrated with previously published materials. Throughout the
research project, many individuals were contacted and information
concerning specific items was obtained. The synthesis of all data
gathered from private individuals, governmental officials, union
and management representatives, the literature review, conference
proceedings, field research, and contract analysis provides the
general framework upon which the findings reported are based.

TABLE 1.1

Summary of Variables Used in Labor Agreements Analysis

Union security issues
  Bargaining unit designation
  Designation of union as exclusive
    representative
  Union security clause
  Provision for dues checkoff and
    administration and cost of checkoff
  Paid time off for officers and members
    for union business
  Superseniority
  Provision for union meetings on property
  Provision prohibiting contracting out
  Provision prohibiting supervisor from
    performing bargaining unit work
Job assignment
  Minimum hour guarantees
  Workweek and scheduled days off
  Work scheduling
    Basis for selection of work
    Requirements for advance posting of work
    Required number of bids per year
    Changes, additions, and deletions of
      regular runs
    Procedures for allocation of overtime
  Extra board
    Scope
    Provisions for rotation
    Payment for administrative error
  Promotion procedure for garage employees
  Layoff procedure
  Provisions for premium pay
    Rate of pay for time worked on a holiday
    Rate of pay for time worked on scheduled
      day off
    Rate of pay for time worked in excess of
      regularly scheduled workday or in excess
      of 8 hours
    Spread time
    Shift premiums
    Training allowances
    Longevity pay
Wages
  Wage rate ranges and steps
    Drivers
    Maintenance employees
  Negotiated wage rates
    Drivers
    Maintenance employees
  Cost-of-living allowance
  Other forms of payment
    Preparatory time
    Court appearances
    Report pay for extra board
    Time spent completing accident reports
    Intervals between pieces of runs
    Attendance of safety meetings
    Check-in time
    Call-in time
    Meal relief
    Relief time

Vacation, sick leave, funeral leave
  Vacation
    Amounts for years of employment
    Eligibility
    Scheduling
    Amount of vacation
    Use of paid vacation
  Sick leave
    Rate of cumulation
    Eligibility requirements
    Use of paid sick leave'
  Funeral leave—amount and eligibility of
    specific relatives
  Holidays
Negotiated impasse resolution procedure
  Steps in negotiated grievance procedure
  Definition of a grievance
  Time limits for appeals and decisions
  Special grievance procedure
  Union rights in the negotiated grievance
    procedure
  Civil service appeals procedure
  Arbitration
    Authority of arbitrator's award
    Scope of arbitration
    Time limits
    One level versus two levels of arbitration
    Selection of arbitrator(s)
    Provision for expense of arbitration
Public interest
  Service
  Safety
  Passenger treatment
  First aid training
  Promptness
  Customer satisfaction
  Safety meetings
Management rights
  Management rights clause
  Management rights with respect to specific
    issues
    Selection of employees
    Layoffs of employees
    Determination of length of runs
    Schedule changes
    Technological changes
    Time standards for runs
    Apprenticeships
    Bidding of runs
Contingent benefits
  Insurance programs
    Hospital—medical-surgical
    Major medical
    Life insurance
    Accident insurance
  Pension, retirement plan

Source: Appendix A of this book.

9

Contract Analysis

Current labor agreements, as well as any side agreements, were solicited from all transit properties in the southeastern study area. With the assistance of the international officers of the Amalgamated Transit Union (ATU) and officials of the American Public Transit Association, all requested labor contracts were received from both local units and local operating managements without exception. In several properties in the nine-state area either there is no union or the collective bargaining unit has not received formal recognition during the study period.

A measure of union influence over the terms of employment can be obtained through an examination of labor contracts. In attempting to quantify the role or influence of unions in mass transit, and factors that might affect their role, it was necessary to develop a format or model that could be utilized in analyzing the provisions of all transit labor agreements. After initial analysis of the labor agreements, a list of issues covered by the contracts, as well as of the way those issues are resolved, was developed. Table 1.1 presents a summary of the variables used in the labor agreement analysis portion of the research, and Appendix A contains the complete list of variables. The model used for the preparation of our 249 variables drew on the earlier efforts of Gerhart, a noted authority in the area of public sector collective bargaining. Due to the transit-specific nature of this research, it was necessary to modify substantially Gerhart's original variable list and expand the categories. This model was utilized to analyze agreements ranging from a 15-page, double-spaced, memorandum agreement to a 90-page, sophisticated contract. While this contract analysis model was specifically designed for analysis of transit contracts, it can, with minor modifications, be utilized to analyze any transportation mode's labor agreements.

By providing an operational measure of the scope of bargaining, based upon the written formal agreement between the parties, it is possible to obtain an understanding of union involvement in the provisions of that agreement. In some instances, one item reflected the resolution of an issue, while in other cases, several variable numbers were necessary to record more accurately the resolution of an issue, that is, to provide some indication of the breadth and depth of union involvement or power. For instance, on the issue of management aid to other unions, only one variable and two response categories were needed; that is, is it or is it not covered by the agreement. On issues of a more complex nature, such as paid vacations, several variables, each containing numerous response categories, were necessary to reflect all of the dimensions of those issues in the contract. As Gerhart notes:

> The information collected reflects not only the breadth
> of bargaining, but also the depth of union penetration. . . .
> The consideration of issue resolution is necessary if
> the underlying concept, i.e., union influence, is to be
> measured meaningfully. Indeed, the scope of bargaining
> is not a very useful concept, . . . unless some consi-
> deration is given to the substantive content of the issues
> included within it.[7]

Our study analyzed the responses to each of the 249 variables and
grouped them into several major categories. These categories
represent chapter discussions in this book, namely, institutional
issues, economic issues, administrative issues, and impasse resolutions.

Additionally, in an attempt to measure the degree of union
involvement or union power evident in contract language, the responses
to each of the 249 variables were recoded, that is, collapsed into
two responses, indicating either "little or no union involvement or
union power" or "relatively higher union involvement or union power."
These two response categories were derived after careful observations
of the initial response frequencies. By recoding all 249 variables
and calculating the proportions of the two responses (one signifying
relatively less union involvement and the other signifying greater
union involvement or power), it was possible to obtain an overall
view of the relative degree of union involvement or power in labor
agreements with respect to particular issues—institutional, economic,
and other issues. This technique provides a measure of power in the
overall collective bargaining climate, and by comparing the proportions of the two responses by organizational structure, city population
size, unit size, and number of buses, it is possible to determine
patterns of union involvement in these major issue categories.

Field Research

After completion of the literature research and collection of
labor agreements in the Southeast, the research design called for
an extensive, confidential on-site interview with local union and
management representatives who had been actively engaged in collective bargaining for the property. The purpose of the interview guide
employed in the field research was to add structure to the interview
process, thereby permitting comparison of the responses to somewhat
standardized questions. Table 1.2 is a summary of the types of
information obtained from the interview guide, and Appendix B contains a copy of the interview guide that was administered in the field
research.

TABLE 1.2

Summary of the Dimensions of the Field Research

Characteristics of sites and respondents
  Descriptive characteristics of visited sites
  Background of the labor and management representatives and the
    collective bargaining relationships
Influences on collective bargaining and impasse resolution
  Structural characteristics in collective bargaining
    Competition with other facilities
    Number of bargaining unit employees and effect on collective
      bargaining
    Classification of bargaining unit employees and effect on collective
      bargaining
  Organizational characteristics
    Private/public ownership (and transition)
    Role of management service companies
  Budgetary influences in collective bargaining
  Length of negotiating
  Attitudes and role of the government in collective bargaining
  Legal constraints on collective bargaining
    State statutes
    Fair Labor Standards Act
  Extent and effect of impasse resolution techniques
Recent negotiation behavior and outcome
  Strategic considerations of the parties
    Composition of management bargaining team, strategy involvement,
      and tactics
    Composition of union bargaining team, strategy involvement,
      and tactics
    "Comparability" agreement between unions and management
    Suggestions for improvement in collective bargaining
    Dimensions and extent of union-management cooperation
    Degree of union involvement in management rights
  Current bargaining issues and their resolutions
Other issues in labor-management relationship
  Union involvement in technological considerations
  Significance of 13(c) provisions for union-management relationships
  Relationship between minorities and collective bargaining
  The dimensions and effect of public interest in collective
    bargaining

Source: Appendix B of this book.

The advantage of the confidential, on-site visits was that they enabled the investigator to resolve any confusion the respondent may have had regarding a particular question, as well as permitting some flexibility by allowing the respondent to discuss various facets of a question. The response by both union and management respondents was outstanding. In all instances, a spirit of cooperation prevailed, and in spite of the length and depth of the questions asked, each individual respondent was fully cooperative and in no instance was any requested information refused. Mail questionnaires were judged not suitable for this project because the many complexities of the labor agreements and labor-management relationships could not be reduced to a simple yes or no or even multiple-choice answers; the response rate to mailed questionnaires of this type has generally been quite low; and there is some uncertainty as to the actual position and relative knowledge of the respondent who completes an anonymous questionnaire.

TABLE 1.3

Dimensions of Transit Properties Studied, 1975-76

| | Range | |
Dimension	Low Value	High Value
Total vehicle miles	540,700	26,985,900
Fixed route miles	159	3,048
Fare box revenues	$360,200	$13,306,200
Operating expenses	$758,300	$33,467,400
Number of buses	38	715
Number of passengers	1,284,600	105,712,700
Number of employees	30	1,438
Size of population	147,000	1,300,000
Current operating cost/mile	$0.78	$1.56
Current labor cost/mile	$0.48	$1.20

Source: Compiled by the authors, based upon information supplied by respondents from 20 on-site interviews.

Prior to pretest of the field interview guide, many individuals commented on the nature and types of information requested. Union and management representatives, as well as government officials from all levels—local, state, regional, and federal agencies—were most helpful in suggesting revisions to the interview guide. The actual 20 sites to be visited were selected to obtain a representative group of properties in the Southeast. The selected sites included transit systems managed as private operations, those publicly operated, and those managed by contract management firms, representing all city sizes, varying unit sizes, and a varying number of buses in operation.

The cities selected were roughly proportionate to the dimensions of the responses received from all cities in the Southeast concerning the labor agreements. Table 1.3 presents the high and low values for the dimensions of the transit properties visited in the field research. The project was designed to visit at least one transit operation in each of the nine states, to include, in proportion to the contracts received, visits to cities of small, medium, and large populations, and to cities covered by all unions represented in the Southeast. While ATU is the dominant union in terms of contracts negotiated and properties represented, this research included properties organized by the Transport Workers Union and several local units of various craft unions, as well as independent employee associations.

Cities visited in the Southeast ranged in size from over 1 million population base to just over 147,000, and unit sizes varied at location from 30 members to 1,438. Fare box revenues ranged from $360,200 to $13,306,200 and operating expenses from $758,300 to $33,467,400 for a fiscal year (1975-76).

ORGANIZATION OF THE STUDY

For the purposes of this study of a nine-state southeastern area, the urban mass transit industry has been defined as all companies engaged in local and suburban mass passenger transportation, over regular routes, and on regular schedules, including charter operations where applicable, and that have agreements covering collective bargaining. The systems in the study area are, whether publicly or privately owned, bus lines. While the area represents the typical problems and issues faced across the nation with respect to collective bargaining in mass transit, the reader is again cautioned that there is no intention to extrapolate the results of this research to all transit operations in the United States. The main purpose of this research is to develop an understanding of the institution of collective bargaining in the mass transit industry.

Chapter 2 presents an overview of the collective bargaining process in mass transit, discussing the background of the agents to the bargaining process as well as their influences on negotiations. The current bargaining behavior is examined in light of the strategies and tactics employed by the parties.

Chapter 3 discusses the institutional issues of labor-management relationships, and through an examination of contract provisions and analysis of on-site interviews, deals with management rights as well as union security issues.

Chapter 4 presents a short discussion of the theoretical constructs of wage determination in bargaining, and develops from the union and management respondents a list of the current issues in bargaining. The structure of economic issues, such as wages, cost-of-living adjustments, premium pay, and other forms of payment, is examined from the development of the contract analysis.

Chapter 5 is a discussion of the administrative issues, such as job assignment, promotion procedures, layoff, and discipline, found to exist in the transit industry in the Southeast.

Chapter 6 focuses on impasse resolutions and develops the patterns of grievance procedures and arbitration.

Chapter 7 contains a discussion of four current issues in the labor-management relationships, including technological changes, Section 13(c) of the Urban Mass Transportation Act of 1964, minorities in transit, and public interest in transit.

Chapter 8 contains a summary and impressions gained from the research concerning issues relating to labor-management relations for the urban transit industry.

NOTES

1. U.S. Department of Transportation, 1974 National Transportation Report (Washington, D.C.: U.S. Government Printing Office, 1975), pp. 233-34.

2. Ibid.

3. Paul F. Gerhart, "The Scope of Bargaining in Local Government Labor Agreements," (Ph.D. diss., University of Chicago, 1973), pp. 4-5.

4. Ibid., pp. 12-16.

5. Margaret K. Chandler, Management Rights and Union Interests (New York: McGraw-Hill, 1964), p. 3.

6. Gerhart, op. cit., pp. 22-23.

7. Ibid.

2

THE COLLECTIVE
BARGAINING PROCESS

This chapter as well as the remaining chapters will approach the concept of collective bargaining from several perspectives. First, this concept represents a continuing joint decision-making process between union and management representatives over terms of employment and working conditions. While many tend to equate collective bargaining with formal contract negotiations and resultant output, we take a much broader view of this concept, namely, negotiation (Chapter 2), administration (Chapter 3—management rights), and interpretation (Chapter 6—grievances) of the labor agreement.[1]

The decision-making process inherent in the collective bargaining relationship is subjected to two somewhat opposing influences. First, collective bargaining can be a rational process, one where union and management representatives resolve their differences in an amicable, objective manner:

> Rationalization means . . . the making of . . . decisions
> through rules, organization and expertness rather than
> through trial by struggle, ideology and hit or miss. More-
> over, the alternatives from among which decisions are
> made are more likely to be "closely related to existing
> reality" than to revolutionary goals.[2]

Our discussion of collective bargaining will include an analysis of several elements conducive to rationality: background of the collective bargaining relationship and participants, length of the formal contract negotiations, presence of experts on union and management bargaining teams, and so on.

The collective bargaining process often also has been viewed as having elements of power; the specific form and content of the labor agreement is often determined by the respective bargaining power of the union and management representatives.[3] Hence, each party to the collective bargaining process attempts to convince the opponent that it will cost more for the opponent to disagree than it will to agree, and that therefore the opponent should agree with the other's position or demands. For example, unions may suggest that a strike or political action will increase management's cost to disagree, while management might counter that a strike will reduce operating costs and thereby reduce deficit expenditures. Thus, our research will also attempt to analyze the degree to which the element of power is found in collective bargaining.

Finally, collective bargaining can be viewed as an interaction process,[4] representing an interdependent relationship between union officials and their rank-and-file constituents, management officials representing differing levels of organizational authority, and government officials at state, local, and national levels who can affect the content of the labor agreement. We will investigate the complex dimensions of these relationships, indicating the apparent advantages and problems they offer the mass transit industry as well as the affected public.

BACKGROUND OF THE LABOR-MANAGEMENT REPRESENTATIVES AND THE COLLECTIVE BARGAINING RELATIONSHIP

In attempting to understand the collective bargaining process, it is first necessary to examine the general atmosphere in which collective bargaining takes place. Of paramount importance is the tradition of collective bargaining found in the mass transit industry. One author has suggested that union organization of the industry in the Southeast occurred almost entirely during two periods, the first occurring after World War I, and the second beginning about 1936 and continuing through the early days of World War II. The first period of union organization appears to be due mainly to voluntary acceptance of the union by management officials. However, many unions organized after 1936 received these recognitions on the basis of the National Labor Relations Act (1935). This form of recognition was not immediately attained after the passage of the act; rather, some transit systems that were not involved in carrying passengers across state lines had to ask the National Labor Relations Board and the courts for clarification of their status under the act. This question was eventually resolved in the Baltimore Transit Case (1943) when the courts determined that a system operating within state lines nonetheless could affect interstate commerce through the secondary effect on port and industrial operations in Baltimore.[5]

TABLE 2.1

Profile of Labor-Management Relationships at 20
Mass Transit Facilities in the Southeast

Collective Bargaining and Background of Union-Management Negotiators	Mean for the 20 selected sites
Years formal collective bargaining has occurred at facility	36
Number of formal labor contracts that have been negotiated at facility	22
Chief union negotiator	
Years of formal collective bargaining experience in mass transit	12
Years of experience in mass transit	20
Chief management negotiator	
Years of formal collective bargaining experience in mass transit	14
Years of experience in mass transit	18

Source: Interview responses gathered in nine-state study area by the authors.

It is safe to say that regardless of the particular impetus, the mass transit industry in the Southeast has been involved with unionized employees and collective bargaining for as long as, or longer than, most other industries in the same geographical area. This tradition is further evidenced by a summary of the collective bargaining relationships found at our 20 selected interview sites; as Table 2.1 suggests, labor-management relationships at the selected facilities have been maintained over a relatively long period of years, with each location averaging over 22 negotiated labor agreements. Additionally, the chief union and management negotiators at these properties have had considerable negotiating experience, averaging 12 and 14 years, respectively, as well as working experience in mass transit operations averaging 20 and 18 years, respectively. All of these factors point to an established collective bargaining relationship; one, as indicated at approximately four-fifths of the locations, where management and union representatives know each other well, respecting each other's competencies as well as their mutual abilities to resolve noneconomic work issues over the years.

INFLUENCES ON COLLECTIVE BARGAINING

Structural Considerations

Collective bargaining "structure" refers to the organizational scope of collective bargaining; more specifically, to the nature and number of bargaining units, either formally or informally recognized, that are either directly involved or influential in the negotiation of the labor agreement. The inclusion or exclusion of various bargaining units in formal negotiations can have a serious impact on the resultant labor agreement. To illustrate, if a municipality negotiated a common labor agreement covering most of its employees (for example, motor pool, recreation department, sanitation department, streets and highways, mass transit), there would probably be few provisions pertinent to the issues and complexities confronting mass transit. However, none of the publicly owned agencies studied included mass transit operations in a centralized bargaining process—the negotiated labor agreement applies solely to mass transit employees. This finding is in part due to the unique legal considerations affecting mass transit as well as the separate governmental administration of the transit properties. A similar situation is found in privately owned mass transit companies; consequently, all of the selected mass transit sites experience decentralized bargaining—management and union officials negotiating a labor agreement pertaining to the exclusive interests of each mass transit property.

Additionally, only five of the 20 locations indicated that they have more than one bargaining unit at the facility, with the majority of these instances occurring at privately owned utilities. None of these locations have experienced "coordinated bargaining"—joint efforts of the units to bring coordinated pressure upon management, or "parity"—each union using the other union's settlement as a starting point for its own negotiation settlement. However, two of the management officials attribute significant impact to the multi-unit bargaining as "it makes it more difficult in trying to please two groups who are quite competitive in their bargaining demands." Another influence in multiunit bargaining is the extent to which mass transit operations affect the total operations of the facility. Management officials at two of the privately owned utility firms indicated that mass transit employees represent a minority of the operation's total employees and are, therefore, subject to the pattern established by the more dominant union.

While the preponderance of mass transit agencies have one bargaining unit representing the exclusive interests of its employees, there are nonetheless informal, internal differences that influence the negotiation process and outcome, as two authorities note:

In an important sense, collective bargaining consists of
no less than three separate bargains—the agreement by
different groups within the union to abandon certain
claims and assign priorities to others; an analogous
process of assessing priorities and trade-offs within
a single company or association; and the eventual
agreement that is made across the bargaining table. [6]

Perhaps the most vivid internal distinction occurs between the bus
operators and craft employees.

A somewhat consistent proportion of craft employees to total
bargaining unit employees is found throughout the investigated properties. More specifically, the average proportion is 19 percent[7]
(range of 15 percent to 23 percent). This proportion is not affected
by the total size of the investigated bargaining units. Craft employees
have traditionally represented a "significant minority" in some labor
organizations—their interests, influence, and obtained settlements
often extend beyond their proportional representation among bargaining
unit employees, creating a structural controversy as old as the labor
movement. [8] Consequently, management and union respondents were
asked if the respective proportions of craft and operator employees
had any effect on collective bargaining practices and settlements.
Half of the management respondents indicated that the union is
"driver oriented." For example, various economic issues—bonus
time, spread time, pay for time not worked, fringe benefits—are
negotiated for the operators, who "dominate the negotiation committees and ratification vote," and are subsequently applied to craft
employees. [9] Two respondents pointed to the low negotiated wage
differential between craft employees and operators to substantiate
their contentions; and a subsequent review of labor agreements
containing both craft and operator classifications indicates an average
wage differential of only 10 percent. However, one management
representative pointed out that the reason for the relatively low wage
differential is that many of the detailed craft assignments, often calling for a higher wage differential, are either contracted out, or the
responsibility of the vendor.

None of the union respondents indicated any problems arising
from this proportional difference. While all but one of the affected
union officials (those having craft and operator classifications in
their units) indicated contract ratification is on the basis of one man-
one vote, four union respondents indicated that at least one position
of the negotiation team is always reserved for a craft employee.
Another union respondent indicated that only craft employees vote
on those issues which pertain solely to craft classifications. Finally,
management and union officials at two locations indicated that special

consideration is given to craft employees because of either jurisdictional problems among the crafts or the fact that few of the craft employees are union members. In summary, some difference of opinion appears to exist between management and union officials regarding the effects of bargaining unit composition upon the negotiated settlement.

A final, potential structural influence on collective bargaining is the amount of service furnished by competitors in the local area. This influence can be twofold: management officials may feel pressured to stabilize or reduce labor costs in order to remain competitive; and union officials may use competitors' wages as a starting point in their negotiation demands. However, one author suggests:

> Most transit firms, therefore, can be classified as monopolies, with each monopolist limited to one locality. The systems are only monopolies in the most literal sense, as they do compete with other modes of transportation—the most important being the private automobile. Nevertheless, transit bargaining structure and processes are directly affected by this industrial and market structure. [10]

Our findings suggest competitive service exerts a minimal influence on the collective bargaining process. Union and management representatives at seven locations indicated that there are privately run competitive bus services that include some charter operations; however, all indicated that these operations are relatively insignificant, and do not affect collective bargaining, with the exception of one union representative who indicated charter revenues detract from total agency revenues. The particular question was left open-ended to determine if agency and union officials would regard any form of paratransit operations as being competitive. The only response to this question pertained to other bus operations, not taxis or jitney service. Apparently, mass transit practitioners do not view these latter services as offering potential, serious competition to their operations.

Organizational Characteristics

Public/Private Ownership

In the late 1940s the overwhelming majority of mass transit operations, particularly in the Southeast, were privately owned. [11] However, as Table 2.2 indicates, [12] the industry has undergone a significant shift to some form of public regulation or ownership. A far more important issue pertains to the significance of this shift in labor-management relationships. Some authors have suggested that the differences between private and public sector bargaining are negligible.[13] Typically cited contentions for this reasoning are that many public employee classifications are not different from their private sector counterparts, in terms of their job responsibilities;

TABLE 2.2

The Transit Industry: Systems Changing Status,
by Size of City and Type of Change,
1955-69

Size of City	Number of Systems		
	Becoming Public[a]	Discontinuing Service[b]	Total
Less than 25,000	6	51	57
25,000-50,000	15	40	55
Over 50,000	74	9	83
Total	95	100	195

[a] All systems still in operation in 1969.
[b] About 7 percent of these may have been publicly owned.
Source: Data provided by American Transit Association.

the collective bargaining issues are somewhat similar; and the determination of the negotiation outcome in both public and private sectors is a function of the respective bargaining power of union and management. Other academicians and practitioners have suggested that the shift from private to public ownership has resulted in profound differences in the labor-management relationship.[14]

Our discussion of this bargaining influence will be largely limited to practitioner response to the following question: "How has the change from private to public ownership affected the collective bargaining process and outcome?" It should be noted, however, that other private-public sector distinctions—for example, budget making, ability to go on strike, essential versus nonessential service, the mass transit agency's relationship to the public interest—will be discussed throughout the book when appropriate.

Four of the sites are privately owned; hence this question is not applicable to their response. However, about one-fourth of the respondents (six management and four union officials) indicated the shift from private to public ownership has had little impact on the collective bargaining process. Perhaps this attitude is best reflected by the comment of one union official: "The key to bargaining is the individual negotiator, not the particular organization." One possible reason for this response is that most or all of the labor agreement provisions—for example, arbitration, the right to strike—were negotiated when the agency was privately owned and were included in the transition to public ownership to facilitate application for federal funding.

However, there were two influences cited that are associated with the transition to public ownership; namely, heightened union expectations for wage increases and diminution of the management negotiator's authority. A related study by Daniel Hamermesh examined 48 publicly operated bus systems for the years 1963-71 and found that government takeover of privately owned facilities was statistically significant in explaining wage increases even when several variables—for example, regional differences, cost of living, the "quality of labor"—were held constant. [15]

The potential wage impact associated with public ownership has not gone unnoticed by some transit managers; for example, Louis J. Gambaccini, vice president and general manager, Port Authority Trans-Hudson Corporation, commented:

> We in the industry certainly do not begrudge labor the gains that were made in the period following public takeovers. Many of these gains were overdue and more than justified by the years of neglect in working conditions even as transportation service was declining. However, labor in the transit industry has more than made up for the erosion of its position in the late days of private ownership. Studies of transit wages reveal that labor costs in the industry have increased dramatically in recent years—the years in which many of these systems came under public ownership. At present, transit wages are significantly higher than wages in the private sector— and these wages have been increasing at a faster pace than the general wage rates in private industry. [16]

The wage "catch-up" afforded by some public takeovers of private mass transit properties has been acknowledged by at least one national union official; however, this individual does not think that management requires an ownership profit incentive to bargain effectively:

> These ancient "market forces" theories may be popular with those seeking an excuse for political interference in

collective bargaining, but the history of transit bargaining under tax supported public operation provides
no evidence that management cannot do its job. [17]

Our investigation only partially supports the relationship found
in Hamermesh's study; more specifically, almost a third of the
respondents (seven management officials and six union officials)
believe the shift from private to public management has resulted in
greater economic benefits. This transition has resulted in greater
access to governmental financial assistance, which, in the opinion
of one management official, increases union bargaining power as
management needs union agreement on certain grant provisions.
Many of the management respondents indicated their "inability-to-
pay-higher-wages" argument under the privately owned system is
not currently accepted by the union in the publicly owned agency
because of the agency's access to government subsidies. Almost
all of the public takeovers were due to the dire financial situation
of the private organization; under public ownership, unions maintain
that, as employees and contributing taxpayers, they receive the same
treatment and consideration available to other public employees. This
sentiment was reflected by one union official:

> We think public transit should be treated the same way
> as fire and police and garbage collection or whatever
> other type city service. I've never had to use a police-
> man. I know they are essential. I've never had to use
> a fireman, but I know they are essential and I pay my
> taxes to support it. And I know there are complicated
> work rules regarding the fire department as well as
> there is in the transit industry, and I know that you can't
> have a man fighting a fire 24 hours a day at 8-hour
> shifts, because we hope there's not that many fires,
> but the man that's a fireman has got to make a living,
> so therefore, he's got to have a day's work and a day's
> pay. The same is true with transit. . . . I don't read
> too much about the deficit operation of the police
> department . . . or the other departments. All we
> hear is how much deficit is in transit. But if we could
> get the people back on the buses and out of the cars,
> I think you would find that all of the cities, especially
> the large cities, would be better off. [18]

An often cited element of public sector bargaining is "sovereignty"—the government is the sole possessor of final power as it
represents the interests of all its constituents. This concept makes

it impossible for labor and management to bargain as equals because
the government must remain the sole authority in resolving labor's
interests in terms accommodative to the larger constituency. [19]
Sovereignty presents a paradox as the public employee working for
a government that guarantees and maintains his democratic rights
finds his employment rights are severely limited. A rationale sometimes cited for this paradox is that "the government employee's
share in the control of his working life should be exercised through
his capacity as a voting citizen of the state rather than as an employee
of the state."[20] Interestingly, none of the union and management
officials indicated any concern over this issue; apparently, sovereignty
is neither discussed nor invoked during collective bargaining or
other aspects of the labor-management relationship. Perhaps this
is attributable to two interrelated factors: the previously mentioned
long-established labor-management relationship at most of these
properties, which tends to remove barriers inherent in sovereignty;
and the private ownership heritage found at most of the mass transit
properties.

Yet another aspect of sovereignty pertains to its exercise in
an independent system:

> The operation of government is organized around a
> system of checks and balances that delimit the exercise
> of power by an individual or group. The check and
> balance system exists because of separation of powers,
> elections and constitutions. Employment and personnel
> policies are shared by legislatures, governmental
> departments, independent agencies, commissions,
> and even political parties. [21]

The diffusion of decision-making authority extended to the labor
relations functions differs among the investigated properties. For
example, most of the chief management negotiators had to consult
with various governmental officials before tentatively agreeing on
any economic issue. At least two of the management officials indicated the morass of approval procedures associated with public ownership has reduced the initiative and interest in labor negotiations they
enjoyed under private ownership.

Management Service Organizations

With the decline and closure of many transit properties, the
mass transit industry has been hard pressed to attract, develop, and
train qualified managerial talent. Added to this managerial demise

has been the conversion of private transit operations into public ownership by cities desiring to maintain some semblance of transit service for their communities. Publicly owned systems are, for the most part, service oriented rather than profit dependent and have the advantage of financial assistance from several levels of government. One major difficulty with public ownership and the attempt to revive existing transit systems has been the lack of qualified local government personnel with existing knowledge, expertise, and experience in transit operations—a deficiency which can be best observed in the areas of collective bargaining and marketing. Services of management service organizations have been utilized by many cities in the Southeast study area as a means of maintaining and improving existing transit operations.

During the past ten years, there has been a nationwide demand for competent, progress-oriented senior and middle managers in the transit industry as a whole, not only in the nine-state study area. The major thrust of the management service organizations has been to provide managerial talent to publicly owned transit systems. In 1962, National City Lines, Inc., formerly the largest operator of urban mass transit systems in the United States, organized National City Management Company (NCM) as a subsidiary to provide professional managerial and consultative services to publicly owned transit operations. In 1970, the American Transit Corporation (ATC) and the ATE Management and Service Company, Inc. followed NCM and are presently offering professional managerial services to transit operations. City Coach Lines, Inc. (CCL) was incorporated in 1959 and through subsidiaries owns and/or operates six city transit systems, two cab systems, and a leasing company. These four organizations dominate the contract management field in the transit industry as well as transit operations studied by this research. The management service organizations provide and support managerial needs of local, publicly owned systems, not only with administrative help at the local level, but through the use of nonresident technicians and specialists. Drawing on the cumulative skills of the management service organizations, the local resident managers are able to provide and sustain programs that otherwise might take several years to develop. In the area of union-management relations, the management service firms can bring immediate assistance and expertise to the bargaining table, generally matching that of the union negotiators.

All management service organizations offer similar, competitively bid services for contract to their clients, typically through a resident manager, a resident management team, or their corporate staff, depending upon the needs of the operation. There appear to be two basic management levels common to transit systems operated by management service firms. The upper level generally assumes

overall responsibility for the system and usually includes top management of the contract firm along with an existing public entity such
as the city council, county governing body, or an authority, board,
or commission specifically created to make final decisions relative
to policy, planning, and financing.

The other managerial level consists of the general manager
(frequently called the resident manager) and his staff. This operational level of management is basically responsible for the day-to-day
administration of the property. In the nine-state study area, the
general manager is always, as are key members of his staff, contracted from the management service organization. The general
manager is responsible to the upper managerial level for implementing
its plans, policies, and directives. The nonresident corporate staff
of the management service firm provides direct assistance to the
resident management team. In the four management service organizations representing publicly owned transit properties studied, a
nonresident corporate staff member is assigned the task of conducting
labor agreement negotiations. Contract interpretations may involve
nonresident corporate staff, depending upon the complexity and
monetary significance of the issue involved.

NCM offers complete management services, including consul-
tation in operational problems for both public and private systems.
In the nine-state area, NCM presently is under contract to manage
the transit systems in the following areas: Lexington, Kentucky;
Miami and West Palm Beach, Florida; Baton Rouge and Shreveport,
Louisiana. The firm offers its clients the opportunity to determine
which contracted services will be performed through the resident
managers, and which specific services will be performed exclusively
at the home office. Day-to-day operations are conducted by the local
resident manager, while the corporate staff assists the transit
authority or city officials either directly or through the local management team. The view of one official of NCM is that the management
service firm should be entirely responsible for the daily administration and operation of the system, with the local manager reporting
directly to the policy-making board.

ATC is a wholly owned subsidiary of Chromallory American
Corporation. ATC's first contract was with the transit operation in
Knoxville, Tennessee, in 1967. Currently ATC employs over 2,700
individuals, operates a fleet of 1,300 buses, and owns and/or
manages over 30 transportation properties in 15 states. ATC is
under contract to manage and/or own and operate transit systems
in the following cities (in the study area): Hattiesburg and Jackson,
Mississippi; Pensacola, Florida; Winston-Salem, North Carolina;
Gretna, Louisiana; and Montgomery, Alabama. In addition to the
range of management service ATC offers its clients the opportunity

to join a national contract for the purchase of insurance, new equipment, and parts and supplies. The management philosophy is to give primary responsibility for operations to the resident manager, while responsibility for policy planning, service levels, and financial decisions is left with the policy body, that is, the transit authority.

ATE operated as a private transit operation prior to 1968; the present company was formed in 1970 and manages some 25 properties. ATE is a management service firm with no ownership of transit properties and is presently under contract to manage the properties in the following cities in the Southeast: Birmingham, Alabama; Nashville and Chattanooga, Tennessee; Louisville and Covington-Newport, Kentucky; and Orlando, Florida. ATE is not a subsidiary of any other operating entity and its top and middle managers, for the most part, are stockholders in the corporation. ATE's method of operation is to develop a resident management team, supported by the corporate staff and utilizing local agencies and services, rather than the home office providing the services. The resident management staff is usually augmented by city-employed transit personnel to form a resident management team, with corporate staff acting as advisors.

With an operating philosophy similar to that of the other management service firms, CCL was incorporated in 1959, and through subsidiaries owns and/or operates six city transit systems in the Southeast: Greenville, South Carolina; Charlotte, Raleigh, Asheville, and Wilmington, North Carolina; and Jacksonville, Florida.

Our findings seem to indicate two major advantages for publicly owned transit properties that utilize contract management services; namely, a method for facilitating financial assistance to the public agencies, and increased operational and labor relations expertise. The advantage in facilitating the acquisition of governmental financial assistance is illustrated by the "Memphis formula." Under this arrangement, the transit system's governmental owners contract with a management service firm, which, in turn, bargains with the unions. Since the management service organization is a private firm, state law prohibiting bargaining by public employees is assumed to be inapplicable. It appears that the two most difficult issues to resolve in dealing with the communities, the issues therefore that present difficulties in negotiation strategies, are the questions of labor costs due to labor agreements and the provisions of Section 13(c) agreements. As one management respondent (a resident manager) noted, "13(c) agreements scare the authority members to death!" It appears that the untested and "feared" costs believed to be associated with the employee protection provisions of Section 13(c) present authority members with a dilemma; however, the continuation of collective bargaining, which may be in opposition to state laws affecting publicly

owned transit systems, does not seem to be of major concern to the
authority members. As one speaker at a conference on labor-management relations in the transit industry stated:

> With our firm, all of the employees are employees of
> our company. Therefore, in many respects, we are
> looking at labor negotiations from a private contract
> standpoint in that we are providing a service to the
> authority of the city and part of the cost of that service
> is going to be the cost of the labor that we are providing.[22]

One study, in reporting on the advantages of contract management
that were considered most important by public officials, notes:
"A management company brings to the operation the expertise and
know-how accumulated from years of experience, including extensive
experience in the negotiation of labor contracts and public take-overs."[23]
In discussions with the professional labor staff members for each of
the four management service firms, each indicated extensive labor
relations experience, including a wide variety of negotiation settings.
In response to on-site interviews, several union respondents (five)
commented, "Negotiations for labor agreements have substantially
improved since a professional bargainer has taken over." It is
interesting to note that this expression of confidence in the profes-
sionalism of contract management firms' labor experts extends to
international union officers. In fact, where a certain degree of
animosity could have been expected in such relationships, just the
opposite seems to be the case. Several explanations have been offered,
ranging from the fact that the experts have "infrequent contact with the
labor-management specialists" to, "they bring a comprehensiveness to
the bargaining table which allows for the 'petty' tactics of aggravation to
be eliminated." Regardless of the reason, it seems apparent that
the local labor respondents have a healthy respect for the labor
specialists and also believe that the management service companies
provide for good labor relations. Not one union respondent felt that
the management service company impeded bargaining, but rather,
bargaining had improved since the management service company had
taken over.

Our research and discussions with three management service
firms seem to confirm the prominence of the role of their labor
experts; in fact, these three firms seem to place great emphasis on
their labor experts' serving as chief negotiators at the bargaining
table. In one instance, it appears that the labor expert has direction
of overall labor-management strategy for the firm and in another
instance, the individual has responsibility for overall direction of
labor relations for his geographical territory. In commenting
on these responsibilities, a panelist representing one of these

three firms, at the abovementioned conference on labor relations in the transit industry, stated:

> I think our responsibility is an educational process in that many of the public authorities or municipalities have individuals in decision-making positions who seem to have a natural reaction to criticize anything which they know little about. The fear, particularly in the South, is that when you mention labor, the municipality officials think strike. In some instances, the municipality believes that in dealing with labor that labor is going to pound the table and then go on strike. So I think that a very big part of our program has to be the education of some of these authorities and municipalities to the fact that labor does have some basic rights and those rights are given to them in a great part in Section 13(c) of the Urban Mass Transportation Act.
>
> We also attempt to determine from an authority whether or not there are any "no-no's." Many of the municipalities object to the cost of living clause on the basis that first of all they cannot then budget because they don't know what the cost of living is going to be. Insurance is a problem, mainly because every labor contract we have has a different provision for insurance. If the municipality objects to the total insurance package, we like to find that out prior to negotiations.[24]

Another view of the responsibility in labor-management relations was expressed by Phil Ringo, the president of ATE:

> In terms of the way our company approaches labor negotiations, it is similar in many respects to what you have heard from these other three gentlemen [representing CCL, ATC, and NCM]. I would stress one thing. We believe very strongly in the prerogatives and the sanctity of the local resident manager. The resident manager negotiates the contract with the union. We do provide back-up assistance. ATE has a full-time staff member who has a labor law background and he provides assistance to the resident manager prior to the negotiations.[25]

Regardless of their particular organizational characteristics, each of the management service companies is somewhat equally confronted

with various collective bargaining influences; for example, the
budget-making process.

Budgetary Influences

Budget making is traditionally a unilateral management activity
necessary for organizational funding, planning, and control of
operational activities. Yet, collective bargaining between labor
and management officials can introduce new considerations that
might alter the traditional view of budget making. More specifically,
managerial speculations regarding the amount of the negotiated
settlement might delay the budget-making process, whereas subsequent negotiation settlements might render initial budgets obsolete.
The purpose of this section is to examine the relative influence that
budget-making procedures have on collective bargaining procedures,
that is, timing of negotiations, contract expiration and settlement
dates, and negotiation settlements.[26]

An initial concern was to determine the relationship of contract
starting and expiration dates to the agency's fiscal year. This practice was found in one-fifth of the selected study sites. Perhaps a
major reason for the rather insignificant relationship between expiration dates and fiscal year is the consensual response that there are
no legal prohibitions regarding the extension of the labor agreement
into other fiscal years; this fact is supported by the observation that
there are multiyear labor agreements at 19 out of the 20 selected
sites. Thus, it appears that neither union nor management officials
regard the fiscal year as a constraint in the collective bargaining
process.

Another potentially important aspect of the budget-making
process is the date management officials must submit their budget
for final approval by government officials (or, in the case of private
companies, other management officials). The assumption is that the
date puts pressure on both management and labor officials to either
resolve their differences or have their concerns excluded from
budgetary sanction. However, respondents at 16 of the 20 locations
indicated that the budget submission date does not generally serve
as a critical pressure point to the parties. The looseness of the
relationship between bargaining and budget making can be attributed
to several factors:

1. Financial characteristics of the particular agency: For
example, three agencies have not operated on a formal budget, with
a fourth agency operating on a day-to-day basis due to the city's
financial situation. Some of the management respondents at the privately owned firms indicated that their transit operations represent

a relatively small part of the firm's total budget, thereby facilitating some flexibility in budget making.

2. Retroactivity is permitted on contract settlements made after the contract expiration date or extension into a new fiscal year. All but one of the respondents, in fact, indicated retroactivity was permissible; however, several of the management representatives indicated that this payment was negotiable and not automatic. Additionally, a few management representatives indicated that the final approval authority could place limits on the amount of retroactivity through ceilings on deficit spending.

3. Flexibility is built into the budget-making and approval process. There appear to be several ways to alter the submitted budget to account for subsequent collective bargaining results. Management officials at five facilities indicated that they can file supplemental budgets, or seek an amended budget, to reflect changes in the collective bargaining process. A few (four) of the locations reported some form of lump sum budgeting whereby wages could be either reallocated within the relevant budget category or transfers could occur from another budget category. Finally, one management official indicated that some "padding" does occur in formulating the budget to take into account possible increased costs of the negotiated settlement.

Consequently, negotiated settlements can alter budget figures at a majority (16) of the locations. However, one agency official indicated that the changes could not exceed the submitted budget's total dollar amount, while three other agency officials indicated that this change could not exceed certain deficit spending limits established by the approval authority.

Our interview findings suggest a situation similar to that expressed by a former director of the budget for New York City:

> The director of the budget is less a part of a unified
> management team than a part of the problem, an adver-
> sary not unlike the union leaders themselves; . . .
> underlying the situation is the belief held by most
> labor negotiators that they know "what it takes" to
> effect a settlement and that, in the large complex
> public body, alleged or actual limits on available
> resources have no effect upon the ultimate settlement,
> and they are, in fact, correct. [27]

We did not formally incorporate this dimension into the interview guide; however, approximately one-fourth of the union and management respondents volunteered the related fact that the agency budget is not introduced into the negotiation sessions. The remoteness of budget making to collective bargaining appears to offer an almost unsolvable dilemma. On one hand, if the budget were a controlling factor in contract negotiations, then unilateral managerial decision making would render collective bargaining a farce. However, if collective bargaining is entirely removed from budgetary constraints, then fiscal responsibilities are abated at taxpayer expense.[28]

Length of Negotiations

The average reported length of negotiations was 59 days; however, the usefulness of this figure is limited as the responses were extremely varied, ranging from 3 to 204 days; and respondents indicating the longer negotiation periods also revealed that substantial time periods elapsed between negotiation meetings. More significant is labor's and management's satisfaction with the length of negotiations. On the surface it would appear that negotiations were not long enough as formal negotiations extended beyond the contract expiration date in over half (11) of these cases. Yet, the vast majority (36) of the respondents believed the negotiation period benefited labor and management equally; the delays being due to either established custom at the facility, or unforeseen scheduling problems with union and management representatives, for example, prior commitments, death of one union leader, flu epidemic.

However, one management representative indicated that the extension of negotiations beyond the expiration date benefited the union as the approving authority became concerned about the possibility of a strike. Two other management representatives indicated longer negotiations translated into more expense for management, such as time spent by management participants and consultant fees, thereby placing some pressure on management to resolve their differences with the union. One union official indicated that the negotiation period was shortened because of the union's inability to comply with legal notification requirements; therefore, the union had to play "catch-up" in the abbreviated negotiation period. It must be emphasized again, however, that representatives at most facilities believe that the length of negotiations is not a particularly crucial influence on bargaining behavior and outcome.

Attitudes and Role of the Government

Many observers of public employee bargaining have contended that public employee unions, unlike their private sector counterparts, feel it beneficial to involve government officials in the collective bargaining process:

> Since public employer-employee agreements or contracts
> are ultimately consummated in the political decision
> making process and not at the bargaining table, the
> incentive for an employee organization to influence
> successfully that process is considerable. Consider
> the impact that a well-organized public employee union
> can exert on a local government election (usually
> characterized by a relatively small voter turnout) and
> subsequent influence on the politically oriented decision
> making process. [29]

Accepting this premise, related union organizations offer political officials, in exchange for special consideration at the bargaining table, two commodities: labor peace; and their own electoral support in the form of endorsements, campaign workers and money, and membership votes. [30] One union particularly known for its encouragement of political support in the collective bargaining process is the TWU Local 100, New York City; the international president of the TWU mirrors the local union's philosophy: "We're interested in politics because a lot of the things that we bargain for involve legislation and the political situation." [31]

On the other hand, some academicians and practitioners suggest a union's political activities could be ineffective and not worth the effort. For example, the president of the American Federation of State, County, and Municipal Employees, when asked about the union's political power, commented:

> First of all, if we're so powerful, why does every mayor
> and governor try to make his political reputation by
> fighting our union? If you sat in this office all day, you'd
> get the impression that every public official in the
> United States thinks he can win his epaulets by declaring
> war on our members. It's true that we do help elect
> public officials. So does the entire labor movement,
> but labor represents only 25 percent of the work
> force . . . against probably 10,000 corporations that
> do the same thing. [32]

We indirectly attempted to assess the relationship between the political and collective bargaining processes by asking union and management officials, "Would involvement of local, state, and federal officials assist or deter collective bargaining?" A somewhat rare consensus

of management and union respondents indicated that local government
officials should remain outside the collective bargaining process.
A major reason given by management and union officials is the relative unfamiliarity that government officials have regarding the complex nature of mass transit operations and subsequent work rules;
at best, time would be wasted educating these individuals on these
complexities; at worst, government officials would tend to make
hasty decisions without realizing their implications.

Some union and management officials also expressed concern
over the political nature of city government.[33] For example, one
union official suggested that politicians try to be "buddy-buddy" with
everyone, while one management official indicated he heard a government official (not affiliated with the cities under investigation) comment, "Well, I hope you give to these drivers who have struggled
all these years." Three other managers from publicly owned agencies
believed that government officials might be overly lenient with the
affected employees; however, an opposite conclusion was reached by
union officials working at two private agencies and one public agency;
they felt the service "owned" the officials; therefore, no better settlement would be gained by their involvement. Two union officials commented that some advantages could be gained by the inclusion of governmental officials in bargaining; more specifically they might uncover
"salary discrimination" against mass transit workers when compared to
other public employees, and be more likely to agree with a settlement
they helped to negotiate. This latter reason was qualified by a
management representative who felt that having an individual with
ratification power in the contract negotiations would not allow management enough latitude in discussing and resolving union demands.

Similar comments were given against the inclusion of state and
government officials in collective bargaining, with a frequently cited
additional concern: that these individuals are too emotionally and
geographically remote to benefit collective bargaining. One union
leader suggested that involvement by "labor relations professionals"
(not political appointees) might alleviate his concern; additionally,
one-fourth of the union and management respondents commented
that the Federal Mediation and Conciliation Service was a favorable
exception to their generalizations. Finally, management and union
officials might be reluctant to involve federal government officials
in the collective bargaining process because they perceive various
government officials as being either relatively unconcerned or
against this activity.

The respondents' preference for excluding government officials
from the collective bargaining process is not necessarily synonymous
with their perception of the attitudes of governmental agencies toward
collective bargaining. Subsequent investigation of these perceived

TABLE 2.3

Attitudes of Various Groups of Individuals toward Collective Bargaining, As Perceived by Unions and Management

Group	General Acceptance of the Collective Bargaining Process	Conflicting Attitudes over the Desirability of Collective Bargaining with Limited Expectations	Predominantly Unfavorable Attitudes toward Collective Bargaining	No Real Concern Either Way Regarding Collective Bargaining
U.S. Department of Labor				
Union respondents	13	1	1	5
Management respondents	15	0	0	5
Operating management officials at facility				
Union respondents	12	5	3	0
Management respondents	18	0	1	1
State governmental agencies				
Union respondents	4	2	8	6
Management respondents	3	5	3	9
Federal Department of Transportation				
Union respondents	6	1	1	12
Management respondents	14	0	0	6
Local government officials				
Union respondents	4	2	13	1
Management respondents	5	8	7	0
Union rank-and-file members				
Union respondents	19	1	0	0
Management respondents	17	2	1	0
The local community				
Union respondents	7	10	2	1
Management respondents	8	6	4	2

Source: Interview responses gathered in nine-state study area by the authors.

attitudes resulted in the information provided in Table 2.3. The table suggests that labor and management officials have favorable attitudes regarding collective bargaining; however, the only outside element widely perceived to have a general acceptance of collective bargaining is the Department of Labor. It is interesting to note that the greatest divergence between union and management respondents concerns the Federal Department of Transportation. One possible explanation for the dominant union response of "no real concern" by the Department of Transportation is the lack of policies and/or communication related to collective bargaining. Perhaps the relatively uncertain responses directed toward state government agencies are due to the multifaceted nature of these agencies. Management and union respondents indicate the two groups having the least acceptance of collective bargaining are local governmental officials and the local community. These responses help to explain the tactical reluctance that both union and management officials have in enlisting their collective bargaining participation and support for the local and its officials.

> Before I paint too rosy a picture of the unions' under-
> standing of the realities of public ownership and operation
> in the 1970's, we are aware that there is a serious
> threat to the continuation of labor/management collective
> bargaining in the mass transit industry today from
> political intervention. Such outside interference, most
> of which is politically motivated, clogs the bargaining
> process and even prevents meaningful negotiations by
> the parties themselves to reach settlements without inter-
> ruption of service or costly interest arbitrations. . . .
> We shall resist any and all threats from third parties
> desiring to undercut union wages, hours, and working
> conditions in our industry, and especially any such efforts
> to place limitations on the process of collective bargaining
> in transit.[34]

Legal Constraints

Our study focused on two potential general legislative constraints on labor relations in the mass transit industry; namely, appropriate state legislation, and extension of the Fair Labor Standards Act to include mass transit employees. At least one observer of mass transit labor relations has suggested the potential importance of the jurisdictional transition to public employee bargaining laws.[35] Labor relations activities at most mass transit locations appear to be unaffected by applicable state legislation. More specifically, only one of the nine states (Florida) has legislation mandating or regulating labor relations activities. Additionally, many of the agencies affected by public bargaining legislation are covered by the Memphis formula (described previously). Twelve of the 20 agencies visited were privately owned and/or operated by management service companies; hence, union and management officials at these agencies did not regard public employee bargaining laws as either potentially or actually affecting their operations.

However, six respondents in states with public employee bargaining laws potentially affecting their operations made two general suggestions for improvement: provide binding arbitration for negotiation impasses to complement the no-strike provision; and make collective bargaining sessions closed rather than open to the public. In states with no public employee bargaining laws, six management officials indicated that strikes should be prohibited; however, two of the management officials and one union official indicated that arbitration of negotiation impasses should be presented as a complement to the no-strike provision. The sentiment behind compulsory arbitration is that unions are at an unfair disadvantage when they are not allowed to strike and have no other institutionalized means of impasse resolution. Four union respondents indicated a desire for one or more of the following provisions in states without collective bargaining legislation: formalized recognition of unions including representation election procedures; mandatory dues checkoff procedure; requirements for good-faith bargaining on the part of union and management representatives; and repeal of the right-to-work provision, that is, installation of contractual provision requiring union membership as a condition of employment.

A somewhat recent and pertinent legal development is the extension of the Fair Labor Standards Act to mass transit employees. Perhaps the most significant change embodied in the 1974 Fair Labor Standards Amendments (Section 13b) pertains to the phase-out of the previously unlimited exemption for mass transit employees by requiring public and private agencies (representing approximately 92,000 employees)[36] to pay overtime for hours worked after 48 hours (effective May 1, 1974); 44 hours (effective May 1, 1975); and 40 hours (effective May 1, 1976). Exemptions still apply in the case of hours voluntarily spent in irregularly scheduled charter activities (Section 7n of the act). Crucial to implementation of these provisions is an understanding of what constitutes "off duty" for mass transit personnel. One author has cited the following Department of Labor provisions as appropriate:

(a) General periods during which an employee is completely relieved from duty and which are long enough

to enable him to use the time effectively for his own purposes are not hours worked. He is not completely relieved
from duty and cannot use the time effectively for his own
purposes unless he is definitely told in advance that he
may leave the job and that he will not have to commence
work until a definitely specified hour has arrived. Whether
the time is long enough to enable him to use the time
effectively for his own purposes depends upon all of the
facts and circumstances of the case.[37]

All of the union respondents indicated their pleasure over the
passage of the 1974 amendments primarily because mass transit
employees were previously working too long at the possible expense
of passenger safety; and implementation of the act will probably result
in additional employment at the agency. Five union officials believed
that the amendments should be implemented; however, they also con-
ceded an eventual loss of pay as new schedules or additional employees
will diminish total hours worked by each employee. One of these union
officials indicated that this fact makes it difficult to placate some of
his members who don't care how many hours they work as long as they
receive a larger paycheck.

The majority (11) of the management representatives expressed
serious concern over the implementation of the 1974 amendments.
An initial concern arises over the timing of the act—it instituted
alterations in multiyear labor agreements negotiated by the local
management and union officials. Thus, some (7) management officials
contend that they negotiated the labor agreement with a realistic pic-
ture of costs, and that the additional costs imposed by the amendments
will adversely affect operations expenditures. Alternatives suggested
by some of these respondents either would have placed the act in
effect after the local agency's bargaining agreement expired, or had
a provision in the amendment stating "regular rate of pay at the
(labor) contract rate of pay."

In stipulating "regular rate of pay" the recent Fair Labor
Standards Amendments have generated confusion among many management officials. More specifically, one respondent believes approximately one-half of the mass transit officials (nationwide), regarding
regular rate of pay as equaling the contract rate of pay, would calcu-
late daily wages in a manner similar to that stipulated in calculation
A in Table 2.4; however, other management officials believe regular
rate of pay should be calculated in a different manner (calculation B
in the table). As of this writing the interpretive confusion is not yet
resolved; however, the American Public Transit Association is
advising its members to equate regular rate of pay with the wage
specified in their labor agreement pending a final decision by the
Department of Labor.[38]

TABLE 2.4

Hypothetical Wage Calculations before and after 1974
Fair Labor Standards Amendments

A. Before Fair Labor Standards Amendments
Wage rate as specified in the labor agreement: $4.41 an hour.
Overtime = 1.5 x $4.41, or $6.61 an hour.

1. 8 hours' payment	$35.28
2. Tripper of 1.5 hours (paid for 2 hours at overtime rate)	13.22
3. Charter run of 1 hour (paid for 2 hours at overtime rate)	13.22
4. Accident report: 15 minutes paid for 45 minutes straight time	3.31
Total daily payment	$65.03

B. One interpretation of Fair Labor Standards Amendments rate
calculation

$$\text{Regular rate of pay} = \frac{\$65.03}{10.75 \text{ hours}}, \text{ or } \$6.05 \text{ an hour.}$$

Overtime rate = 1.5 hours x $6.05 = $9.08 an hour.
Pay Item A1 at $6.05 an hour
Pay Items A2 = 4 at 1.5 hours x $6.05, or $9.08 an hour

Source: Compiled by the authors.

Many management respondents indicated that the potential
increased costs can be mitigated by either hiring additional employees
or scheduling interval runs to straight runs; the former alternative
probably would increase costs to a greater extent, and the latter alternative possibly affect public preferences or operations scheduling.
Two additional management officials expressed concern over the
fact that employees would be receiving lower weekly wages, a situation
which, in turn, affects pensions as well as increases pressure for
higher wages at the bargaining table. Finally, a few management
officials indicated that the provisions will be difficult, if not impossible,
to implement unless "off duty" is further defined by governmental
agencies or the courts. While three management officials expressed
positive attitudes over the amendments, a general conclusion is that
most management officials expressed some opposition to these
provisions either directly or indirectly, when other questions were
asked about the desired degree of government involvement in the
collective bargaining process.

Current Bargaining Behavior

An initial dimension of current bargaining behavior is the composition of the management and union negotiating teams and the bargaining tactics used by each. Whereas the number of union members on the bargaining team averages five for the investigated properties, there appears to be no figure common to most properties (the range is from two to 13 union members on the bargaining team). However, most (19 out of 21) of the union bargaining teams include at least one international representative of the union whose function in the vast majority of these situations (16) is to serve as chief spokesman in the formal hearings. The use of the international representative has increased over the years;[39] however, it should be strongly emphasized that this somewhat centralized element does not abnegate the local membership's interest in collective bargaining.

The mass transit unions investigated in our study appear to represent "a body politic in which authority flows from the bottom up."[40] As noted in another study:

> The organizational structure of the labor union is referred to as democratic, because its chief officers are elected either by the general membership of the union or by their delegates at national union conventions, rather than appointed by their predecessors or their fellow union officials. Top union officers are, therefore, responsible and accountable to the membership and, in the last analysis, must satisfy them if they are to stay in office. The final authority, therefore, rests in the hands of the members, not the officers.[41]

All of the union respondents indicated that the membership has direct input in the formulation and/or approval of negotiation proposals, which often (11 cases) involves a threefold procedure: members initiate proposals in a union meeting; the union negotiation committee combines these proposals with input from the international representative because of his familiarity with national bargaining issues; and the membership votes on proposals before they are presented to management.

The management bargaining team typically has fewer representatives, averaging four members, with a narrower manpower range (from two to five members). In a vast majority (16) of the properties studied, the resident manager is a member of the formal negotiation team. However, in 11 of the 12 management service properties visited, the role of chief spokesman in contract negotiations applies to a nonresident management service representative. Many (9) of the properties also include the director or superintendent of operations on the negotiating team, while a few (3) companies include the maintenance superintendent. It should be mentioned, however, that all of the properties reserve the option to call in operations and maintenance personnel if a related, complex issue is being discussed in negotiations.

All respondents were asked how the composition of the bargaining team affects negotiations; however, no clear pattern for improvement emerged. For example, four of the management respondents believed the union's negotiating team was too large, which results in some confusion and waste of time. On the other hand, management officials at five properties were satisfied with large union negotiating committees for one of two reasons: a strong representative team can sell the package it has negotiated to the membership, or the interchange and arguments generated by a large number of union participants can "tip their hand" to management. One union member favored the use of a large negotiating team as an "educational device" for the union's younger, inexperienced officers. Finally, no management respondents had any objections to the role of the international representative; in fact, some believed this individual performed valuable service with his expert knowledge of labor problems as well as his ability to keep the members in line. The only problem pertained to rescheduling of some meetings due to the international representative's busy schedule.

TABLE 2.5

Tactical Considerations in Collective Bargaining

Degree to Which Management and Unions Use Certain Tactics in a Typical Contract Negotiation	Management [a]		Union [b]	
Lobbying with councilmen and/or other local government officials	1.9	2.3	2.0	1.1
Enlisting the support of the press	1.5	1.9	1.7	1.4
Enlisting public opinion	1.5	1.4	1.8	1.6
Lobbying with legislators and/or other state government officials	1.1	1.6	1.3	1.3

[a] Mean responses of 20 management officials.
[b] Mean responses of 20 union officials.

Note: Figures represent mean response based on a five-point scale where 1 = never, 2 = seldom, 3 = sometimes, 4 = frequently, and 5 = always.

Source: Interview responses gathered in nine-state area by the authors.

To provide insight into the use of bargaining tactics, the union and management respondents were asked to describe the degree to which certain tactics were used in typical contract negotiations. The results of this question are reported in Table 2.5.

A review of Table 2.5 reveals that while each group of respondents tends to attribute greater use of each tactic to the other group, there is general agreement regarding the extent to which each tactic is used by both groups. A generalization can be made: that neither the union nor management officials employ these tactics on a very frequent basis. To the extent that lobbying with local government was used, many respondents qualified this tactic to mean, "apprising governmental officials of the situation" instead of "pressure tactics."[42] Presumably, the reluctance to engage in lobbying reflects the aforementioned perceived attitude that government officials are not responsive to the labor relations aspects of mass transit. The even lower responses for the remaining two categories of tactics are understandable in terms of perceived neutral-to-antiunion attitudes of the local community and mass media. The respondents' attitudes are apparently well founded, as empirical studies have indicated that there is highly critical public opinion regarding the actions of unions and their leaders, and "to the public as a whole, communications media tend to project an unfavorable image of organized labor."[43]

The relative aversion to employing these tactics is further illustrated by respondents' assessment of the tactics' effectiveness when they were employed at the location. A number of union and management officials (two and eight, respectively) maintained that lobbying, while laying groundwork for receptive atmosphere, either is not effective or its effectiveness cannot be measured. However, five union officials and one management official believed that management's lobbying efforts are "very effective in negotiations." With a few scattered exceptions, the surveyed respondents indicated that the effects of the remaining tactics, when employed, have been negligible. Hence, tactical considerations in negotiations do not typically extend beyond the primary bargaining agents in their attempt to reach a joint settlement of the issues.

Jointly developed ground rules can affect collective bargaining negotiations in terms of structuring the behavior and priorities of the participants. Union and management respondents at five locations indicated that there are no initial jointly agreed-upon ground rules governing the contract negotiation procedure. The most commonly cited ground rule at 13 locations pertains to dealings with the press— either the press would not be contacted until negotiations broke down or management and union officials would cooperate in issuing a joint press release. Apparently many union and management respondents have not had good experience with the press, a situation vividly

illustrated in the 1970-71 negotiations between the City of New York
and the uniformed forces:

> All of this should have been brought to the bargaining
> table. . . . Collective bargaining is an educational
> process. It also allows you to let off steam. But, almost
> nothing was done at the table; instead both sides took
> to television, advertising, and the loud and dramatic
> press releases.
> Mayor John Lindsay made his first major offer not
> at the table but over television. It was an offer of "a cost
> of living" increase; but nobody knew what he was talking
> about: past cost of living, future cost of living, Consumer
> Price Index, budget director's price index? All of this
> should have been brought to the table, fought over, and
> resolved. Instead he sharpened the situation, created
> greater animosity, and literally destroyed any possibility
> of decent collective bargaining. . . .
> The amateurs of the media keep insisting that collec-
> tive bargaining ought to be open to the public eye. They
> invoke the citizen's tax burden as the major reason for this.
> Experts such as Theodore Kheel and Arvid Anderson know
> the best way to insure trouble is to bring collective bar-
> gaining into the public arena. Instead of labor and manage-
> ment representatives talking to each other, they will talk
> to the public and to their principals only. Invariably,
> the wrong things will be said.
> Management will talk of the "irresponsibly high
> demands" of the workers, and about how services will
> have to be cut back or taxes raised. Understandably the
> media will respond in a sympathetic way. The only
> problem is that the media are not responsible for the
> operation of government.
> The labor leader now has to talk tough. The strike
> threat becomes almost obligatory, because he is now put
> in an impossible squeeze. When the union leader goes
> public he first must talk to the people he represents, and
> retain their confidence. Understandably, the public responds
> not to the facts of the situation but to the militant rhetoric.
> Everybody loses in the process, a process that has little
> or nothing to do with collective bargaining.[44]

Respondents at two locations indicated that the general public is not
to be included in negotiations, while management and union officials
at two other locations agreed not to inform their respective constituents

of the progress of negotiations until concrete agreement is nearly
reached. Most of the respondents gave the general impressions that
they have found an informal and flexible approach to be most successful, for example, scheduling meetings to accommodate the other
demands of union and management officials; and that a comprehensive
set of formalized ground rules might unduly restrict the parties from
reaching a joint agreement.

A final dimension of collective bargaining behavior refers to
practitioner suggestions to improve the collective bargaining process.
Fifteen of the 20 management respondents offered specific suggestions
to improve collective bargaining. Nine of these suggestions pertain
to union efforts in negotiation; more specifically, reducing the size
of the union's bargaining team, and clarifying and/or eliminating
some of the original proposals before collective bargaining commences.
Some management respondents felt this latter problem is due to the
union leaders' desire to please all union members:

> Union has to bring up each member's problem indivi-
> dually. Many of the problems are contradictory which
> takes up time and resolves nothing. The union ought
> to get an overall picture and resolve any contradictions
> before presenting their proposals.

Management representatives at six facilities also believed that arguments regarding wages should be tied to productivity and/or ability
to pay instead of cost of living. Three respondents, while admitting
the cost-of-living basis affords some advantages to the employees,
also indicated that the guarantee of quarterly cost-of-living payments
minimizes the "up-front" offer, which, in turn, makes the contract
difficult for the union to sell to the membership. It should be mentioned that the respondents, when asked about precise productivity
and ability-to-pay measures, admitted this would be a difficult concept to define in a manner equitable to both parties.

Eleven of the 19 union respondents offered specific suggestions
by which collective bargaining could be improved. The major sugges-
tion from five union respondents pertained to mitigating some unfavorable tactics employed by management; more specifically, three
respondents maintained that management should try resolving issues
in a more direct and prompt manner as well as not changing their
mind after tentative agreement has been reached by both parties.
One union official believed that management should resolve the economic issues first and that the noneconomic issues would then fall in line,
while two other officials commented that binding arbitration is essential in negotiation impasses when the no-strike clause is in effect.
The final three suggestions pertained to keeping the members better

informed during negotiations as well as reducing the number of union participants on the negotiating team.

NOTES

1. Harold W. Davey, Contemporary Collective Bargaining, 3d ed. (Englewood Cliffs, N.J.: Prentice-Hall, 1972), p. 3.

2. Jack Barbash, "Rationalization in the American Union," in Essays in Industrial Relations Theory, ed. Gerald G. Somers, (Ames: Iowa State University Press, 1969), p. 147.

3. Neil W. Chamberlain and James W. Kuhn, Collective Bargaining, 2d ed. (New York: McGraw-Hill, 1965), pp. 162-90.

4. Myron L. Joseph, "Approaches to Collective Bargaining in Industrial Relations Theory," in Essays, ed. Somers, pp. 59-60.

5. Frederick Meyers, "Organization and Collective Bargaining in the Local Mass Transportation Industry in the Southeast," Southern Economic Journal 15 (April 1949): 429-30.

6. Derek C. Bok and John T. Dunlop, Labor and the American Community (New York: Simon and Schuster, 1970), p. 225.

7. This proportion is almost identical to that found in a nationwide survey of mass transit properties. See Darold T. Barnum, "From Private to Public: Labor Relations in Urban Transit," Industrial and Labor Relations Review 25 (October 1971): 97.

8. Davey, Bargaining, p. 32

9. This situation is not limited to mass transit operations. For example, see Arvid Anderson, "The Structure of Public Sector Bargaining," in Public Workers and Public Unions, ed. Sam Zagoria (Englewood Cliffs, N.J.: Prentice Hall, 1972), p. 39.

10. Barnum, "From Private to Public," p. 99.

11. Meyers, "Organization," p. 425.

12. Barnum, "From Private to Public," p. 99.

13. For example, see A. Bilik, "Close the Gap: NLRB and Public Employees," Ohio State Law Journal 31 (Summer 1970): 456-89.

14. For a concise statement of these potential differences, see Jay F. Atwood, "Collective Bargaining's Challenge: Five Imperatives for Public Managers," Public Personnel Management 5 (January-February 1976): 24-32.

15. Daniel S. Hamermesh, "The Effect of Government Ownership on Wages," in Labor in the Public and Nonprofit Sectors, ed. Daniel S. Hamermesh (Princeton: Princeton University Press, 1975), pp. 227-38. For a similar study having opposite conclusions, see Darold T. Barnum, "Collective Bargaining and Manpower in Urban Transit Systems" (Ph.D. diss., University of Pennsylvania, 1972), pp. 227 and 301.

16. Louis J. Gambaccini, "A Common Purpose: Labor and Management in the Future of Public Transportation" (Speech delivered at the Conference on Unions, Management Rights, and the Public Interest in Mass Transit [jointly sponsored by the Program of University Research of the U.S. Department of Transportation and the University of North Florida] ,Jacksonville, March 22, 1976).

17. D. V. Maroney, Jr., "Collective Bargaining in Mass Transit" (Speech delivered at the Conference on Unions, Management Rights, and the Public Interest in Mass Transit, Jacksonville, March 22, 1976).

18. Remarks made by a union panelist at the Conference on Unions, Management Rights, and the Public Interest in Mass Transit, Jacksonville, March 23, 1976.

19. Neil W. Chamberlain, "Public vs. Private Sector Bargaining," in Collective Bargaining in Government: Readings and Cases, ed. J. Joseph Lowenberg and Michael H. Moskow (Englewood Cliffs, N.J.: Prentice-Hall, 1972), pp. 11-16. See also William H. Holley, Jr., "Unique Complexities of Public Sector Labor Relations," Personnel Journal 55 (February 1976): 73.

20. Louis V. Imundo, "Some Comparisons Between Public Sector and Private Sector Bargaining," Labor Law Journal 24 (December 1973): 812.

21. Ibid., p. 813. See also Michael H. Moskow, J. Joseph Lowenberg, Edward Clifford Koziara, eds., Collective Bargaining in Public Employment (New York: Random House, 1970), pp. 16 and 211.

22. Remarks of Joe Poquette, president of CCL, serving as a member of the Management Service Panel, at the Conference on Unions, Management Rights, and the Public Interest in Mass Transit, Jacksonville, March 23, 1976.

23. M. M. Bakr, D. Robey, and T. S. Miller, "Role and Effectiveness of Contract Management in the Transit Industry," Report prepared for the Urban Mass Transportation Administration, U.S. Department of Transportation (Milwaukee: Marquette University, 1974), p. 37.

24. Remarks of M. R. Biddle, regional vice president of ATC, serving as a member of the Management Service Panel, at the Conference on Unions, Management Rights, and the Public Interest in Mass Transit, Jacksonville, March 23, 1976.

25. Remarks of Phil Ringo, serving as a member of the Management Service Panel at the Conference on Unions, Management Rights, and the Public Interest in Mass Transit, Jacksonville, March 22, 1976.

26. These analytical variables were suggested by two related articles: Milton Derber, Ken Jennings, Ian McAndrew, and Martin Wagner, "Bargaining and Budget Making in Illinois Public Institutions,"

Industrial and Labor Relations Review 27 (October 1973): 49-62; Kenneth O. Warner, "Financial Implications of Employee Bargaining in the Public Service," Municipal Finance 40 (August 1967): 34-39.

27. Frederick O'R. Hayes, "Collective Bargaining and the Budget Director," in Public Workers, ed. Zagoria, p. 91.

28. This dilemma was further amplified at our Conference on Unions, Management Rights, and the Public Interest in Mass Transit. Some managers indicated that fiscal realities place the budget in a crucial collective bargaining role. However, they also acknowledged that the budget cannot be controlling as it is subject to alteration, which, in turn, can take place after union wage demands are made.

29. Atwood, "Collective Bargaining," p. 25.

30. R. D. Horton, Municipal Labor Relations in New York City: Lessons of the Lindsay-Wagner Years (New York: Praeger, 1973), p. 134.

31. Michael Marmo, "Public Employee Unions—The Political Imperative," Journal of Collective Negotiations in the Public Sector 4 (1973): 370-71.

32. Does This Man Have the U.S. By the Throat?" Skeptic, (May-June 1976) p. 54.

33. For a vivid example of political considerations affecting collective bargaining, see A. H. Raskin, "Politics Up-Ends the Bargaining Table," in Public Workers, ed. Zagoria, pp. 122-46; and A. H. Raskin, "Mayor and Governor: Knee-Deep in Trouble," in Collective Negotiation for Public and Professional Employees, ed. Robert T. Woodworth and Richard B. Peterson (Glenview, Ill.: Scott, Foresman, 1969), pp. 288-92.

34. Maroney, "Collective Bargaining."

35. Barnum, "From Private to Public," p. 110.

36. Gerald M. Feder, "Highlights of the New Wage and Hour Law," Bureau of National Affairs, Collective Bargaining Negotiations and Contracts, Special Supplement (Washington, D.C., April 25, 1974), p. 19.

37. Ibid.

38. APTA (American Public Transit Association) Bulletin, April 30, 1976, p. 1.

39. Barnum, "From Private to Public," p. 101; Meyers, "Organization," p. 430. Our findings parallel those in Barnum, "Collective Bargaining," p. 76: "Currently, an international representative is present at about 90 percent of all contract negotiations, and in most cases acts as the chief negotiator."

40. Davey, Bargaining, p. 6.

41. Marten Estey, The Unions: Structure, Development and Management, 2d ed. (New York: Harcourt, Brace & World, 1976), p. 51.

42. Our findings regarding the ineffectiveness of lobbying parallel related national observations for the industry; Bok and Dunlop, Labor, p. 318. For a thorough discussion of the lobbying tactics, see Moskow, Lowenberg, and Koziara, eds., Collective Bargaining, pp. 265-68.

43. Bok and Dunlop, Labor, p. 36. See also, Paul Hartman, "Industrial Relations in the News Media," Industrial Relations Journal 6 (Winter 1975-1976): 4-18.

44. Victor Gotbaum, "Collective Bargaining and the Union Leader," in Public Workers, ed. Zagoria, pp. 83-84.

3

Collective bargaining is often concerned with preserving the respective strengths and functions of the union and management organizations. Some practitioners contend that the issues are inversely related—greater union security diminishes management prerogatives. While the issues may be related, each is substantively different and does not necessarily affect the other.

DIMENSIONS OF UNION SECURITY

The institutional issue of union security consists of two broad elements: the attraction and retention of union members; and explicit managerial support given to the union and its leaders. A primary reason the union desires union security provisions in the labor agreement is the limited statutory protection assigned to the union. In the private sector, an incumbent union is protected from a subsequent election involving a rival union for a mere one-year period after its initial recognition.[1] Similar public sector protection is found in only one of the nine southeastern states with the remainder of the states silent on this issue. Consequently, a union, after winning an employee representation election, has little or no protection from rival unions or a decertification election. A second reason behind union security is that full employee membership in the union strengthens the union's tactical and financial positions in its dealings with management representatives. Without union security, an antiunion employer could either replace prounion employees with more docile or antiunion employees, or play an antiunion faction against a prounion faction.[2] Finally these provisions are sought for philosophical reasons. Many union leaders have charged critics of union security with being

inconsistent; the critics believe compulsory union membership vio-
lates the freedom of the individual workers, while at the same time
advocating collective bargaining, which gives the union the power
to negotiate working conditions for all employees. Contract language
dealing with union security issues can be introduced into the labor
agreement by means of several provisions. An analysis of the labor
agreements in our study area reveals the union security provisions
shown in Table 3.1.

TABLE 3.1

Union Recognition and Security Provisions

Contractual Category and Resolution	Number of Agreements with Resolution
Bargaining unit	
No reference	1
Members only	2
All employees in unit	32
Those employees authorizing union to represent them	2
Exclusivity	
No reference	3
Employee explicitly retains right to self-representation	1
Union explicitly represents members only	1
Union is "exclusive" representative	30
Union is designated formal representative	2
Union security—members	
No reference	11
Agency shop	1
Union shop	7
Quasi-union shop	7
Provision for union shop if federal and/or state laws change	3
Open shop	8

Source: Analysis of labor agreements in nine-state study area
compiled by the authors.

The preponderance of the responses to the first two items in Table 3.1 suggests the unions exclusively represent all employees in the bargaining unit. However, three out of the five public sector labor agreements, as opposed to 3 percent of the private sector and management service labor agreements, limit the bargaining unit to union members only, or to those employees authorizing union representation. Perhaps this response is attributed to the public sector's legacies of sovereignty and the civil service system. A somewhat common union security clause found in the labor agreement analysis is the quasi-union shop. This provision is found in states with right-to-work laws and initially indicates union membership is a condition of employment. However, a disclaimer is also placed in the labor agreement indicating the provision is null and void if it conflicts with state or federal law. The apparent purpose of this provision is to encourage new employees to become members of the union even though there is no legal obligation to do so. While less than 19 percent of the labor agreements have explicit union shop

TABLE 3.2

Managerial Actions Affecting Union Security

Contractual Category and Resolution	Number of Agreements with Resolution
Discrimination	
No reference	21
Clause prohibits discrimination and/or other acts that would discourage union membership	16
Management aid to other unions	
No reference	37
Prohibited	0
Contracting-out work	
No reference	28
Contracting out prohibited or restricted	7
Unilateral management right	2
Supervisor performing bargaining unit work	
No reference	26
Prohibited or restricted	11

Source: Analysis of labor agreements in nine-state study area compiled by the authors.

provisions, the proportion of employees who are union members appears quite high. For example, the average proportion of employees who are union members at our 20 interview sites is 92 percent. This high proportion is probably attributable to the established nature of union-management relationships found in the southeastern mass transit properties.

While the vast majority of investigated mass transit unions have attracted and retained most of the bargaining unit employees, there are nonetheless potential managerial actions that can reduce or eliminate the number of union members. For example, see Table 3.2 for managerial actions affecting union security.

The large number of agreements with "no reference" to the first two issues in Table 3.2 could carry little significance. Possibly, the subject matter of these issues is so remote from practitioner experience that there has been little need for subsequent formalization into the labor agreement. However, a "no-reference" response to "contracting out" and to "supervisor performing bargaining unit work" can mean a potential problem for the union in that resultant transfer of work could reduce the potential, if not actual, number of union members. A cross-item analysis of these variables, in Table 3.3,

TABLE 3.3

Contracting Out and Supervisory Performance
of Bargaining Unit Work, by Number of
Employees in Organization
(number of agreements with provision)

Contractual Provision	100 Employees or Less		More than 100 Employees	
	No Reference	Restricted or Prohibited	No Reference	Restricted or Prohibited
Contracting out	18	0	10	6
Supervisor performing bargaining unit work	15	3	9	7

Source: Analysis of labor agreements in nine-state study area compiled by the authors.

with number of employees in the mass transit organization reveals some interesting differences. It appears that those agencies with more employees are more vulnerable and/or concerned about potential erosion of bargaining unit jobs, and reflect this attitude in

TABLE 3.4

Managerial Support of Union Officers and Activities
(number of agreements with provision)

Contractual Provision	No Reference	Provided without Management Restrictions (or contract silent on restrictions)	Provided with Restrictions	Prohibited
Paid time off for stewards—grievances	31	2	2	2
Paid time off for union officials—negotiations or meetings	28	0	5	4
Superseniority—stewards	36	1	0	0
Superseniority—other officers	36	1	0	0
Use of bulletin boards	16	14	7	0
Premises provided on the property for union meetings	37	0	0	0
Access to premises for international representatives	34	2	1	0
Dues checkoff provision	3	0	33	1

Source: Analysis of labor agreements in nine-state study area compiled by the authors.

appropriate labor agreement provisions. However, caution should be taken in interpreting these findings, as "no reference" does not mean these issues are void of restrictions. It should also be noted that none of the interviewed union representatives expressed reservations or problems with these provisions.

Finally, there are several labor agreement provisions that can support union leaders and administration of union activities, as shown in Table 3.4. A review of this table suggests that many accommodative aspects of the union-management relationship are not formalized in the labor agreement. However, it must again be remembered that "no reference" does not equal prohibition; none of the interviewed union representatives expressed any dissatisfaction over the privileges and perquisites cited in the table. The notable exception to this contractual ambiguity is "dues checkoff," a provision where dues are automatically taken out of the employee's paycheck and sent to the union. This provision is essential to the union as it insures continuous, dependable revenues with a minimum of membership objections. The overwhelming majority of the labor agreements reflect this dimension of union security.

MANAGEMENT RIGHTS: SCOPE AND LIMITATIONS

The issue of management rights in a unionized setting can be placed into proper perspective with the following questions: "How is the management of labor in American industry affected by trade unions and collective bargaining?"[3] and "To what extent can management unilaterally decide where people work and what they are going to do?"[4] This is perhaps the most controversial issue in the labor-management relationship; managerial officials' defense of their prerogatives has historically been steeped in intense emotion. Currently, many management officials maintain that their "property rights" enable them to unilaterally determine the disposition of issues not specifically covered by the labor agreement. However, in the case of private sector establishments, one authority noted:

> As for inherent property rights, the contention is that management has been authorized by the stockholders to manage the enterprise, including the right to direct employee activity. This is not the case. Management's legal rights are restricted to deciding how the property or assets of the firm will be utilized. These rights do not include the employee. There is no question that management can organize, arrange and direct the machinery, materials, and money of the enterprise; however, it has no comparable right to direct the employee.[5]

Indeed, legislation has given the unions legal sanction and encouragement in challenging management's vested authority. Thus, the organization (either privately or publicly owned) becomes a "debating society" where employees, through their union representatives, challenge managerial directives and policies. A few issues are sealed off from bilateral consideration or joint decision making between management and the union. However, the vast remainder (either specified in or excluded from the written labor agreement) are subject to management's procedural authority or administrative initiative. Management reserves the right in all instances to act on the basis of its interpretation of the labor agreement, as illustrated by the following comments by Arthur Goldberg:

> The union cannot direct its members to their work stations or work assignments. The union does not tell people to go home because there is not work. The union does not notify people who are discharged to stay put. . . .The union does not start or stop operations unless perhaps some urgent safety matter is involved and there is some contractual or other basis for such action. [6]

Unions do not usually want to be "partners with management," as this practice could foster concern from their constituents. However, unions do desire the option to challenge or appeal management's procedural rights through at least four avenues: contract negotiations, joint union-management committees, the negotiated grievance procedure, or informal discussions.

Our labor contract analysis and interviews attempted to determine the extent of union involvement in managerial decisions; more specifically, the extent and substance of those issues under management's unilateral domain. The results of these attempts are presented in Table 3.5 and Table 3.6. We also attempted to ascertain from the interview respondents their definitions of managements' and unions' unilateral rights.

A review of Table 3.5 indicates that mass transit management has sole discretion on a number of administrative issues. If contractual silence is considered to furnish the same discretion as a contractually specified unilateral management right, the combined categories represent a very substantial portion (over 70 percent) of the total for eight of ten issues. The two exceptions (employee layoff procedures and bidding of runs) do not usurp management's right to direct the operation; rather, they reflect the assignment of employees after management has made the major issue determination.

The interview response (Table 3.6) served as a check on our contract analysis while also indicating the degree of potential union

TABLE 3.5

Extent of Union Influence in Administrative Decisions
(number of agreements referring to issue)

Issue	No Reference or Contract Silent	Contract Specifies Unilateral Management Right	Contract Specifies Procedures
Selection of employees	20	16	1
Layoffs of employees—determination of when needed	9	25	3
Layoffs of employees—procedures	5	3	29
Length of runs*	17	9	9
Scheduling changes—routes*	21	9	5
Scheduling changes—times*	20	9	6
Technological changes	29	7	1
Time standards—run times*	24	7	4
Apprenticeships	33	1	3
Bidding of runs*	6	0	29

*Total for three issues is not 37, as bus operator's classification is not found in all labor agreements.

Source: Analysis of labor agreements in nine-state study area compiled by the author.

TABLE 3.6

Extent of Union Influence in Administrative Issues
(number of responses)

	Unilateral Management Right	Contract Provision Pertaining to Issue	Union Can Grieve and/or Management Has Obligation to Confer	Management Must Union Approval for Issue	Union Has Right to Negotiate Issue
Selection of employees					
Union respondents	19	0	1	0	0
Management respondents	20	0	0	0	0
Layoffs of employees— determination of when needed					
Union respondents	16	1	2	0	1
Management respondents	17	1	2	0	0
Layoffs of employees— procedures					
Union respondents	6	12	2	0	0
Management respondents	5	12	3	0	0
Length of runs					
Union respondents	11	6	2	1	0
Management respondents	11	9	0	0	0
Scheduling changes (routes)					
Union respondents	13	3	3	0	1
Management respondents	14	3	3	0	0
Scheduling changes (times)					
Union respondents	13	5	2	0	0
Management respondents	15	4	0	1	0
Technological change					
Union respondents	16	0	3	0	1
Management respondents	20	0	0	0	0
Time standards (run times of routes)					
Union respondents	11	0	6	0	3
Management respondents	7	3	10	0	0
Apprenticeship					
Union respondents	11	3	5	0	1
Management respondents	16	3	1	0	0
Bidding of runs					
Union respondents	0	20	0	0	0
Management respondents	1	19	0	0	0
Spread times					
Union respondents	0	19	0	0	1
Management respondents	1	19	0	0	0
Implementing of affirmative action program					
Union respondents	13	0	4	1	2
Management respondents	14	1	5	0	0
Application for capital grants					
Union respondents	17	0	1	2	0
Management respondents	20	0	0	0	0
Revenue charges (fares and advertising)					
Union respondents	20	0	0	0	0
Management respondents	19	1	0	0	0

Source: Interview responses gathered in nine-state study area by the authors.

challenge to managerial authority. The interview results parallel
those obtained in Table 3.5. Another, perhaps more significant
observation, is that both union and management respondents appear
to attach some permanence to the unilateral management rights.
More specifically, relatively few union and management representatives apparently believe the union can negotiate or alter a unilateral
management right even though many of these rights have not been
formalized into the labor agreement, and grievances at many of the
locations are defined to include working conditions not specified in
the contract. The exception to this conclusion pertains to time standards. Thus, it appears that many of the issues are removed from
bilateral decision making, including the previously cited avenues of
union appeal.[7]

Both union and management respondents were also asked, in
an open-ended question, to indicate what management's unilateral
rights are. Six union respondents indicated that anything not covered
by the contract is a unilateral management right; however, this statement was amended by two other union officials who stated "they
[management officials] have no rights that can't be negotiated away."
The majority (11) of the union respondents preferred to equate management rights with the contractually designated management prerogatives;
more specifically, the provision containing items such as route
scheduling and hiring of employees. Five management officials indicated they have the unilateral right to run the operation in the best
interests of the system. Several other management officials (6)
suggested two general sources of management rights: the management
rights clause in the labor agreement; and residual rights, by which
"the right to manage anything not in the contract is a management
prerogative and subject to management discretion." The largest
number of management respondents preferred to answer this question
in terms of one or more of the following specific categories: determination of routes, training, pay, fares, work rules, hiring and firing
of employees (the latter particularly in the case of probationary
employees), selection of supervisory personnel, and determination
of bus assignments to various runs.

Most of the union and management respondents suggested that
the union's unilateral right is to insure that contract provisions will
be adhered to, a right accomplished through two additional and
interrelated rights: collective bargaining for its members (as indicated
by seven management and 15 union respondents); and requesting
meetings, either informally or through the grievance procedure, with
management over issues and concerns raised by union members (as
indicated by five management and two union officials). Management
and union officials at seven facilities indicated that the union has
unilateral rights in two additional areas: seeking formal recognition

from management officials; and the union's internal affairs—"the right to determine dues, which members will serve as officers of the union, and the right to select the negotiating team." Additionally, one-fourth of the respondents (six union and four management officials) indicated they are not aware of any unilateral union rights.

The findings generated from these interview questions as well as the more comprehensive contract analysis suggest that management has a relatively unencumbered hand in dealing with operations at the mass transit facilities. While no questions specifically asked about the effects of union involvement on managerial discretion, it is important to note that no management official volunteered any concern over the issue during the rather lengthy interview.

UNION INVOLVEMENT IN
INSTITUTIONAL ISSUES—OVERVIEW

To determine the overall degree of union involvement in institutional issues as evidenced in contract language, the responses to each of the 33 variables dealing with institutional issues were recoded as response 1, indicating little-to-no union involvement, or response 2, indicating relatively high union involvement.[8] To illustrate, variable 22 reads as follows:

<u>Supervisor Performing Bargaining Unit Work</u>

0	No reference
1	Prohibited or restricted
2	1 + provision for penalty payment

The responses to this variable were recoded as follows:

Variable Number	Response Number	Recode
22	0	1
	1	2
	2	2

Thus, those contracts with response 0 were judged to exhibit relatively less involvement than those contracts with responses 1 or 2.

By recoding all 33 institutional variables and calculating the proportion of number 1 and 2 responses, an overall view can be gained of the relative degree of union involvement with respect to administrative issues. In addition, by comparing the proportions of number 1 and 2 responses by organizational structure, city population size, unit size, and number of buses, we can check for patterns in union power or involvement. The results are presented in Table 3.7.

TABLE 3.7

Relative Degree of Union Involvement in Institutional Issues by Comparison Category

Category	Number in Category	Proportion of Number 1 Responses (little-to-no union involvement)	Proportion of Number 2 Responses (relatively high union involvement)	Analysis of Variance in F-Ratio
Organizational structure				
Privately owned	10	.7627	.2373	2.83
Publicly owned—Management services company	21	.7098	.2902	
Publicly owned and operated	5	.6563	.3437	3.37*
Population				
Less than 250,000	17	.7537	.2463	
250,000 to 500,000	11	.6960	.3040	
More than 500,000	8	.6683	.3317	
Unit size (employees)				
Less than 100	18	.7500	.2500	3.43*
100 to 200	7	.6741	.3259	
More than 200	9	.6739	.3261	
Number of buses				
Less than 50	17	.7684	.2316	8.40*
50 to 100	7	.6473	.3527	
More than 100	11	.6792	.3208	
Overall proportions		.7171	.2829	

* Indicates significant difference at .05 level.

<u>Source:</u> Analysis of labor agreements in the nine-state study area compiled by the authors.

As can be seen from Table 3.7, the overall degree of union involvement in institutional issues is relatively low, a finding confirming our interview response. Yet three of our independent variables—unit size, number of buses, and population—account for statistically significant explanations of variations in union involvement. More specifically, union involvement is significantly less (at the .05 level) at properties having less than 100 employees than at those properties having more than 200 employees. Union involvement in these issues is also significantly less at properties having less than 50 buses than at those properties having more than 50 buses. It thus appears that the size of the organization, as measured by these two variables, exerts some pressure to formalize the unions' rights in the labor agreement. A third variable, population, also differentiates the degree of union involvement in institutional issues; more specifically, unions in higher-population areas (over 500,000 individuals) tend to have greater involvement in these issues than unions in low-population areas (less than 100,000 individuals). It is assumed that population size affects the collective bargaining outcome in this instance by influencing the size or magnitude of the agency's mass transit operations. Finally, while organizational structure does not explain overall involvement in institutional issues, it should be noted that there is significantly less union involvement at privately owned companies than found in publicly owned and operated agencies. Perhaps this finding stems from the observation cited in Chapter 2—unions representing mass transit employees in some private companies have relatively less influence where there is another numerically dominant union found at the same property. Perhaps the bargaining power of these unions is also lessened, as a cessation of mass transit activities at some of these properties would affect a relatively small portion of the firms' overall operations.

NOTES

1. It should be mentioned that this period can be extended if there is a preexisting written labor agreement covering more than a one-year time period.

2. Daniel H. Pollitt, "Union Security In America," The American Federationist 80 (October 1973): 16.

3. Sumner Slichter, James J. Healy, and E. Robert Livernash, The Impact of Collective Bargaining on Management (Washington, D.C.: Brookings Institution, 1960), p. 4.

4. Neil W. Chamberlain, "The Union Challenge to Management Control," Industrial and Labor Relations Review 17 (January 1963): 185.

5. Stanley Young, "The Question of Managerial Prerogatives," Industrial and Labor Relations Review 17 (January 1963): 242.

6. Paul Prasow, "The Theory of Management-Reserved Rights—Revisited," in Industrial Relations Research Association Proceedings of the Twenty-Sixth Annual Winter Meeting (Madison: Industrial Relations Research Association, 1974), p. 76.

7. It should also be noted that one potential appeal alternative, joint union-management committees, is somewhat limited, as only six out of the 37 analyzed labor agreements contain related provisions.

8. The 33 variables dealing with institutional issues are shown in Appendix A and correspond to variable numbers 1 to 22, and 229 to 239.

The economic issues are the heart of the labor agreement,
especially in mass transit operations where employee compensation
accounts for approximately 60 to 80 percent of total operating expenses.
Indeed, our investigation of southeastern transit properties shows
economic issues dominate current collective bargaining negotiations.
Economic issues indicate to the employee how much pay he will get
for work on a given job, and to the employer how much it will cost—
in money—to get desired performance. There is often a tendency to
view employee compensation narrowly in terms of wages. However,
the wage is merely the most obvious and often the most variable
part of employment compensation. A substantial portion of the economic issues consists of contingent benefits such as sick leave, insurance
programs, pension programs; provisions for premium or extra
pay; and payment for time not worked—for example, vacation and jury
duty.

The purpose of this chapter is to discuss the current major
bargaining issues in the mass transit industry in the Southeast along
with their resolutions, and to analyze the economic issues contained
in the labor agreements. In addition to a general overview of each
issue, efforts are made to compare issue resolutions by such factors
as property size, organizational structure (publicly owned and
operated, management-service operated, or privately owned and
operated), bargaining unit size (number of employees in the bargaining
unit), and city size.

CURRENT ISSUES IN NEGOTIATIONS

Union and management respondents were asked the open-ended
question, "What were the major issues during your last contract

negotiations?" It was anticipated that an industry such as mass
transit, with a declining output, would have different labor problems/
issues than an expanding industry; for example, that job security
issues would be relatively more important than wage demands. One
would expect, even in inflationary times, that wages and wage demands
would be moderated in a situation where price (fare) increases, often
necessitated by wage increases, resulted in fewer riders and
fewer jobs. However, wages were mentioned as a major, if not the
major, issue by all union and management respondents at 20 on-site
interviews in the Southeast. As shown in Table 4.1, the issues listed

TABLE 4.1

Issues in Contract Negotiations in the Southeast, 1975-76

Issue	Number of Properties Where Issue Is Current	
	Union Respondents	Management Respondents
Wages	20	20
Cost-of-living adjustments	14	14
Vacation provisions	9	8
Health benefits (including insurance and sick-day provisions)	13	14
Pension provisions	6	6
Other issues (for example, length of work week, spread time)	12	12

Source: Interview responses gathered in nine-state study area
by the authors.

most often by respondents from those surveyed properties are
economic in nature. An explanation for this emphasis on economic issues, aside from inflation, would appear to be the long
history of collective bargaining in the transit industry; that is,
most labor agreements in the study area reflect established and somewhat detailed criteria for promotion, layoff, and selection of runs,
with systemwide or departmental seniority as the prime criterion.
A merit system considering the critical issues of promotion, security,
and run selection is somewhat difficult to attain because of the inherent
inability to measure superior performance. With seniority issues
so critical and because of the proportion of minority workers in the

study area, it was anticipated that work conditions or seniority issues would have been listed by respondents as one of the prominent issues in the most recent negotiations. However, only one property listed the progression scale for operators as an issue; and one other property listed a minor problem with the classification and jurisdiction concerning maintenance work. One of the respondents representing an employee association listed the scope of the "right-to-manage" clause as one of several issues; and while several union respondents discussed the tactic of "no fare," they did not believe a no-fare policy to be an issue for contract negotiations. One respondent did note that since the transit system "had gone to an exact fare, management did make an issue of the allowed 30 minutes checkup time." Management contended that the exact fare eliminated the need for the 30-minute checkup time at the end of the run. In this instance, the union was successful in maintaining the provision and based its argument on the 10-minute prestart time without pay, applied to the split shifts required of all drivers, which was seen as largely offsetting the 30-minute checkup time.

Perhaps this economic emphasis reflects the opinion expressed by several union respondents that federal and local financial assistance given to the transit industry, belongs, in part, to the transit employees both as a factor of production in the creation of transit services and as taxpayers. As noted earlier, the research was directed toward discovering how the unions were dealing with problems directly connected with the production process and where the union had been having a substantial impact upon the security and job satisfaction issues—problems such as the content or requirement of a job, methods of operation, and rates of operation and work loads. It was found that almost overwhelmingly union officials seem to emphasize wages and cost-of-living adjustments, along with other economic issues, as the most current problems and the major items of concern in negotiations. Only in a few cases was there a response that dealt with a noneconomic issue, such as grievance procedures or checkoff of dues. Neither management nor union respondents listed issues such as technological changes, innovations, contracting work out, productivity or safety as issues at the most recent negotiations. For the most part, "other issues" mentioned by the respondents in Table 4.1 concerned conversion of the straight-time portion of the workweek from 44 or 48 hours to 40 hours as required by the 1974 Fair Labor Standards Act Amendments and the corresponding adjustment to pay (listed by eight respondents); the problem of a daily guarantee for employees on the extra board to provide those employees with an eight-hour equivalent (listed by one respondent); and the issue of spread time, that is, the request that spread time be treated as a rate and not flat time, and be applied to "trippers"—short runs (listed by one respondent).

Since collective bargaining agreements in the transit industry place no limitations on management's freedom to hire employees in the labor market, the union does not act as the hiring agent; and since the requirements for entry into the transit industry, particularly as an operator, do not call for great skills, the union does not desire to set forth joint agreements on qualifications. Again, the long history of collective bargaining in the transit industry has allowed for each side to become well acquainted and for the major difficulties to be worked out. Most agreements contain a number of provisions with respect to wages, which will be discussed later in this chapter. However, it should be mentioned that jointly negotiated welfare programs are now commonly a part of the labor agreement and, as shown in Table 4.1, are one of the major issues listed by respondents as part of the negotiations during the latest contract bargaining. Pension plans were listed at six properties as being major issues during the last negotiations, with the problems listed as the contribution policy of management and the extension of coverages.

WAGE DETERMINATION THEORY

In order to provide greater insight into the analysis of wage compensation, a short discussion of wage determination is presented below. There is no attempt here to develop a complete theory of wage determination in the mass transit industry, as such an undertaking is beyond the scope of this study. Additionally, with available data, we are unable to adequately test a wage determination model.

There are many wage theories, some economic and some institutional, but all attempt to explain the process of wage determination. Generally, economic wage theories tend to view employees and employers as economic agents, trying to maximize wages and profits, respectively. When employees organize, the union becomes the economic agent, attempting to maximize the wage bill for its members. The union's efforts are typically constrained by a desire to maintain membership, a constraint which discourages pushing wages so high that employment is significantly reduced. Economic theories focus on productivity as the principal determinant of wages. Institutional wage theories, on the other hand, emphasize the importance of market structures, for example, existence of monopoly powers, and administrative and political forces, in the determination of wages, and pay less attention to productivity as a wage determining factor. According to Richard Lester, "The more mixed the economy becomes, the less controlling is the market mechanism and the greater tends to be the influence of group psychology, public opinion, and political, social, and institutional factors."[1]

Lester adds that any theoretical formulation that allows for multiple motivation and includes the influences just mentioned must necessarily be "eclectic and unprecise, devoid of simple solutions and subject to zones of indeterminacy."[2] Relatively little attention has been devoted to the public sector in the formulation of wage theories. However, there are some marked differences between private and public sectors, particularly with respect to employer goals and, frequently, output characteristics. The public employer generally responds to political motivations, and is less likely to be concerned about agency survival or relative labor costs and product price vis-a-vis his competition than his private counterpart.

The output or product of public employees and the price of this product often make application of economic wage theory difficult if not impossible. In order to assign a value to the productivity of a public employee, it is first necessary to determine the price of the product or service, and the output of the public employee. In many cases, this information is not obtainable. Current conditions in the mass transit industry illustrate these problems well. It is not an easy matter to identify the output of a mass transit system or to measure the productivity of transit employees. Without elaborating, the services provided by a mass transit system affect many people in addition to the riders, and it is precisely these external effects that make the output uncertain. Furthermore, to the extent that the system receives governmental financial assistance and does not rely solely on voluntary purchases for revenue, the price of mass transit services is also unclear.

Because of these inherent problems, many public agencies must rely heavily on wage comparisons as a means of setting wages. This practice, commonly referred to as the prevailing-wage principle, is given a legal basis by the Federal Salary Reform Act of 1962, which requires that federal pay rates be comparable to private enterprise pay rates for the same levels of work. Application of the prevailing-wage technique is not a simple statistical undertaking devoid of discretion but involves elements of negotiation. According to Derek Bok and John Dunlop, the final decision is influenced by the geographical area from which comparable wages are selected, the particular firms and occupations included, the data of the survey, and the methods of combining the survey data.[3]

An examination of the application of the prevailing-wage principle leads Walter Fogel and David Lewin to conclude that public sector wage rates tend to be higher than private sector rates for low-skill and craft jobs for the following reasons: government employees tend to exclude small firms from their wage surveys, giving an upward bias to the results of such surveys; where private sector wage rates are considered relatively low, the public sector tends to pay wage rates higher than existing private rates; where private sector wage

rates are considered relatively high, the public sector tends to pay
rates at least equal to private rates; in setting wage rates, public
sector agencies do not take into account, that is, adjust public wage
rates downward to offset, favorable nonwage aspects of public sector
employment sector employment such as greater job security. [4]

The conclusion that an upward bias exists in wages for low-skill
and craft jobs in the public sector is contradicted, however, in a
study by James Annable, Jr., [5] Annable concluded that the range
of acceptable wages for any given public employee is generally more
narrow, and eventually lower, than for his private sector counterpart.
For the public employer, the upper limit of the acceptable range of
wages is determined by the desire to maintain stable or decreasing
tax levels. The lower limit is determined by the minimum wage at
which the public employer can attract sufficient labor to provide
stable or increasing levels of service. Pressures forcing these two
boundaries to be very close to each other come essentially from the
interaction of two facts: the outputs of most public agencies are
largely labor-intensive services; and the productivity growth trend
in the service-producing sector is less than half that of the goods-
producing sector (approximately 1.1 percent per annum and 2.4 percent per annum, respectively). If the minimum wage required to
attract qualified labor is set by the private sector, it is likely that
this wage will increase at a rate roughly equal to the growth rate in
the goods-producing sector. Since wage gains not offset by productivity increases must result in increases in per unit labor cost, the
public employer must choose between paying higher labor costs for
stable levels of public service or stabilizing labor costs by permitting
public services to deteriorate. Since public output is labor intensive,
any rise in labor costs results in higher taxes. The public employer,
according to Annable, faces a dilemma that gives the employer very
little flexibility in setting wages and exerts constant downward pressure
on public employee wages. He suggests that the unionization of labor
is probably the only effective means available to public employees to
combat this severe wage constraint.

On a priori grounds, we would expect that both of the hypotheses
discussed earlier about public sector wage levels have some applicability to the mass transit industry. First, the decade of the 1960s was
characterized by a substantial growth in per capita earnings. Significant increases in private sector earnings would have exerted upward
pressure on public sector wages. Comparability was unavoidable.
Secondly, continued declining ridership and fare box revenues coupled
with the labor intensity of mass transit services would have made
wage increases impossible without large increases in tax subsidies.
If subsidy levels are to be stabilized or if transit services are to be
expanded, it seems likely that the transit employer's range of acceptable wages must become subject to the same constraints discussed by

Annable. However, this pressure upon the employee wage levels may be mitigated by the source of external financial assistance—that is, because of the inability to adequately associate increasing taxes, at say the federal level, with the wage level, municipal employers may feel less constrained in permitting wage increases. Also, it seems likely that unions will vigorously pursue wage increases comparable to those received by workers in other industries.

TRANSIT WAGES—THEORY AND REALITY

Data furnished by the Bureau of Labor Statistics (BLS) tend to support the effectiveness of transit unions in obtaining substantial wage increases. Nationally, union wage rates for local transit operating employees averaged $6.25 per hour on July 1, 1975, an average increase of 11.3 percent over the previous year.[6] Between 1960 and 1975, union hourly wage rates of transit operating employees increased approximately 160 percent, and between 1965 and 1975, the average annual rate of increase was 7.9 percent.[7]

While these wage rate increases indicate substantial gains enjoyed by unionized transit operating employees, it must be noted that a significant part of these wage rate increases resulted from the cost-of-living escalator clauses found in most contracts. In fact, of the 11.3 percent average increase between July 1, 1974 and July 1, 1975, only 1.5 percentage points represented an increase in real wages.[8]

Wage rates of unionized local transit operating employees in the Southeast tend to be somewhat lower than their national counterparts. According to the BLS survey, the average hourly wage rate for unionized operating employees in the Southeast was $5.32 on July 1, 1975, or $.93 below the national average rate. The rate of increase in transit wages between July 1, 1974 and July 1, 1975 in the Southeast was 11.1 percent, approximately the same as the national average.[9]

It is unlikely that traditional market forces such as productivity increases or increased demand for transit services explain these wage gains. As Darold Barnum points out, "The fact that transit wages have rapidly increased at the same time that productivity and profits have decreased is just one more indication that these [productivity and profits] have not been controlling criteria."[10] He suggests that comparisons with other transit systems are likely to be an important criterion.

Comparability As a Basis for Wage Determination

In order to determine the extent to which comparability is used as a basis for wage determination, we examined the contracts for provisions pertaining to wage comparisons, and asked union and management officials specific, related questions. The only wage-setting practice specified in the contracts is a cost-of-living adjustment. None of the contracts contains a provision requiring the use or consideration of a wage survey, a wage formula, or the payment of a prevailing wage rate.

In the on-site interviews, union and management officials were asked, "To what extent was comparability used in the negotiation of the present labor agreement, e.g., wages and specific noneconomic issues?" Exactly one-half of the respondents indicated that comparability is extensively used in economic issues, whereas only one respondent indicated that comparability is extensively used in non-economic issues. Perhaps more significant is the perceived effect that comparability has in persuading each side to accept the other's position. A sizable number (16) of the respondents indicated that comparability is used only as "a talking point" to "illustrate rationales behind union and management demands." One management official appeared to sum up this statement with the following remark: "You can get a list and I can get a list. You won't convince me and I won't convince you, so let's work with what we have here."

The interview respondents were then asked, "How was comparability defined by management and union in the most recent negotiations?" The results of this question are presented in Table 4.2. An analysis of the table reveals some interesting conclusions. First, overall response for management and unions indicates relatively few differences of opinion regarding the extent to which each item is used in comparability. One minor exception to this conclusion is that management respondents maintained they and union officials place slightly more comparability emphasis on other bargaining units at the same facility than do union respondents. In discussing this, management officials indicated that unions compare wages and working conditions to those of other public employees, for example, secretaries, truck drivers, firefighters; perhaps unions regard the question in more narrow terms (as intended) to mean other bargaining units at the specific mass transit facility. However, both union and management respondents are in general agreement regarding the extent to which comparability is used by the other party in collective bargaining.

The two most commonly used dimensions of comparability are geographical proximity and size of company. Impressions obtained from the respondents indicate that these dimensions tend to follow a pattern—the union often compares the facility with nearby facilities while management either uses another geographical comparison, or counters that union comparisons are not taking into account the size of the respective facilities.

TABLE 4.2

Union's and Management's
Definitions of Wage Comparability

Dimension of Comparability	Use of Dimension by Management		Use by Union	
	Yes	No	Yes	No
Geographical				
Union respondents	16	4	15	5
Management respondents	16	4	13	7
Cost of living				
Union respondents	5	15	10	10
Management respondents	5	13	13	7
In terms of other bargaining unit at same facility				
Union respondents	4	16	5	15
Management respondents	7	13	8	12
Size of company				
Union respondents	11	9	13	7
Management respondents	16	4	14	6
Revenues				
Union respondents	6	14	7	13
Management respondents	9	11	7	13
Best negotiated settlement, by specific issue, by other parties				
Union respondents	7	13	12	8
Management respondents	7	13	13	7

Source: Interview responses gathered in nine-state study area by the authors.

Both management and union officials indicate that unions are more prone to use "best negotiated settlement, by specific issue, by other parties." This seems understandable since contract specification usually reflects union involvement while contract silence reflects managerial prerogatives. Therefore, comparisons of contractual provisions would appear to favor labor organizations in collective bargaining.

Finally, the respondents were asked, "Have management and union reached agreement on how comparability is to be defined? If so,

what is the definition and the relative priorities attached?" Only one
of the locations indicates a joint definition of comparability—the union
and management representatives at this location have agreed to limit
comparability to the county in which they are located. The remainder
of the sites do not have joint definitions of comparability and representatives are doubtful that this objective could be accomplished. This
sentiment is typified by one management representative who states:

> No agreement has been reached by either side and there-
> fore [comparability] is not a part of the negotiations on
> an agreed upon basis. Neither side can agree upon which
> topics or parameters are acceptable, much less the values
> or weights.

It would appear, therefore, that comparability is used fairly
extensively in wage determination, particularly with respect to
geographical comparisons and size-of-company comparisons. The
finding that union and management do not agree on a common definition of wage comparisons is not surprising. Both groups, especially
management, are reluctant to resort to formulas for wage determination and thus relinquish the flexibility provided by collective bargaining over wages. In other words, both groups prefer to keep the
scope of bargaining as broad as possible.

In the discussion that follows, wages in the transit industry
in the Southeast are described. Since wages are typically the most
important part of employee compensation and, likewise, of total
operating expenses, and since rising costs have been one of the
primary reasons for the shift to public ownership, efforts are made
to determine the impact of public ownership on wages.

Transit Wages in the Southeast

Wage Rate Ranges

The actual wage received by an operator or a garage employee
depends on several factors—the negotiated wage for each job classification, the pay differential for each range within each job classification,
and finally the amount of the cost-of-living adjustments, if provided
for in the contract.

Transit operators traditionally have been paid on the basis of
a graduated system of wages, that is, a starting rate, intermediate
step rates, and a top rate. Some firms, in the past, did not pay
operators the top rate until ten years of service; and before 1920,
progressions of 25 years were not uncommon. [11] After a firm had

been unionized, the ATU generally reduced the wage progression to one year. Our research found that wage rate ranges for operators varied widely, with the most typical arrangements having two or three steps and reaching the maximum wage in 6 to 12 months. While these two alternatives covered more than 75 percent of the contracts with wage rate ranges, one contract provided for eight steps while three contracts specified ranges that covered 36 months. Only one contract made no reference to wage ranges for operators. Thus, the one-year rate can be considered the job rate for unionized firms in the transit industry.

Approximately 55 percent of the contracts (17) covering maintenance employees contain wage rate ranges for craft employees and only about 20 percent (5) contain wage rate ranges for apprentices. Twelve of the 17 contracts specifying ranges for craft employees stipulate either three or four steps. However, the number of months covered by the steps varies fairly evenly from six to 36. The number of steps contained in wage rate changes for apprentices varies from three to eight, and the time required to reach maximum wage varies from 18 to 48 months.

Progression through the ranges for drivers, craft employees, and apprentices is an automatic function of time in all contracts containing wage rate ranges, with one exception. One contract stipulates that the basis for progression through the ranges for drivers is "merit"; however, this concept is not defined by the labor agreement.

Negotiated Wage Rates

There is wide variation in negotiated wages[12] for both operators and craft employees. Table 4.3 presents wage information for both operators and craft employees for January 1976. Of the contracts that cover operators for January 1976, negotiated wages range from a low of $3.00 per hour to a high of $5.96 per hour. The mean negotiated wage for operators is $4.40 per hour. Negotiated wages for craft employees for January 1976 range from $3.35 per hour to $6.77 per hour, with a mean wage of $4.90 per hour.

As shown in Table 4.3, craft employees' negotiated wage is higher in every case than operators' negotiated wage, although the size of wage differential varies widely. The differential ranges from $1.835 per hour to $0.11 per hour, with the mean differential being approximately $0.55 per hour.

TABLE 4.3

Wages at Various Transit Properties—Negotiated and Actual,
Effective January 31, 1976

Negotiated Base Wage as of January 1976		Cost-of-Living Adjustment Provision			Actual Wage (negotiated base wage plus Cost-of-Living Adjustment for January 1976)	
Operators	Craft Employees	Index and Base	Frequency of Adjustment	Rate	Operators	Craft Employees
3.00	3.35	*	*	*	3.00	3.35
3.40	4.35	*	*	*	3.40	4.35
3.50	4.27	CPI-1967	Quarterly	0.5 = $.01	3.90	4.67
3.57	4.01	CPI-1957-59	Quarterly	0.6 = $.01	4.29	4.73
3.65	4.65	*	*	*	3.65	4.65
3.84	3.99	CPI-1957-59	Quarterly	0.5 = $.01	4.49	4.64
3.87	4.77	*	*	*	3.87	4.77
4.02	4.32	CPI-1967	Quarterly	0.5 = $.01	4.52	4.82
4.05	†	*	*	*	4.05	†
4.10	4.45	CPI-1967	Quarterly	0.4 = $.01	4.72	5.07
4.11	4.55	CPI-1957-59	Quarterly	0.6 = $.01	4.43	4.87
4.11	5.11	CPI-1957-59	Quarterly	0.5 = $.01	4.47	5.47
4.19	†	*	*	*	4.19	†
4.19	†	*	*	*	4.19	†
4.25	†	CPI-1967	Quarterly	0.5 = $.01	4.48	†
4.32	4.86	CPI-1957-59	Quarterly	0.5 = $.01	4.70	5.24
4.49	4.70	CPI-1967	Quarterly	0.4 = $.01	5.19	5.40
4.68	4.88	CPI-1957-59	Quarterly	0.5 = $.01	4.87	5.07
4.75	4.90	CPI-1957-59	Quarterly	0.4 = $.01	4.995	5.145
4.935	†	*	*	*	4.935	†
4.935	6.77	*	*	*	4.935	6.77
5.00	†	CPI-1967	Quarterly	0.4 = $.01	5.51	†
5.00	5.38	CPI-1957-59	Quarterly	0.5 = $.01	5.65	6.03
5.06	5.26	CPI-1957-59	Quarterly	0.6 = $.01	5.29	5.49
5.16	5.45	CPI-1957-59	Quarterly	0.5 = $.01	5.30	3.59
5.48	5.59	CPI-1967	Quarterly	0.4 = $.01	5.99	6.10
5.62	5.95	CPI-1957-59	Quarterly	0.5 = $.01	5.81	6.14
5.96	6.34	CPI-1967	Annual	0.6 = $.01	5.96	6.34

Note: Asterisk indicates no provision; dagger indicates unit not covered by contract; CPI indicates Consumer Price Index.

Source: Analysis of labor agreements in nine-state study area compiled by the authors.

Cost-of-Living Adjustments

Approximately 60 percent of the contracts (23) contain provisions
for cost-of-living adjustments. This preponderance is not surprising
in view of the international unions' policy that any contract that does
not contain a cost-of-living adjustment provision must be for less
than two years' duration. All contracts with such provisions use the
Consumer Price Index (CPI) as the basis for the adjustment, although
the combination of particular base years and conversion rates used
varies substantially among the properties. The most commonly
specified base years and conversion rates are as follows: 1957-59
base period, 0.5 = $0.01 (eight contracts); 1957-59 base period, 0.6 =
$0.01 (four contracts); 1967 base year, 0.4 = $0.01 (five contracts);
and 1967 base year, 0.5 = $0.01 (four contracts). Using the November
1975 CPI figures from both base periods (1957-59 and 1967), it is
interesting to note that a 1 percent increase in the index results in
a 1 percent adjustment in operators' wage rates in only two contracts,
and in a more than 1 percent increase in one contract, with the remainder of the contracts receiving a less than 1 percent wage adjustment.
A 1 percent increase in the index results in a less than 1 percent wage
adjustment for craft employees in all contracts.[13]

Cost-of-living adjustments are made on a nonretroactive and,
for the most part, quarterly basis, although two contracts stipulate
that seven adjustments are to be made over a two-year period. Only
one contract provides for an annual adjustment. Also, with two
exceptions where the contracts are silent, the cost-of-living provisions
guarantee that there can be no decrease in the negotiated wage rate
if the index declines below the base index.

Actual Wage Rates

The actual wage rates presented in Table 4.3 include any cost-
of-living adjustments. The mean actual wage rate for operators is
$4.67 per hour and for craft employees is $5.21 per hour.[14] The
variation in actual wages is substantial, with operators' wage levels
varying between $3.00 per hour and $5.99 per hour, and craft employees' wage levels between $3.35 and $6.77 per hour.

To examine the impact of public ownership on wage levels, Table
4.4 presents wage information by organization structure. As shown
by the table, the highest average wages for operators and craft
employees are paid by publicly owned, management service company-
operated firms ($4.91 and $5.38 per hour, respectively). The lowest
mean wages for both operators and craft employees are paid by privately owned bus operations ($4.39 and $5.19 per hour, respectively).

TABLE 4.4

Actual Wage by Organization Structure, January 1976

Organization Type	Number of Firms	Mean Wage Per Hour (dollars)	High (dollars)	Low (dollars)
Private ownership	10			
Operators		4.39	4.935	3.00
Craft employees		5.19	6.77	3.35
Publicly owned and operated	5			
Operators		4.54	5.99	3.40
Craft employees		5.23	6.10	4.35
Publicly owned— management service company	21			
Operators		4.91	5.96	3.40
Craft employees		5.38	6.34	4.65

Source: Analysis of labor agreements in nine-state study area compiled by the authors.

However, the range of wage rates is so large for all three organizational types that tests for statistical differences among the mean wages reveal no differences at the .05 level of significance. It appears, therefore, that actual wages paid by privately and publicly owned transit operations are not significantly different. This conclusion is supported by findings of Barnum in a test to determine the impact over time of change from private to public ownership on transit wage rates. After examining the wage trends of eight systems that became publicly owned between 1958 and 1968, he concludes that "going public often changes the wage trend, but the change is not consistently higher or lower."[15]

A more revealing breakdown of wage rates appears to be that by city size. Table 4.5 shows wage rates for operators and craft employees for small, medium-sized, and large cities. There is no difference in the mean wage rates for operators and craft employees in cities of less than 500,000 population ($4.51 and $5.08 per hour, respectively). There is some variation in the range of wage rates paid in the small and medium-sized cities, however, with both categories exhibiting fairly wide ranges. Large cities with more than 500,000 population pay substantially higher wages for operators—

TABLE 4.5

Actual Wage by City Size, January 1976

City Size	Number of Cities	Mean Hour Per Hour (dollars)	High (dollars)	Low (dollars)
Less than 250,000	17			
Operators		4.51	5.29	3.40
Craft employees		5.08	6.77	4.35
250,000 to 500,000	11			
Operators		4.51	5.65	3.00
Craft employees		5.09	6.03	3.35
More than 500,000	8			
Operators		5.81	5.99	5.51
Craft employees		6.14	6.34	5.99

Source: Analysis of labor agreement in nine-state study area compiled by the authors.

29 percent higher—and craft employees—20 percent higher. Furthermore, the range of wage rates for both operators and craft employees is much narrower in large cities. Variations in wage rates for transit employees appear to be more a function of city size than organizational structure.

Provisions for Premium Pay

With only three exceptions, operators who work in excess of eight hours per day or who work in excess of a defined workday or workweek are paid at one and a half times the base hourly rate. This provision applies also to craft employees. In over 85 percent of the contracts (30), operators receive one and a half times the base hourly rate for work performed on the operator's scheduled day off. A similar provision for craft employees is present in more than 75 percent of the contracts (23).

Operators receive the base hourly rate, that is, no premium, for work performed on a holiday, in addition to holiday pay for time not worked, in 80 percent of the contracts (28). Only six contracts specify operator pay at one and a half times the base hourly rate for holiday work. Approximately the same number of contracts (6) provide for craft employees who work on a holiday to receive the base hourly rate (again, in addition to regular holiday pay for time not worked). Most of the contracts make either no reference to or no distinction in the rate of pay for work performed on a holiday when the holiday falls on a scheduled day off. Of those which do, for operators, six provide for pay at the rate of one and a half times the base hourly rate, two at twice the base hourly rate, and one at two and a half times the base hourly rate. The provisions are similar for craft employees.

Slightly more than 50 percent of the contracts have provisions for operators to receive pay at one and a half times the base hourly rate for split runs that extend beyond a specified allowable spread time. The most commonly specified (11 contracts) allowable spread time before premium pay begins is 12 hours, with four contracts specifying shorter spread times and four contracts specifying a longer spread time. Split shifts and spread time seldom concern craft employees, as evidenced by the fact that there is reference to this issue in only two contracts.

Only three contracts provide for shift premiums for operators while eight contracts contain shift premium provisions for craft employees. Shift premiums range from $0.05 per hour to $0.15 per hour and are usually paid for work between 12 P.M. and 6 A.M. More than 60 percent of the contracts (22) provide for training allowances to be paid to operators. Finally, only two contracts contain provisions for longevity pay, that is, a bonus for employees who have completed a specified number of years, one providing less than $100 annually, the other more than $500 annually.

Miscellaneous Forms of Payment

In addition to pay for time worked, drivers, and in a few cases craft employees, receive other forms of payment, that is, some payment for time not worked. While other payment may result from numerous activities, the most common sources for other payment are preparatory time (provided in 85 percent of the contracts), court appearances (73 percent of the contracts), report pay for extra operators (63 percent of the contracts), and time spent completing accident reports (59 percent of the contracts). Payment for intervals between pieces of runs, attendance of safety meetings, check-in time, meal relief, and relief time is specified in approximately 25 to 35 percent of the contracts. The majority of the contracts containing references to payment for preparatory time, time spent completing accident reports, and intervals between pieces of runs exempt such payments from computation of overtime. With all other categories, however, the majority of the contracts are silent with regard to inclusion in overtime computation.

Forms of Indirect Compensation

In the preceding discussion, the term "wage" has been defined narrowly to mean direct monetary payments. Increasingly, nonmonetary benefits are a substantial portion of total employee compensation. The costs of fringe benefits such as paid holidays and medical and hospitalization plans are measurable; they represent dollar outlays by the employer for the services of labor and, therefore, are part of the unit cost of labor. In the post–World War II period, nonmonetary compensation or fringe benefits have increased in importance. In fact, there are indications that employee preference for compensation in the form of benefits has been increasing. Between 1950 and 1966 the percent of organized workers covered by health and insurance plans in the labor agreement increased from 47 to 91. The corresponding increase for pension plan coverage during the same period is 34 to 71 percent. [16]

The principal advantages to the employee of fringe benefits as a form of compensation are substantial economies of scale that may be achieved in purchasing such services as insurance; tax advantages derived because employer contributions to nonwage programs are not taxable; and possibly a sense of security derived from certain benefits that are automatically provided. Employers might prefer nonwage benefits to wage increases because such benefits probably reduce labor turnover and therefore reduce recruiting and training costs; and various kinds of added costs that increase with wages—for example, Social Security taxes, overtime, pension contributions, vacation pay, and holiday pay—would not be incurred if an equal expenditure for uniform nonwage benefits were made instead. [17] There are indications that union leaders prefer fringe benefits relatively more than rank-and-file members, primarily because negotiated fringe benefits permit differentiation of labor agreements. Unions are quite competitive in terms of negotiated settlements. Nonwage benefits permit union leaders to use items other than direct wages for comparison.

According to one industry practitioner, improvements in benefits for mass transit employees began during World War II under wage and price controls. Transit employees, unable to increase wages, pushed for nonmonetary benefits. The heavy emphasis on fringe benefits has continued, he said, since World War II, with the result being a very substantial fringe benefit package for most transit employees today. Analysis of the labor agreements fails to confirm his contention and reveals considerable variation in fringe benefits among southeastern transit workers.

Vacation Benefits

The description of vacation benefits found in the contracts focuses on several relevant aspects of vacation determination. First, the amount of vacation time the employee receives and the increase in vacation time with years of service are determined. Second, the types and variation of eligibility requirements for vacation are noted. Third, the issue of vacation pay is discussed. Finally, the allowable uses of vacation time are considered.

Over half of the contracts (20) provide for paid vacation of one week after one year of employment. Sixteen of the remaining contracts provide for two weeks' paid vacation after one year of employment. After two years of employment, 35 of the contracts specify two weeks' vacation, with two contracts providing more than two weeks. After three years of employment, 30 percent of the contracts allow three weeks' paid vacation. The maximum paid vacation provided is five weeks in 56 percent of the contracts (21) and four weeks in 36 percent (14 contracts); of the two remaining, one provides for six weeks and the other more than six weeks.

There is substantial variation in the eligibility requirements for vacation. The most prevalent requirement (15 contracts) is that the employee must have worked 75 percent of the previous year to be eligible for full vacation. Nearly 30 percent of the agreements (11) express eligibility requirements in terms of minimum days or hours to be worked. These requirements range from 1,000 hours to 1,500 hours to one year. Eight contracts make no reference to vacation eligibility requirements. Vacation scheduling is based on seniority in 80 percent of the agreements (30), with half of these specifying managerial restrictions. In only three contracts is vacation scheduling a unilateral management right.

Vacation pay for operators in based on regularly scheduled run time prior to vacation in 80 percent of the agreements (28). The most common basis for determining vacation pay for extra operators and craft employees is the contractually defined workweek or workday, with 65 percent of the agreements (23) specifying this method for the former group and 70 percent (21 contracts) for the latter.

The allowable use of paid vacation varies considerably. Twenty-one percent of the contracts (8) permit paid vacation to be used for either severance or retirement, and 10 percent prorate accumulated vacation in the case of layoffs. An additional 14 percent (five contracts) add pay in lieu of vacation to the alternatives. Only three contracts restrict the use of paid vacation to vacation.

Sick Leave

The important issues in sick leave provisions are the rate and amount of sick leave accumulation; eligibility requirements for sick leave; and permissible uses for sick leave. The maximum rate of cumulation of paid sick leave is one day per month in 18 of the contracts (nearly 50 percent) while four contracts have a maximum rate of cumulation of a half day per month. Somewhat surprisingly, nearly one-third of the contracts (12) contain no reference to the rate of cumulation of paid sick leave. The maximum amount of paid sick leave that may be accumulated varies relatively evenly among five categories ranging from 30 days or less to 121 days or more.

Minimum eligibility requirements are contained in nearly 60 percent of the contracts (22). The most prevalent eligibility requirement is one year (9 contracts), with the remainder varying from two months to six months. In addition to minimum eligibility requirements, many contracts (19) stipulate that paid sick leave begins only after a specified number of days of illness. Most of these contracts specify the first day as a noncovered day (8 contracts) or the first three days as noncovered days (8 contracts).

Only one contract permits using paid sick leave for vacation, while two permit using it for retirement and severance. One contract requires that days used for funeral leave be charged against accumulated sick leave.

Paid Funeral Leave

Paid funeral leave has essentially two dimensions: relatives whose death qualifies for paid funeral leave for the employee, and the number of days of leave allowed for each relative's death that qualifies. Three contracts do not contain any provisions for paid funeral leave. Of those that do, nearly 75 percent (25 contracts) allow three days for funerals involving parents or legal guardians, while approximately 24 percent (8 contracts) allow only two days; 88 percent of the contracts provide for three days' paid leave for the funeral of a spouse or a child. Three other contracts allow only two days' paid funeral leave in these cases while one permits seven days' funeral leave in the death of a spouse or a child. Just over 60 percent of the contracts (21) provide for three days' funeral leave in deaths involving siblings while six contracts allow for two days in death of a sibling. Five contracts that contain provisions for paid funeral leave do not specify sibling deaths as qualifying. Nearly one-third of the contracts (11) with paid funeral leave provisions do not consider deaths of relatives-in-law as qualifying while approximately

38 percent (13) provide for three days' leave for the funeral of a
relative-in-law. The majority of the contracts (23) with funeral
leave do not specify deaths of grandparents as qualifying, although
five contracts allow three days for the funeral of a grandparent.
Only two contracts contain provisions for paid funeral leave in deaths
of relatives beyond those already mentioned, for example, aunts,
uncles, cousins; and these two contracts provide two days' leave for
the funeral of any such relative. To summarize, most of the contracts
specify either four eligible categories of deaths of relatives for funeral
leave (10 contracts), five eligible categories (13 contracts), or six
eligible categories (6 contracts).

Paid Holidays

While there is some variation in the number of paid holidays
per year, the majority of the contracts specify either six paid holidays (12 contracts), seven paid holidays (10 contracts), or eight paid
holidays (six contracts). The smallest number of paid holidays
allowed is four (two contracts) while the greatest number is 12
(two contracts). Only one contract differentiates between operators and craft employees, allowing eight paid holidays for
operators and nine for craft employees.

Contingent Benefits

Contingent benefits include those forms of nonmonetary compensation that offer protection or financial assistance to the employee
in the event of contingencies—that is, insurance protection. There
are several types of insurance benefits that the union may bargain
for: hospital-medical-surgical insurance, major medical, accident
insurance, life insurance, and pension plans, to name just a few. In
addition to a variety of programs, coverage can apply to the employee
only or to the employee and his family. In analyzing all of the 37 contracts, we found contract language on contingent benefits to be the
most ambiguous and difficult to analyze of the topics considered.
Possibly because of the complexity of costs and benefits of insurance
and pension plans, these items were either not negotiated or dealt
with outside the labor agreement.

Most of the labor agreements (28) contain a provision for hospital-medical-surgical insurance for employees. Just over 20 percent
of these contracts (6) provide plans fully paid by the employer while
50 percent provide for employer contribution of less than 100 percent.
For the most part, contract language beyond this basic coverage is

vague. Hospital-medical-surgical plans for the employee's family are not provided in 35 percent of the contracts. However, an additional one-third of the contracts (12) contain a reference to a general insurance plan, not specifying types of coverage or extension to family. Major medical is provided in approximately 27 percent of the contracts (10) but may also be provided by some of the general plans. Over 50 percent of the contracts (20) contain life insurance programs for employees, with over one-third of these being fully paid by the employer. Again, other general company plans may actually provide life insurance coverage without specifying this coverage in the labor agreement.

Approximately 70 percent of the labor agreements (26) contain provisions for a retirement plan. For the most part, references are lacking in detail with respect to the level of contributions by the employer and/or employees as well as with respect to the benefits received or formulas for calculating benefits. Of the few programs that are explicit, employee pension benefits are expressed in absolute terms, for example, $50.00 per month, rather than in terms of a percentage of wages or a formula including years of service and wages. Because of the vagueness of contract language for pension plans, it is probably very beneficial to employees in the mass transit industry to be covered by recent federal pension reform legislation.

UNION INVOLVEMENT
IN ECONOMIC ISSUES—OVERVIEW

To determine the overall degree of union involvement in economic issues as evidenced in contract language, the responses to the 87 variables dealing with economic issues were recoded as response 1, indicating little-to-no union involvement, or response 2, indicating relatively high union involvement or union power. [18] To illustrate, variable 68 reads as follows:

Vacation Scheduling

0	No reference
1	Bid by seniority
2	Unilateral management right
3	Bid by seniority with restrictions
4	Management will give full consideration to seniority but at discretion of department head

The responses to this variable were recoded as follows:

Variable Number	Response Number	Recode
68	0	1
	1	2
	2	1
	3	2
	4	1

Thus, those contracts with response 0, 2, or 4 were judged to exhibit relatively less union involvement than those contracts with response 1 or 3.

By recoding all 87 variables and calculating the proportion of number 1 and 2 responses, an overall view can be gained of the relative degree of union involvement with respect to economic issues. In addition, by comparing the proportions of number 1 and 2 responses by organizational structure, city population size, unit size, and number of buses, we can check for patterns in union involvement. The results are presented in Table 4.6.

As indicated in Table 4.6, union power or involvement is relatively low with respect to economic issues. The proportion of number 1 responses varies between 55 and 65 percent, with the overall proportion of number 1 responses being 62 percent. When the proportion of number 1 and 2 responses is analyzed according to organizational structure, population, unit size, and number of buses, the results provide further support for the conclusions from the analysis of wages; namely, the only category in which there is not significant difference in the proportion of number 1 and 2 responses is organizational structure. All of the remaining categories contain differences significant at the .05 level. Cities of more than 500,000 population are characterized by relatively greater union involvement or power with respect to economic issues than cities with less than 250,000 population. Mass transit firms with bargaining units containing more than 200 individuals tend to exhibit relatively greater union power or involvement with respect to economic issues than those with bargaining units of less than 200 people. Similarly, mass transit firms with more than 100 buses tend to exhibit relatively more union power or involvement with respect to economic issues than firms with less than 100 buses.

Obviously, population, unit size, and number of buses are highly correlated. The finding of significant differences in all of these categories is not surprising, once a significant difference is found in one of them. What is interesting, however, is that size, not public ownership, tends to better explain union power or involvement in economic issues including wages.

TABLE 4.6

Relative Degree of Union Involvement in Economic Issues by Comparison Category

Category	Number in Category	Proportion of Number 1 Responses (little-to-no union involvement)	Proportion of Number 2 Responses (relatively high union involvement)	Analysis of Variance in F-Ratio
Organizational structure				1.848
Privately owned	10	.6676	.3324	
Publicly owned—management services company	21	.6103	.3897	
Publicly owned and operated	5	.5915	.4085	
Population				3.573*
Less than 250,000	17	.6534	.3466	
250,000 to 500,000	11	.6257	.3743	
More than 500,000	8	.5577	.4423	
Unit Size (employees)				3.977*
Less than 100	18	.6491	.3509	
100 to 200	7	.6482	.3518	
More than 200	9	.5559	.4441	
Number of buses				4.357*
Less than 50	17	.6515	.3485	
50 to 100	7	.6517	.3483	
More than 100	11	.5624	.4376	
Overall proportions		.6236	.3764	

* Indicates significant difference at .05 level.

Source: Analysis of labor agreements in the nine-state study area compiled by the authors.

NOTES

1. Richard A. Lester, "A Range Theory of Wage Differentials," Industrial and Labor Relations Review 5 (July 1952): 485.

2. Ibid.

3. Derek C. Bok and John T. Dunlop, Labor and the American Community, (New York: Simon and Schuster, 1970), pp. 318-20. For a cogent discussion of some of the merits and problems of using comparability as a wage-determining criterion, see Neil W. Chamberlain, "Comparability Pay and Compulsory Arbitration in Municipal Bargaining," in Collective Bargaining in Government: Readings and Cases, ed. J. Joseph Lowenberg and Michael H. Moskow (Englewood Cliffs, N. J.: Prentice-Hall, 1972), pp. 342-46; and Stephan A. Koczak, "Collective Bargaining and Comparability in the Federal Sector," in Industrial Relations Research Association Proceedings of the Twenty-Eighth Annual Winter Meeting, ed. James Stern and Barbara Dennis, (Madison: Industrial Relations Research Association, 1976), pp. 197-204.

4. Walter Fogel and David Lewin, "Wage Determination in the Public Sector," Industrial and Labor Relations Review 27 (April 1974): 410-31.

5. James E. Annable, Jr., "A Theory of Wage Determination in Public Employment," The Quarterly Review of Economics and Business 14 (Winter 1974): 43-58.

6. U.S. Department of Labor, Bureau of Labor Statistics, Union Wages and Hours: Local-Transit Operating Employees, July 1, 1975, Bulletin 1903 (Washington, D.C.: U.S. Government Printing Office, 1976).

7. Ibid., p. 5. This calculation is based on the wage rate index of union hourly wage rates for local transit operating employees, table 1.

8. Ibid., pp. 2-3.

9. Ibid., p. 8. There is some discrepancy between the BLS definition of the Southeast and the definition used in this study. The BLS definition includes Alabama, Florida, Georgia, Mississippi, North Carolina, South Carolina, and Tennessee. This study also includes Kentucky and Louisiana.

10. Darold T. Barnum, "Collective Bargaining and Manpower in Urban Transit Systems" (Ph.D. diss., University of Pennsylvania, 1972), p. 297.

11. Melvin Lurie, "The Measurement of the Effect of Unionization on Wages in the Transit Industry" (Ph.D. diss., University of Chicago, 1948), p. 14.

12. Negotiated wage for operators represents the top of the wage rate range. Negotiated wage for craft employees represents the top of the wage rate range for the highest craft-wage job category.

13. These conclusions are based on the following calculations. Depending on the base period, the CPIs for November 1975 are 165.6 (1967 = 100) and 192.6 (1957-59 = 100). A 1 percent increase in the index results in an increase of 1.656 points (1967 = 100) or 1.926 points (1957-59 = 100). The size of the wage adjustment would be as follows:

Conversion Rate	Cents-Per-Hour Adjustment
.4 (1967 base)	4.14
.4 (1957-59 base)	4.815
.5 (1967 base)	3.312
.5 (1957-59 base)	3.852
.6 (1967 base)	2.76
.6 (1957-59 base)	3.21

By comparing the cents-per-hour adjustment with a 1 percent change in the appropriate negotiated wage, it readily can be determined if the negotiated wage increases at a faster or a slower rate than the CPI, or at the same rate.

14. Comparisons are not made here between the negotiated and actual wage rate because the difference depends both on the size of any cost-of-living adjustment and the newness of the negotiated wage rate. Furthermore, these mean hourly wage rates are not comparable to the BLS reported transit wages cited earlier because the geographical sample areas are different; the size of cities included in the sample is different; and the hourly wage rate computations may differ.

15. Barnum, "Collective Bargaining," p. 292.

16. Allan M. Cartter and F. Ray Marshall, Labor Economics, rev. ed. (Homewood, Ill.: Richard D. Irwin, 1972), p. 335. For a good discussion of employee and employer opinion surveys regarding fringe benefits, see Richard A. Lester, "Benefits as a Preferred Form of Compensation," Southern Economic Journal 33 (April 1967): 488-95.

17. Ibid. pp. 336-37.

18. The 87 variables dealing with economic issues are shown in Appendix A and correspond to numbers 23 to 28, 30 to 49, 54 to 57, 59 to 83, 86 to 92, 98 to 108, 113 to 116, 125 to 133, and 247.

5

ADMINISTRATIVE
ISSUES

The administrative issues in the labor agreement deal with provisions relating to job assignment, promotion procedure, layoff procedure, and discipline. These topics detail many of the conditions of work and are extremely important to both management and the union. This is especially true in the mass transit industry where employee and customer preferences for routes and run times vary widely; thus, degree of flexibility in work scheduling is of vital importance to management.

This chapter describes the administrative issues covered in the labor agreements and their resolutions. Also, as in the preceding chapter on economic issues, the contracts are examined to determine the extent to which issue resolutions vary according to property characteristics such as organizational structure, city population, unit size, and number of buses. Finally, our interview guide contained several open-ended questions designed to uncover various labor relations problems at the properties. This input will also be analyzed when appropriate.

JOB ASSIGNMENT

Although operators are only represented by one title and their duties are uniform, there are several job titles and job descriptions for craft employees. This difference between operators' and craft employees' jobs is reflected in the labor agreements. Approximately 29 percent of the contracts (10) contain no specific reference to job titles or duties for operators and the remaining 71 percent make reference only to job titles, with no mention of job duties. Specific reference to job titles and duties for craft employees is contained in nearly 50 percent of the labor agreements (14). Of the remaining 15 contracts covering craft employees, 14 list job titles and one contains no reference to job titles or duties. Apparently, the lack of contractual precision regarding job duties does not result in any difficulties at the properties, as interview respondents were silent on these issues. More specifically, with only one exception, none of the examined properties indicated jurisdictional disputes between operators and maintenance classifications or among the various maintenance classifications.

In a majority of the contracts (19), operators are guaranteed between eight and eight and a half hours for a regularly scheduled run. Five contracts guarantee between eight and a half and nine hours, while the remainder either express the guarantee differently—for example, 42 to 52 hours per week—or make no reference to a minimum hour guarantee for a regularly scheduled run. For extra operators, minimum hour guarantees are generally dependent on the extra operator making all of his required daily report periods. Although most contracts (21) do not specify the required number of daily show-ups for extra board, all those which do (14), require two daily show-ups. The guaranteed report pay for extra board is not mentioned in 11 contracts; however, 19 contracts list report pay as one hour. Only five contracts contained provisions for payment of a premium for show-ups in excess of the required minimum. It is likely that the large number of "no references" with respect to required report periods and report pay is the result of satisfactory informal agreements between management and the union regarding the operation of the extra board; and our interviews revealed no evidence to refute this.

Contract language concerning the workweek and scheduled days off varies. While contracts specifying a five-day workweek exceed 75 percent of the total in the case of regular operators and 60 percent in the case of craft employees and extra operators, fewer than 25 percent designate that the workweek must provide two consecutive days off. Somewhat surprisingly, six contracts make no reference to scheduled days off for extra operators or for craft employees.

The selection of regular runs by operators is based almost unanimously on seniority, with over 90 percent of the contracts (32) specifying seniority as the sole determinant. Approximately 77 percent of the contracts (27) require advance posting of regular runs for rebidding (pick list), with 62 percent (22) specifying the amount of advance notice required. The contracts vary as to the required number of picks for regular runs per year. Slightly more than 50 percent of the contracts (18) require at least three general bids annually; 22 percent (8) require at least two, while 20 percent (7) require at least four per year. Any changes, additions, or deletions

of regular runs are open to the general bidding procedure in 62 percent
of the contracts (22). Several contracts (5) allow a general bid only
if the change occurs a specified number of days prior to a regularly
scheduled general bid.

Allocation of overtime opportunity, charter runs, and special
service is not covered in the majority of the contracts. Of those
contracts which do address the issue (18), 12 provide for preference
to be given to extra operators. Only one contract provides for
advance posting of charter runs, and then only if the charter cannot
be filled off the extra board.

One topic exhibiting substantial variety in contract language is
the scope and operation of the extra board. Approximately 25 percent
of the contracts (9) restrict the extra board solely to extra operators.
However, over 30 percent of the contracts (11) require regular operators to report to the extra board in certain circumstances—for example,
after a lose-out or after being released from jury duty—and 14 percent (5) specify that regular operators are eligible for the extra
board on their time off.

Contract provisions for rotation of the extra board are highly
individualized. Roughly one-half of the contracts (18) provide for
daily rotation of extra operators on the basis of assignment, with
nine of these contracts specifying a minimum number of hours
required for rotation. Some of the contracts (4) provide for rotation
on a first-in, first-out basis, and others (3) provide for rotation on
the basis of seniority. Evidence of the uniqueness and probably the
informality that often characterize the operation of the extra board
is given by the fact that more than 22 percent of the contracts (8)
have no specific provision for rotation of the extra board. Similarly,
policy for dealing with refusal of assignments by extra operators is
most often dealt with informally, as over 60 percent of the contracts
(22) have no reference to penalty for refusal.

Forty percent of the contracts (14) have provisions for payment
for administrative error in connection with the operation of the extra
board. Most of these (10) provide for differential payment or credit
for the amount of time involved in the runaround. Only four contracts
provide for full payment or credit.

Procedures for distributing overtime opportunities for craft
employees are not provided in over half of the contracts (16). Roughly
one-third of the contracts (11) provide for distribution of overtime,
specifying, for example, that there be an attempt to equalize overtime
hours, with only one of these providing for payment in the case of management error. Similarly, there are no provisions for bidding by craft
employees for holiday work in 70 percent of the contracts (21). Twenty
percent (6) provide for bidding on the basis of seniority. While no
contracts provide for bidding for new jobs, roughly one-half of the
contracts (14) require posting of new job openings.

Promotion Procedure

The major factor in the promotion procedure for craft employees is seniority. Slightly more than one-half of the contracts (16) that cover craft employees specify seniority as the basis for promotion if other factors are equal, while 20 percent (6) specify seniority as one of several factors. For purposes of promotion, seniority is most often defined as seniority within job classification or line (14 contracts), or within the maintenance department only (9 contracts). None of the contracts specified a procedure for promotion for operators, nor do operators receive contractual encouragement to pursue promotions through the craft line.

Layoff Procedure

Seniority is also the major factor in determining layoff procedure for both operators and craft employees. Eighty-five percent of the contracts (30) specify seniority as the sole determinant in layoff procedure for operators, while 80 percent (24) specify seniority as sole determinant in these cases for craft employees. Surprisingly, two contracts contain no reference to layoff procedure for either operators or craft employees. Operators' rights for bumping to maintenance classification are not referred to in 65 percent of the contracts (23), with only three contracts permitting bumping on any job on the property. Bumping rights for craft employees are specified for any job within the job line in roughly one-third of the contracts (11), for any job in the department in only two contracts, and for any job on the property in only three contracts. Forty percent of the contracts (12) contain no reference to bumping rights for craft employees.

With very few exceptions (3), the contract is silent regarding the determination of when layoffs are needed (9 contracts) or the contract designates this as a unilateral management right (25 contracts). Only six of the contracts contain provisions requiring management to give advance notice of a permanent layoff.

Discipline Rights

The rights of management and the union with regard to discipline are not clearly spelled out in most of the contracts. Virtually all of the contracts provide for new employees to serve a probationary period, which most frequently lasts 60 or 90 days. Just over percent of the contracts (19) stipulate that management's right to discharge employees during the probationary period is unilateral, with

the remainder containing no reference. Management has a relatively
free hand with respect to discipline, as evidenced by these findings:
barely 50 percent of the contracts stipulate "just causes" for discipline, with the remainder giving management the right to determine
just cause; fewer than 40 percent of the contracts (14) provide for a
statute of limitations for employees (that is, maximum time in
which employee is accountable for actions) with respect to discipline;
and only two contracts contain a reference restricting indefinite
suspensions.

Discipline issues also assume some prominence as one indicator
of union-management cooperation at the mass transit properties.
While one of the interviewed management officials suggested high
union cooperation in maintaining discipline among the operators,
management officials at four properties suggested union officers
"played politics" in discipline cases—the union officials regarded
discipline issues as campaign tactics for reelection. On the other
hand, union officials at four locations believed that management was
inconsistent and arbitrary in applying "miss-out" penalties to operators. Two union representatives believed overall labor-management
cooperation could be improved if management was not discriminatory
in "playing favorites" on disciplinary matters, whereas management
officials at six locations maintained union-management cooperation
could be enhanced if unions would assume a more objective and
"less advisory role" in these matters.

Somewhat related to discipline is the issue of physical
examinations. To illustrate, an employee can be disciplined
for refusal to take a physical examination, and a physical exam
can be used to support a discipline decision. Although most
contracts (24) do not contain a reference to preemployment phy-
sicals, in those that do the company generally bears the expense. When a current employee's physical fitness is questioned,
most contracts (19) provide for the company to pay for the first
examination and for the company and the employee (the union in
four contracts) to share the costs if more than one opinion or
exam is required. Thirty-three percent of the contracts (12)
contain no reference to the handling of physical fitness determination exams. Apparently, preemployment fitness is not an issue
with the union while fitness determination after employment is.

Past-Practice Clause

A provision common to many labor agreements is a past-
practice clause, which prohibits, or at least limits, management's
right to alter any past practices. In essence, it constrains

management's ability to make changes that affect employees even though the labor agreement may not specifically deal with the area in which the change would be made. A good indication of the degree of harmony in the mass transit industry (at least in the Southeast) is that none of the contracts contains a provision stating that past practices shall not be unilaterally changed. The overwhelming majority contain no reference at all (29 contracts) while a few (6) stipulate that past practices are superseded by the labor agreement.

UNION INVOLVEMENT IN
ADMINISTRATIVE ISSUES—OVERVIEW

To determine the overall degree of union involvement in administrative issues as evidenced in contract language, the responses to each of the 44 variables dealing with administrative issues were recoded as response 1, indicating little-to-no union involvement, or response 2, indicating relatively high union involvement or union power.[1] To illustrate, variable 137 reads as follows:

Distribution of Overtime
Opportunity—Garage employees

0	No reference
1	Company attempts to equalize but no penalties for management error
2	Company attempts to equalize, with penalties for management error
3	Other provision (specify), e.g., seniority emphasized more than equalizing overtime hours

The responses to this variable were recoded as follows:

Variable Number	Response Number	Recode
137	0	1
	1	2
	2	2
	3	2

Thus, those contracts with response 0 were judged to exhibit relatively less union involvement than those contracts with response 1, 2, or 3.

By recoding all 44 variables and calculating the proportions of number 1 and 2 responses, an overall view can be gained of the

TABLE 5.1

Relative Degree of Union Involvement in Administrative Issues by Comparison Category

Category	Number of Category	Proportion of Number 1 Responses (little-to-no union involvement)	Proportion of Number 2 Responses (relatively high union involvement)	Analysis of Variance in F-Ratio*
Organizational structure				
Privately owned	10	.6624	.3376	1.466
Publicly owned—management services company	21	.5951	.4049	
Publicly owned and operated	5	.6238	.3762	
Population				1.062
Less than 250,000	17	.6444	.3556	
250,000 to 500,000	11	.5932	.4068	
More than 500,000	8	.5949	.4051	
Unit size (employees)				0.920
Less than 100	18	.6431	.3569	
100 to 200	7	.6031	.3969	
More than 200	9	.5919	.4081	
Number of buses				0.674
Less than 50	17	.6341	.3659	
50 to 100	7	.6157	.3843	
More than 100	11	.5866	.4134	
Overall proportions		.6178	.3822	

* None of the F-ratios is significant at the .05 level.

<u>Source:</u> Analysis of labor agreements in the nine-state study area compiled by the authors.

relative degree of union involvement with respect to administrative issues. In addition, by comparing the proportions of number 1 and 2 responses by organizational structure, city population size, unit size, and number of buses, we can check for patterns in union power or involvement. The results are presented in Table 5.1.

It is clear from the table that there is no discernible trend or pattern in the degree of union involvement in administrative issues. None of the F-ratios is significant at the .05 level, indicating no significant differences within each comparison group as to the proportions of number 1 and 2 responses. The overall proportion of number 1 responses is .6178. There is very little variation among the categories from this overall figure. These results tend to support the description found in contract provisions; that is, resolutions of administrative issues are fairly uniform throughout the industry, regardless of ownership type, management type, or size.

NOTE

1. The 44 variables dealing with administrative issues are shown in Appendix A and correspond to numbers 52, 53, 58, 111, 117 to 123, 134 to 160, 171 to 175, and 245.

6

IMPASSE RESOLUTIONS: GRIEVANCES AND COLLECTIVE BARGAINING

Impasses can occur over two forms of industrial disputes. One form, grievances, or disputes of "right," protests alleged violations of the labor agreement. The union, in these instances is not seeking a new or altered working condition; instead, the dispute represents an attempt to enforce already attained rights and work rules found in the existing labor agreement. Grievances are usually resolved with the use of local union and management officials, without a major interruption of work activities. The other dispute category, "interest" disputes, pertains to the formal collective negotiations process; here the impasse occurs because one party seeks to obtain a somewhat permanent change in working conditions, and includes this alteration in the collectively bargained labor agreement. This type of dispute receives relatively more publicity particularly when operations are halted, government officials are involved in its resolution, or the impasse resolution techniques conflict with state laws.

The two dispute categories are not mutually exclusive—grievances are typically a significant factor in shaping and extending the collectively bargained labor agreement:

Contract negotiation is the part of the collective bargaining iceberg that shows above the surface. The larger and more important part of the iceberg, seldom seen, is the administration of collective agreements. A contract is no better than its administration. The test of the soundness of a union-management relationship lies in how effectively the parties implement their contract in the troublesome process of living together under the agreement. [1]

Grievance settlements, over a period of time, establish a common law that supplements or even modifies the terms of the negotiated agreement. While arbitrators often frown on an attempt by either labor or management to gain a concession through the grievance procedure that was denied in prior contract negotiations, they nonetheless consider grievance settlements in situations where appropriate contractual language is unclear or nonexistent. Also, the review of employee grievances by union officials is a common tactical procedure in formulating bargaining demands for formal labor agreement negotiations. In many cases the grievance procedure actually represents a continuation of the formal contract negotiations as many of the actions, strategies, and objectives of labor and management representatives prevalent in the formal negotiations are also reflected in grievances preceding the signing of the labor agreement.[2] However, the fundamental differences inherent in the two dispute categories, including their means of resolution, warrant separate consideration in this chapter.

IMPASSE RESOLUTION: GRIEVANCES

The grievance procedure has been considered by many students and practitioners of industrial relations to be a most important aspect of the labor-management relationship. Some consider the grievance procedure to be a "social invention of the greatest importance for our democratic society,"[3] while others regard this process as the "most significant mechanism for accommodating labor-management conflict."[4] Grievances assume initial importance in their close association with potential union membership, as two authorities note:

> Employee representation plans by the score were defeated
> and absorbed by the CIO in the early stages because the
> plant representatives could not get favorable settlements
> of grievances. The telephone workers' unions were built
> on grievances, without the aid of professional organizers.
> The grievance builds the union; over a period of time,
> practically every employee will be drawn into a grievance
> transaction affecting his job.[5]

As the quotation suggests, grievance handling and resolution continues to remain a significant function of the union organization even after it has been established as the exclusive bargaining representative for a specified group of employees. Most, if not all, union members are interested in those policies and actions that directly affect their unique work situations; their assessment of the union's effectiveness will, therefore, be in part determined by their perception of union responsiveness toward any potential problems arising from these policies or actions. However, many specific problems of this nature cannot be resolved during formal collective bargaining negotiations where time constraints and efficient decision making require discussions of problems pertaining to large numbers of employees. Therefore, if union officials wish to demonstrate their intent or desire to represent their constituents' particular job interests, they will probably do so through the use of the grievance procedure.

Similarly, management officials are often concerned about the grievance procedure, but for somewhat different reasons. Management tends to view grievances from a production cost standpoint as grievances can involve a loss of production time when hourly employees, production managers, and management staff representatives devote their attention to grievance adjudication. Management's grievance answer might also establish a precedent applicable to a larger number of employees with a potentially increased financial cost to be incurred by the company. Grievances that are viewed by employees as being unnecessarily delayed or handled unfairly might result in lost production output through resultant employee action, for example, work stoppages,[6] industrial sabotage.

Finally, it is contended that grievances can serve as a valuable communication tool—relaying employee desires and problems to union and management officials. This view of grievances, however, should be tempered with the realization that the sheer number of grievances is not necessarily indicative of the quality of the labor-management relationship at the facility.[7] It is quite conceivable that some of the grievances are either insincere or filed by a small number of the employees.

> It requires subtle and skillful discrimination to interpret grievances properly. An increase in the number of grievances may indicate an approaching union election, the replacement of several old, experienced grievance representatives with new ones, an intraunion factional fight, a crackdown by a plant superintendent upon long-standing lax enforcement of production standards, the appearance of a new, young foreman, or a failure of managers to abide by the agreement. If few grievances are being processed in a firm, the management cannot safely conclude that union relations are good; they may also indicate that the foremen are giving the company away to the union.[8]

Notwithstanding the motives or the scope of the grievances, management officials can still obtain through the grievance procedure some insight into employee attitudes.

GRIEVANCE DEFINITION AND
THE GRIEVANCE PROCEDURE

Grievances can be defined either in general terms, that is, any
employee complaint or concern, or in more restrictive terms, that
is, concerns regarding the interpretation or application of the labor
agreement. One advantage of a specific grievance definition is that
it might restrict invalid grievances; however, a corresponding disadvantage is negative repercussions resulting from supervisory
refusal to accept the grievance unless it protests a specific contractual
violation. The reviewed labor agreements are almost equally divided
between a nonexistent or general grievance definition (45 percent), and
a definition that limits grievances to alleged contractual violations
(55 percent). Management service and privately owned properties
tend to place greater emphasis on a restricted grievance definition;
however, 80 percent of the publicly owned properties provide a
general grievance definition. Perhaps this finding can be attributed to
greater visibility of public employee complaints and the desire of
government officials to demonstrate corresponding responsiveness
to their constituency. Grievance definitions can be further refined
by specifying in the labor agreement certain issues to be excluded
from the grievance procedure. However, none of the reviewed labor
agreements contained any such exclusions.

TABLE 6.1

Steps Specified in the Negotiated Grievance Procedure

Maximum Number of Steps in Negotiated Grievance Procedure	Number of Locations and Percent of Total
2	2 (5.6)
3	18 (50.0)
4	12 (33.3)
5	4 (11.1)

Source: Analysis of labor agreements in the nine-state study
area compiled by the authors.

Almost all (36 out of 37) properties have a contractual provision
for a grievance procedure. The grievance procedure is relatively
independent of competing jurisdiction of civil service appeal systems; only two of the locations operated under management service

ownership explicitly indicate civil service appeals systems for topics excluded from the negotiated grievance procedure, while one other agency (publicly owned) has civil service appeals procedures serving as a step in the negotiated grievance.

A review of Table 6.1 indicates some variation in the number of steps in the grievance procedure. The number of grievance steps is not associated with three of four independent variables, namely, city size, type of ownership, and number of buses. However, there is a somewhat positive association between unit size (number of employees in the unit) and the number of steps in the grievance procedure; more specifically, 39 percent of the properties having less than 100 bargaining unit employees have four or five grievance steps, while 55 percent of the properties having 200 or more employees have this number of steps. Perhaps larger unit size brings greater concern for precedent-setting implications of grievances; and increased numbers of union officers who, in turn, might have to be accommodated through an extended grievance procedure.

A crucial aspect of the grievance procedure is the point of grievance initiation. If procedural time limits commence with the date of the incident, then it is conceivable that tardy realization that the incident merits grievance procedures may negate subsequent grievance processing. On the other hand, if the time limit commences with the "date of discovery," unions will have a relatively unencumbered hand in processing grievances within specified time limits. The labor agreements are equally divided over the grievance initiation issue; more specifically, 50 percent of the contracts indicate "date of incident," with an equal number indicating "date of discovery." None of our independent variables assists in explaining these differences.

Another aspect of the grievance procedure pertains to the extent to which time limits for union appeal and management decision are specified in the contract. Little or no restriction placed on union appeal time limits would give the union a strategic advantage in grievance resolution in that they could have more time to develop their contentions; similarly, the union could defer grievance processing until management was more vulnerable or receptive to grievance resolution in the union's favor. Time limits placed on management's grievance decision would tend to insure a relatively prompt reply to the employee's concern, a situation that can enhance employee morale:

> A quick hearing and reply can be more important than back pay in some grievances. If through tardy recognition of his complaint a worker suffers a loss of dignity and self-respect, management cannot easily recompense him. Workers are, perhaps, as interested in assurance of justice

before the act as in justice through the grievance
procedure after the act. They want a manager to hear
and explicitly to consider their interest before he
acts, as well as afterward. How better can a foreman
or a superintendent show his consideration than by giving
the workers or their steward a hearing, listening to their
gripes, views, or proposals? He may still proceed
exactly as he intended originally, but the workers have
had a kind of accounting and a recognition of their concern. [9]

A vast majority (61 percent) of the labor agreements specify time
limits for all grievance appeals, while a much smaller number (19
percent) of the labor agreements place similar time restraints on
the grievance decisions. It should be mentioned, however, that almost
90 percent (32) of the labor agreements specify at least some time
limits for grievance decisions, the exception in many of these agreements being unrestricted time for the arbitrator's decision. However, there is substantial variation in some of these time limits, as
shown in Table 6.2.

TABLE 6.2

Length of Time Limits in
Negotiated Grievance Procedures

Total Maximum Time Limit Stipulated for Management's Last Decision (before arbitration or other external procedure)	Number of Locations and Percent of Total
Total time limit not stipulated	10 (29.4)
10 days or less	7 (20.6)
11 to 20 days	6 (17.6)
21 days or more	10 (29.4)

Source: Analysis of labor agreements in the nine-state study
area compiled by the authors.

Indeed, the table reflects varying maximum time periods for
resolving grievances. The only independent variable associated with
this variance is unit size; more specifically, 44 percent of the properties having 200 or more bargaining unit employees have maximum

grievance processing time of 21 days or more. Perhaps this increased time is needed, or at least the need for the time is anticipated, to resolve the greater number of grievances from the larger bargaining unit. It should be mentioned that grievance time limits can be extended by mutual labor-management agreement at approximately 35 percent of the publicly owned and management service-operated properties but at none of the privately owned properties.

The private-public ownership distinction may explain another difference in grievance processing. One union official who was involved in the public takeover of a private agency noted:

> In the private operation's grievances management did not
> have to run to some other source and get an approval.
> Today, in our situation, this is not the case, and I sus-
> pect it is not the case in many of the other local unions
> who have to deal with their managements in the transit
> authority concept. We deal up through the layers of
> authority through the general manager. The general
> manager in the transit authority concept, as we have
> with our management company, will not make a decision
> on something until they go to some other management
> official. I don't know who they go to—they may go to
> the transit authority, they may go to the people who are
> above them in the other private management arrangement.
> Many times this causes disenchantment within the local
> membership . . . because the delay comes about in such
> a way as to make an expeditious settlement of a grievance
> almost impossible. Delay breeds disunity and discord.
> This is one of the big problems that a labor union officer
> has to be confronted with. If you don't have a handle on
> your membership and can't exercise some degree of
> control over the situation you will lose it and the next
> thing you know, you have an unfortunate situation that
> both management and labor does not want to have, so
> this is something that is a very serious matter. Manage-
> ment and labor need to focus attention upon this area of
> concern because if we allow it to run, it's just like pouring
> gasoline on a fire or having a spark, or fire, get started
> and the next thing you know it is running out of hand, and
> that fire department that was mentioned earlier may not
> get there in time to put it out and you have a total disaster. [10]

The final step in most (95 percent) of the contractually specified grievance procedures is binding arbitration. This high percentage reflects the heritage of private sector ownership—the percentage is comparable to that found in most private sector industries while considerably higher than that in most public sector operations.[11] The vast majority (83 percent) of the applicable provisions do not specifically exclude certain issues from arbitration; however, some labor agreements prohibit arbitration over some adverse actions, contract negotiations, and jurisdictional questions under statutes or civil service laws. All but one of the properties, either expressly in the arbitration provision or through contractual silence, allow the arbitrator to resolve questions of arbitrability. However, approximately one-fourth of the arbitration provisions, found mostly at the management service properties, indicate that the arbitrator has no power to "add to or subtract from the contract."

There are two different forms of arbitration found in the reviewed labor agreements. Slightly over half the properties having grievance arbitration use a two-step arbitration procedure. Management and union representatives each choose an arbitrator at the first-level arbitration hearings; the decision of the first-level arbitrators is binding if the arbitrators are in agreement over the issue's resolution. If the arbitrators do not reach agreement, then arbitration proceeds to the second level where a third, neutral arbitrator resolves the issue, either alone or as a third member of the arbitration panel. The other half of the labor agreements feature only one arbitration level where the neutral arbitrator, chosen by the management and union representatives, either solely resolves the issue or has the deciding vote on a three-member panel (neutral arbitrator, union arbitrator, management arbitrator). In all cases, management and the union each pay the cost of their respective arbitrators and witnesses and share the expense of the neutral arbitrator.

A significant issue in grievance resolution is the average amount of time taken to resolve a grievance. One empirical study analyzing several thousand arbitration decisions found that the average time lapse from grievance date to arbitration award was 8.5 months.[12] As previously cited in this section, only 37 percent of the labor agreements require management's final grievance decision to be reached 20 days or less before the grievance can be appealed to arbitration. Another dilatory factor pertains to the relatively unspecified time limits placed on the arbitrator's final decision. For example, 11 percent of the contract provisions allow the arbitrator over 31 days to reach a decision whereas 71 percent of the contracts place no time limit on the final arbitration decision. Thus, it can potentially take a very long time to arrive at the final grievance disposition. However, our interviews at 20 mass transit locations did not uncover this lack of decision limits as a problem.

Finally, the negotiated grievance procedure (steps and time limits) is somewhat common to all grievance topics. Only 17 percent of the labor agreements contain "special" grievance procedures, with the vast majority of these procedures pertaining to employee discipline issues.

Employee and Union Rights in the Grievance Procedure

Unions coming under the jurisdiction of the National Labor Relations Act have the implicit duty to act fairly toward the employees they represent. However, a 1953 Supreme Court decision[13] qualified this obligation by indicating that the union does not have to process all employee grievances; in fact, processing dichotomous employee grievances on a particular issue could hinder or destroy the union's effectiveness as well as go against the intent of the National Labor Relations Act. A more recent Supreme Court decision extended this reasoning:

> Some have suggested that every individual employee should have the right to have his grievance taken to arbitration. Others have urged that the union be given substantial discretion (if the collective bargaining agreement so provides) to decide whether a grievance should be taken to arbitration, subject only to the duty to refrain from patently wrongful conduct such as racial discrimination or personal hostility.
> Though we accept the proposition that a union may not arbitrarily ignore a meritorious grievance or process it in a perfunctory fashion, we do not agree that the individual employee has an absolute right to have his grievance taken to arbitration regardless of the provisions of the applicable collective bargaining agreement.[14]

Therefore, it is not surprising that none of the privately owned mass transit properties expressly allows the employee to continue the grievance after the union aborts. Also, none of the investigated contracts expressly prohibits the union's screening of employee grievances to determine whether the grievance is justified.

Employee appeal rights in the public sector are often subject to many local and state laws. However, two recent (1972) Supreme Court decisions suggest that a public employee may have appeal rights irrespective of constraints posed by the state, municipality, or labor agreement.

Roth-Perry, in addition to holding that public employees with liberty or property interests in their jobs could not be dismissed without a hearing, also held that a public employee could not be dismissed, regardless of his status, for an unconstitutional reason. When a litigant complains of a deprivation of liberty or property, the remedy he seeks is an administrative hearing. When a litigant complains that he has been dismissed for an unconstitutional reason, however, his remedy lies with a federal court.

Often, the distinction between the remedies sought is blurred; federal courts hold trial-type hearings in both situations.

The federal courts have therefore become a de facto "super civil service commission" for all public employees. A public employee, discharged for a reason he considers to be arbitrary and perhaps denied access to an administrative hearing, can use the back door to

TABLE 6.3

Contractual Provisions Dealing with the
Rights of Unions in the Grievance Process
(number of agreements)

Contractual Provision	Contractual Specification of Rights		
	Contract Silent	Not Allowed	Allowed
Union official has right to initiate the grievance even if not the aggrieved	28	1	8
Involvement of the union grievance committee in the negotiated grievance procedure	16	0	21
Number of union stewards specified in the labor agreement	36	0	1
Movement and time limitations are placed on the union stewards and representatives in investigating grievances	34	0	3
Compensation for stewards and representatives for time lost in grievance duties during working hours	28	2	7
Use of outside union officials in appeals procedure	31	0	6
Union receives a copy of the final grievance decision	24	0	13

Source: Analysis of labor agreements in the nine-state study area compiled by the authors.

the federal court. He needs only to add to his due process claim a count alleging dismissal for an unconstitutional reason. Invariably, the court determines that
it must give the litigant a full hearing, regardless of
whether it finds that he has a Roth-protected liberty or
property interest.[15]

Perhaps the four labor agreements (found only at management service
properties) allowing employees to continue appealing after union
rejections of the grievances reflect the reasoning and/or influence
of the aforementioned judicial decisions.

Table 6.3 summarizes the contractual rights of unions and
union officials in the grievance process. Perhaps the only conclusion
to be drawn from the table is the lack of contractual formalization of
the union's grievance procedure rights. While it is impossible to
interpret contractual silence as favoring the union, some of our
open-ended interview questions—for example, "What steps could be
taken to improve overall management-union cooperation in the administration of the contract at your facility?"—failed to uncover any
union or management dissatisfaction with the grievance process. Therefore, we interpret contractual silence on the preceding issues to
mean an informal accommodation of the union's rights in the grievance
process.

IMPASSE RESOLUTION: INTEREST DISPUTES

Arbitration

Arbitration of negotiation impasses is similar to grievance
arbitration in that a binding decision is made by a neutral party or
tripartite panel, consisting of labor and management representatives
and a neutral third party, after hearing and analyzing union and
management contentions. The ATU has perhaps encouraged arbitration
of negotiation impasses longer and with more fervor than any other
union in the American labor movement.

In its first constitution in 1892 the Amalgamated [ATU]
stated that one of its objectives was to "encourage the
settlement of all disputes between employees and employers by arbitration." It was later made mandatory that the
locals offer to arbitrate disputes before striking . . .[16]

Current comments from the ATU newspaper reflect this enthusiasm:

> Arbitration is a procedure to be used as a last resort,
> taking the place of a strike, particularly, where we
> are prohibited by law from striking due to the industry's
> transfer from private to public ownership. [17]

> The Amalgamated feels that arbitration appeals to the
> people's support; that if its cause is just and reasonable,
> it will stand up to fair-minded arbitration; if it is not
> a reasonable demand, then it won't. [18]

Another advantage of arbitration is that it offers management and
union representatives a face-saving alternative—the technique allows
each side to demonstrate to its constituents a steadfast attitude
regarding labor issues while, at the same time, accepting an outsider's decision. Finally, arbitration has the advantage of finality
while insuring uninterrupted mass transit services. It should
be mentioned, however, that this advantage may be realized more
by state government officials than by their local counterparts,
who are concerned about the "ripple" effect of arbitration
settlements being eventually passed on to other employee
classifications. [19]

However, arbitration of interest disputes is not without its
corresponding disadvantages. [20] Perhaps the most serious charge
leveled against arbitration is that this technique can discourage
contract negotiations. [21] For example, management officials, antici-
pating the possibility of interest arbitration, might not present their
true final wage offer to the union, fearing that the arbitrator will use
this figure as a starting point in the eventual compromise. Similarly,
the union will hold to an inflated wage demand, realizing that the
arbitrator will alter the figure downward in attempting to reach a
settlement acceptable by both parties. [22] One way to avoid this
disadvantage is "either-or" arbitration where the arbitrator, either
on an issue-by-issue basis or for the entire labor agreement proposal, cannot compromise management and union negotiation proposals. [23] Our investigation did not uncover any use of the either-or
arbitration technique at the mass transit properties.

In commenting on impasse resolutions, a management service
representative noted:

> We as a firm strongly oppose interest arbitration and
> have so stated in every 13(c) agreement that we have
> ever signed. We feel that we have been able to deal on
> each one of the properties that we manage with the local
> and the international union for many years and have been
> able to resolve our own problems—the local problems

from the membership standpoint—and to put that
into a third party, in our judgment, is an error.[24]

This external role can raise legal questions when governmental
sovereignty is transferred in its entirety to a pro tem appointed
board.[25] A related problem occurs when the arbitrator is unfamiliar
with the issues found at the mass transit locations, a situation which
one observer suggests presents the union with an advantage:

> The reason use of voluntary arbitration declined after
> 1952 was that management increasingly found it an
> unacceptable technique for resolving impasses. Manage-
> ment's primary objections, according to Alfred Kuhn,
> were that the arbitrators had unlimited powers, the
> arbitrators were biased, the three-man arbitration
> boards did not try to determine what was objectively
> right but engaged in "horse trading" among themselves
> in order to reach a settlement, it cost too much, and
> its use impeded collective bargaining.
>   Of all the objections to the present practice of
> arbitration, the one which appears most frequently . . .
> is that the Amalgamated [ATU] has outsmarted, out-
> bargained, and in general used more effective strategy
> than has management.
>   The main reason was that the ATU had centralized
> control and a highly professional team of advocates,
> while management had little coordination and less
> experience. The ATU's advocates, the Labor Bureau
> of the Midwest, proved easily superior to management's
> local counsels. As one employer stated:
>   "The battle array still presents a highly organized
> team of specialists lined up on the union side against a
> capable but overburdened group of managers opposing
> them. . . . The crux of this: Management unorganized
> is no match for labor organized."[26]

Whatever the reason, the use of interest arbitration in mass transit
has declined over the years, as evidenced by the statistics shown
in Table 6.4. Our investigation mirrored the decline of this technique;
for example, only four of the analyzed labor agreements contained
provisions for arbitration of negotiation impasses.[27] Similarly,
interest arbitration has been employed on only three occasions, at
only two of the interviewed properties. Unfortunately, little information regarding the effectiveness of this technique could be obtained;
one of the arbitrations occurred in 1947, and the other two arbitration

TABLE 6.4

Transit Industry: Arbitrations And Strikes,
Ten-Year Totals, 1920–69

Period	Arbitrations	Strikes	Total	Arbitrations As Percent of Total
1920–29	117	153	270	43
1930–39	60	29	89	67
1940–49	260	375	635	41
1950–59	74	482	556	13
1960–69	15	532	547	3

Source: Darold T. Barnum, "From Private to Public: Labor Relations in Urban Transit," Industrial and Labor Relations Review 25 (October 1971): 108.

cases were, at the time of the interview, unresolved. It should be mentioned that all management and union officials involved with the current arbitrations were uncertain and apprehensive over the outcome. Finally, one interviewed management representative succintly expressed reasons for not using this technique:

> Arbitration is an abdication on the part of the union and management of any control over their situation. If the company is private, going to arbitration means giving away your responsibilities to the stockholders. If the company is public, going to arbitration means giving away your responsibilities to the taxpayers.

Mediation

Mediation can occur before or after the contract expiration date; in other words, any time management and/or labor representatives, believing there is an impasse, seek the mediator's assistance. Most mediators are government officials, employed by the Federal Mediation and Conciliation Service, and serve in an advisory capacity at the will of the labor and management representatives—the mediator is indeed an invited guest, one who can be asked to leave at any time by one or both of the negotiating teams.

The mediator's role is to assist the parties in making their own agreements, ones with which they can live. In many cases the mediator's success derives from his role—the mediator sometimes steps

into a situation where negotiations have broken off and both labor
and management representatives are reluctant to reconvene negotiations for fear that to do so will be interpreted as a sign of weakness.
The mediator can call for resumption of collective bargaining, with
both sides indicating to their respective constituents that they are
honoring the government official's advice. Thus:

> . . . the mere entrance of a mediator into a dispute is
> in some ways a face-saving device. In an ambiguous
> situation, the implication that the battle was so hard
> fought that a mediator had to be brought in may be help-
> ful. More important perhaps, the mediator may share
> some of the responsibility for the outcome and thereby
> decrease the responsibility of the parties. He might do
> this, for example, by making recommendations for a
> settlement for which he will take responsibility and, if
> need be, pursuant to this end, public responsibility.[28]

Perhaps the mediator's personality characteristics are most
responsible for the success or failure of the impasse resolution technique. One such personality trait is persuasiveness:

> The mediator's stock-in-trade is persuasion applied
> through the use of pressure in order to modify attitudes
> and behavior. Pressure refers to those techniques
> which tend to cause one party or the other to reconsider
> its position. Pressures could be economic, social, and
> political, referring to opinions of the public, and unions
> and employees other than those directly involved, and
> personal, involving attributes of the mediator that facili-
> tate agreement such as his prestige and knowledge of the
> industry. Pressures used in mediating a public sector
> case tend to be more personal, social, and political, but
> less economic.[29]

A closely related personal characteristic is the ability to inspire
trust. Often the mediator holds separate caucuses with the union
and management bargaining teams and obtains confidential information regarding final offer and acceptance positions. This information
can facilitate eventual agreement; however, if improperly divulged,
it can destroy labor-management negotiations.

The mediator can also help negotiations by providing a fresh
viewpoint, which allows the parties to pursue new and related
courses of action. This characteristic assumes that the mediator
is knowledgeable about the situation, an assumption that cannot be

taken too lightly. [30] There are relatively few mass transit operations under a mediator's jurisdiction; this, coupled with the unique and complex mass transit issues, for example, spread time, intervals in an operator's schedule, extra operators, places the mediator at a relative disadvantage.

Unfortunately, it is difficult, if not impossible, to gauge the effectiveness of mediation as an impasse resolution technique:

> The principal reason so little is written about mediation may be attributed to its success. Mediation is inherently a private activity. When employed successfully, it remains hidden from public view. Only when mediation falters and fact finding is initiated is there an opportunity, and then only indirectly, to assess the mediation process. [31]

Additionally, since many mass transit properties are subject to the legal requirement of collective bargaining, virtually all disputes must be settled at some point, whether before or after a strike. It is therefore conceivable that the settlement would ultimately occur with or without outside assistance from the mediator. [32]

Only five of the labor agreements analyzed in our study explicitly recognized mediation in the resolution of negotiation impasses. However, this is one clear instance where contractual silence must be interpreted cautiously, as our interviews revealed mediation is the most commonly used (70 percent of the interviewed properties) impasse resolution technique.[33] Only one management and four union representatives expressed neutral-to-negative reactions over this form of impasse resolution. Additionally, management representatives at six locations and a union representative at one location qualify the mediator's success on the basis of his personal capabilities. These respondents have experienced both good and bad mediators and suggest no inherent benefits rest with mediation; instead, the potential success of this technique rests solely on the performance of the individual mediator. The most often cited handicap of the mediator is his unfamiliarity with the complexities inherent in mass transit operations. The remainder of the respondents indicated mediation has been very effective for at least two reasons: it has helped keep negotiations going on, or, in some cases, helped break the stalemate between the parties; and mediators have educated the parties, particularly those new to the complexities of collective bargaining.

Job Action

Perhaps the most publicized form of job action is the strike—a concerted cessation of service by employees intended to force management to acquiesce to the union's bargaining demands. Many of the policy dimensions surrounding the strike tactic will be discussed in Chapter 7; the purpose of this section is to examine the frequency and relative effectiveness of this technique. It should be mentioned that this technique has a paradoxical relationship to the labor movement in mass transit. On one hand, the 1966 New York transit strike has been cited as the impetus for strikes in the public sector as the benefits obtained from this technique were viewed by many public employees as outweighing possible disadvantages.[34] However, one transit union has continually gone on record as opposing strikes:

> We must also keep in mind the one thing that we must always have, and that is the public on our side, because the public, in one way or another, pays our wages. In most cases we must depend on the public for our very livelihood and we certainly cannot expect their support if we continue to abuse their needs. We have learned, often the hard way, that illegal strikes encourage stiff anti-strike legislation.[35]

> It is a documented fact that strikes cause a permanent loss of business. Customers turn to other modes of transportation when transit workers strike, and they more often than not continue to avoid public transportation after work resumes. Thus, peaceful settlements of disputes—as through arbitration—generally work to everyone's advantage.[36]

As can be seen from the following quotation, the strike tactic can offer a fundamental strategic advantage to a public sector union:

> Public officials are more susceptible than private employers to public (hence, political) pressure to settle a negotiation dispute. The high visibility of public services, ready accessibility of public officials, and sole-source character of most public services contribute to the generation of this public pressure. Such pressure stems from the reality that these public officials run periodically for reelection to their current office or for election to a higher office. As has been observed . . . voters will tend to choose political

leaders who avoid inconveniencing strikes over those
who work to minimize the costs of settlements at the
price of a strike.[37]

However, a more fundamental question emerges regarding the applicability of the strike to the mass transit industry. At least one observer of mass transit's industrial relations activities infers the shift
from private to public ownership may abnegate the strike option as
well as other collective bargaining rights.[38] One purpose of our
research was to inquire into the extent and effectiveness of strikes
in the mass transit industry in the Southeast. Only nine of the analyzed labor agreements either were silent or had a general prohibition
regarding this impasse technique. The large remainder of the labor
agreements prohibited strikes during the term of the labor agreement;
presumably, this contractual provision at least implicitly recognizes
the strike option during a negotiation impasse occurring after the
labor agreement expires. Interviews at the 20 selected mass transit
locations revealed 15 strikes at eight locations, with nine of the
strikes occurring before 1960, and four strikes occurring since 1970.
However, there are few legal restraints on strikes at the properties
as only five of these locations had legislation prohibiting strikes at
their properties. The shift from private to public ownership of mass
transit agencies had not had a retarding effect on the ability to
strike as most of the locations studied have retained under current
Section 13(c) negotiated provisions the formerly established right to
strike. Our findings parallel those resulting from a study of California legislation; more specifically:

> In the transit authority legislation in question, the right
> of collective bargaining was given, but no mention was
> made of rights to engage in concerted activities as there
> had been in the earlier case. The court nevertheless
> determined that the collective bargaining rights granted
> in the legislation contemplate and imply a right to strike.
> The court also distinguished the proprietary activity of
> the transit workers from other public employees when
> it stated that "we deal only with government operation of
> a normally private, proprietary activity; . . . our
> holding in no way extends to 'public employees such as
> policemen, firemen and public officers exercising a
> portion of the state's sovereign powers.'" This case
> may have implications for transit district employees in
> other jurisdictions.[39]

Management and union representatives, at five and four locations,
respectively, acknowledged that strike activity at their location

resulted in a permanent loss of wages and revenues, as well as in adverse public opinion.

One mass transit official indicated the following potential disadvantages of the strike tactic:

> I think that in the future the classical nature of collective bargaining will change significantly with respect to public transportation. In a deficit situation, clearly the use of economic warfare by either side is irrational. The strike no longer exerts economic pressure, since, in deficit operations, not operating saves money. On the other hand, if in the past the strike has been used as a means of inconveniencing the public in an effort to bring political pressure on management to settle at any price, its use for that purpose in the future will be increasingly pointless. We are at a point where localities simply do not have the means to give in to such pressure even if they want to. As a practical necessity, localities will have no choice but to resist further escalation of operating costs. Strikes will not only have devastating operating results, but will erode the vital political support on which subsidies depend. In the future such strikes will more likely result in punitive legislation than economic gain. [40]

However, two union officials stated that strike action was sometimes necessary to let management know the union will take a firm stance on some issues and not be pushed around.

Strikes are not the only form of job action that can be employed to bring pressure on management. Slowdowns, that is, following the rules to the letter, sickouts, refusals to do nonessential work, and so on, often assume the pressure of a strike while not depriving union members of wage losses associated with a strike. Our interview investigation revealed few job actions of this nature; more specifically, only one property indicated this experience and the management representative at this property regarded the tactic as being "ineffective."

Finally, our interviews attempted to determine the extent and desirability of the involvement of local, state, and federal officials in negotiation impasses. [41] None of the properties had experienced such participation. However, almost all of the management and union representatives doubted the potential effectiveness of governmental involvement, excepting that of mediators, in negotiation impasses, the reasons being twofold: the political nature of these officials; and their limited knowledge of mass transit operations.

UNION INVOLVEMENT IN
IMPASSE RESOLUTION—OVERVIEW

To determine the overall degree of union involvement in impasse resolution as evidenced in the contract language, the responses to each of the 58 variables dealing with impasse resolution were recoded as response 1, indicating little-to-no involvement, or response 2, indicating relatively high union involvement.[42] To illustrate, variable 177 reads as follows:

	Grievance Definition
0	No negotiated grievance procedure
1	No definition
2	General definition, e.g., matter of concern, complaint, working conditions
3	Definition stating interpretation, application, or violation of agreement

The responses to this variable were recoded as follows:

Variable Number	Response Number	Recode
177	0	1
	1	2
	2	2
	3	1

Thus, those contracts with responses 0 and 3 were judged to exhibit relatively less union involvement than those contracts with responses 1 and 2.

By recoding all 58 impasse resolution variables and calculating the proportions of number 1 and 2 responses, an overall view can be gained of the relative degree of union involvement with respect to impasse resolution. In addition, by comparing the proportions of number 1 and 2 responses by organizational structure, city population size, unit size, and number of buses, we can check for patterns in union power or involvement. The results are presented in Table 6.5.

By comparing this table with the data in Tables 3.7, 4.6, and 5.1, it can be seen that unions have a higher degree of involvement in impasse resolution than in institutional, economic, and administrative issues. This finding is not surprising as unions have traditionally emphasized impasse resolution procedures as a means of justifying their organizational existence to their constituents. However, it is

TABLE 6.5

Relative Degree of Union Involvement in Impasse Resolution Issues by Comparison Category

Category	Number in Category	Proportion of Number 1 Responses (little-to-no union involvement)	Proportion of Number 2 Responses (relatively high union involvement)	Analysis of Variance in F-Ratio*
Organizational structure				
Privately owned	10	.5719	.4281	1.714
Publicly owned—management services company	21	.5558	.4442	
Publicly owned and operated	5	.6262	.3738	
Population				
Less than 250,000	17	.5655	.4345	0.804
250,000 to 500,000	11	.5929	.4071	
More than 500,000	8	.5483	.4517	
Unit size (employees)				
Less than 100	18	.5631	.4369	1.368
100 to 200	7	.6166	.3834	
More than 200	9	.5600	.4400	
Number of buses				
Less than 50	17	.5645	.4355	0.094
50 to 100	7	.5765	.4235	
More than 100	11	.5706	.4294	
Overall proportions		.5700	.4300	

* None of the F-ratios is significant at the .05 level.

Source: Analysis of labor agreements in the nine-state study area compiled by the authors.

117

somewhat surprising to find none of our variables accounting for statistically significant variation among these issues. We initially assumed that the agency's size (number of employees and number of buses) would be positively associated with the inclusion of more detailed impasse resolution procedures in the labor agreement—the potentially greater number of grievances processed in larger agencies would result in a higher degree of contractual formalization of impasse resolution procedures and related union rights. Similarly, we expected to find different organizational structures having somewhat unique administrative preferences for impasse resolution, with these preferences being incorporated into the labor agreement. However, the inability of these variables to differentiate union involvement suggests that applicable labor agreement provisions may more likely reflect the impasse resolution experience (both grievances and negotiation impasses) found at the particular property. Unfortunately, there is virtually no research on impasse resolution, particularly grievances and arbitration in the mass transit industry. Significant insights into this area can be attained only through future research.

NOTES

1. Harold W. Davey, Contemporary Collective Bargaining, 3d ed. (Englewood Cliffs, N.J.: Prentice-Hall, 1972), p. 141. See also, Robert B. McKersie and William M. Shropshire, Jr., "Avoiding Written Grievances: A Successful Program," Journal of Business 25 (April 1962): 139.

2. For example, see James W. Kuhn, Bargaining in Grievance Settlement (New York: Columbia University Press, 1961); and M.S. Ryder, "Some Concepts Concerning Grievance Procedure," Labor Law Journal 7 (January 1956): 15-18.

3. William F. Whyte, The Grievance Process (Lansing: Industrial Relations Research Center, 1956), p. 6.

4. Van Dusen Kennedy, "Grievance Negotiation," in Industrial Conflict, ed. Arthur Kornhauser, Robert Dubin, and Arthur Ross (New York: McGraw-Hill, 1954), p. 287.

5. Joseph Kovner and Herbert Lahne, "Shop Society and the Union," Industrial and Labor Relations Review 7 (October 1953): 61. See also Joel Seidman et al., The Worker Views His Union (Chicago: University of Chicago Press, 1958), pp. 182-83.

6. For example, see Alvin Gouldner, Wildcat Strike (New York: Harper & Row, 1965), pp. 49 and 109; and McKersie and Shropshire, loc. cit.

7. Michael H. Moskow, J. Joseph Lowenberg, and Edward Koziara, eds., Collective Bargaining in Public Employment (New York: Random House, 1970), p. 115.

8. James W. Kuhn, "The Grievance Process," in Frontiers of Collective Bargaining, ed. John Dunlop and Neil W. Chamberlain (New York: Harper & Row, 1967), pp. 259-60.

9. Kuhn, "The Grievance Process," p. 257.

10. Remarks made by a union panelist at the Conference on Unions, Management Rights, and the Public Interest in Mass Transit, Jacksonville, March 23, 1976.

11. Moskow, Lowenberg, and Koziara, eds., Collective Bargaining, p. 247; Winston Crouch, "The American City and Its Organized Employees," in Collective Bargaining in Government: Readings and Cases, ed. J. Joseph Lowenberg and Michael H. Moskow (Englewood Cliffs, N. J.: Prentice-Hall, 1972), pp. 72-80; and George T. Sulzner, "The Impact of Impasse Procedures in Public Sector Labor: An Overview," Journal of Collective Negotiations in the Public Sector 4 (1975): 3.

12. Pearce Davis and Gopal C. Pati, "Elapsed Grievance Time, 1942-1972," Arbitration Journal, March 1974, p. 21. For an example of the potential of expedited grievance arbitration, see Michael F. Hoellering, "Expedited Grievance Arbitration: The First Steps," in Industrial Relations Research Proceedings of the Twenty-Seventh Annual Winter Meeting, ed. James Stern and Barbara Dennis (Madison: Industrial Relations Research Association, 1975), pp. 324-31.

13. Ford Motor Co. v. Huffman, 345 U.S. 31 (1953).

14. Vaca v. Sipes, 386 U.S. 171 (1967). See also, Charles J. Morris, ed., The Developing Labor Law (Washington, D.C.: Bureau of National Affairs, 1971), p. 738.

15. "The Due Process Rights of Public Employees," New York University Law Review 50 (May 1965), p. 351. See also, Paul D. Staudohar, "Individual and Collective Rights in Public Employment Appeals Procedures," Labor Law Journal 26 (July 1975), pp. 435-38.

16. Darold T. Barnum, "From Private to Public: Labor Relations in Urban Transit," Industrial and Labor Relations Review 25 (October 1971): 104. The author also indicates that the other major transit union, TWU, has never been enthusiastic over interest arbitration. For a historical perspective of the ATU's constitutional arrangements for arbitration of interest disputes, see Emerson P. Schmidt, Industrial Relations in Urban Transportation (Minneapolis: University of Minnesota Press, 1937), p. 175. For a historical, case study approach to transit-interest arbitration, see Dallas Young, "Fifty Years of Labor Arbitration in Cleveland Transit," Monthly Labor Review (May 1960): 464-71.

17. In Transit, March 1974, p. 2.

18. In Transit, May 1974, p. 13.

19. Sam Zagoria, "The U.S. Cities Tackle Impasses," in Industrial Relations Research Association Series: Proceedings of the 25th Anniversary Meeting, ed. Gerald G. Somers (Madison: Industrial Relations Research Association, 1973), pp. 51-52.

20. For example, see Raymond A. Smardon, "Arbitration is No Bargain," Nation's Business 62 (October 1974), pp. 80-83.

21. Sulzner, "The Impact," p. 10; R. Clark, Jr., "Legislated Interest Arbitration—A Management Response," in Industrial Relations Research Association Proceedings of the Twenty-Seventh Annual Winter Meeting, p. 320. It should be mentioned that there is little in the way of empirical confirmation of this disadvantage. See for example, J. Lowenberg, "Compulsory Arbitration for Police and Firefighters in Pennsylvania in 1968," Industrial and Labor Relations Review 23 (April 1970): 337-70; and J. Lowenberg, "The Effect of Compulsory Arbitration on Collective Negotiations," Journal of Collective Negotiations in the Public Sector, May 1972, pp. 177-90.

22. This arbitration problem has been evidenced in the mass transit industry; see Darold T. Barnum, Collective Bargaining and Manpower in Urban Transit Systems (Ph.D. diss., University of Pennsylvania, 1972), pp. 154-55.

23. Joseph R. Grodin, "Either-Or Arbitration for Public Employee Disputes," Industrial Relations 11 (May 1972): 260-66; Gary Long and Peter Feuille, "Final Offer Arbitration: Sudden Death in Eugene," Industrial and Labor Relations Review 27 (January 1974): 186-203; and Fred Witney, "Final Offer Arbitration: The Indianapolis Experience," Monthly Labor Review 96 (May 1973): 220-25.

24. Remarks made by a management service panelist at the Conference on Unions, Management Rights, and the Public Interest in Mass Transit, Jacksonville, March 23, 1976.

25. Charles M. Rehmus, "Legislated Interest Arbitration," in Industrial Relations Research Association Proceedings of the Twenty-Seventh Annual Winter Meeting, p. 307; and K.A. Houseman, "Compulsory Arbitration in the Public Sector: Constitutionality and Enforcement Issues," Public Personnel Management 2 (May–June 1973), pp. 194-99. For an altered arbitration process, which attempts to mitigate the outsider disadvantage, see Joseph Grodin, "Arbitration of Public Sector Labor Disputes: The Nevada Experiment," Industrial and Labor Relations Review 38 (October 1974): pp. 89-102.

26. Barnum, "From Private to Public," p. 105.

27. Neither the contract analysis nor the interview data reflected any indication of the final offer arbitration technique in resolving negotiation impasses.

28. Carl Stevens, "Mediation and the Role of the Neutral," in Frontiers of Collective Bargaining, ed. Dunlop and Chamberlain, pp. 283-84.

29. Paul D. Staudohar, "Some Implications of Mediation for Resolution of Bargaining Impasses in Public Employment," Public Personnel Management 2 (July-August 1973): 300; and Hugh C. Lovell, "The Pressure Lever in Mediation," Industrial and Labor Relations Review 6 (October 1952): 22.

30. Ibid., p. 300; and Eva Robins, "Some Comparisons of Mediation in the Public and Private Sector," in Collective Bargaining in Government, ed. Lowenberg and Moskow, pp. 323-29.

31. Sulzner, "The Impact," p. 6.

32. Staudohar, "Some Implications," p. 302.

33. There was no particular relationship between property ownership and use of mediation; indeed, a somewhat unexpected finding was that four out of the five public agencies interviewed in this study have employed this technique.

34. Arnold M. Zack, "Impasses, Strikes, and Resolutions," in Public Workers and Public Unions, ed. Sam Zagoria (Englewood Cliffs, N.J.: Prentice-Hall, 1972), p. 102.

35. In Transit, March 1974, p. 2.

36. In Transit, April, 1974, p. 12.

37. Jay F. Atwood, "Collective Bargaining's Challenge: Five Imperatives for Public Managers," Public Personnel Management 5 (January-February 1976): p. 25; H. H. Wellington and R. K. Winter, Jr., "Structuring Collective Bargaining in Public Employment," Yale Law Journal 79 (April 1970): 847; and John Dunlop, "The Function of a Strike," in Frontiers, ed. Dunlop and Chamberlain, pp. 103-04.

38. Darold T. Barnum, "National Public Labor Relations Legislation: The Case of Urban Mass Transit, Labor Law Journal 27 (March 1976): 168.

39. Paul D. Staudohar, "Quasi-Strikes by Public Employees," Journal of Collective Negotiations in the Public Sector 3 (Fall 1974): 367.

40. Louis J. Gambaccini, "A Common Purpose: Labor and Management in the Future of Public Transportation" (Speech delivered at the Conference on Unions, Management Rights, and the Public Interest in Mass Transit, Jacksonville, March 22, 1976).

41. For a description (including advantages and disadvantages) of state governmental officials in collective bargaining, see Jean T. McKelvey, "The Role of State Agencies in Public Employee Labor Relations," Industrial and Labor Relations Review 20 (January 1967): 182-97.

42. The 58 variables dealing with impasse resolution are shown in Appendix A and correspond to numbers 163 to 216, and 240 to 243.

CHAPTER

7

CONTEMPORARY LABOR-
MANAGEMENT ISSUES
IN MASS TRANSIT

The preceding chapters have discussed various aspects of the collective bargaining process and their results. However, there are various, rather significant issues which are not only expressed in collective bargaining, but also pervade the overall labor-management relationship at mass transit properties. The purpose of this chapter is to address the following: the impact of technological changes on labor; Section 13(c) of the Urban Mass Transportation Act of 1964; minorities and transit; and the public interest in mass transit.

THE IMPACT OF TECHNOLOGICAL CHANGE ON
LABOR-MANAGEMENT RELATIONS

The issue of technological change has frequently been prominent in collective bargaining, not because of its intrinsic interest to both labor and management, but because of its potential impact on the nature of labor-management relations.[1] Our investigation approached this topic in a twofold manner. First, we examined the extent of technological change in the mass transit industry; more specifically, the recent technological innovations as well as their possible effects on mass transit employees. Secondly, an attempt was made to determine union involvement in technological change.

Extent of Technological Change in Mass Transit

Technological change can embrace improved physical facilities, changes in methods of operation, as well as innovations in hardware. Both union and management interview respondents expressed a general

122

feeling that there have not been significant technological changes at their property; one management official expressed this feeling by commenting, "We have had the same rubber tire bus operation for the past forty years."

Each respondent was asked to specify recent technological changes occurring at their property; the following list represents the more commonly cited technological changes (in the order of their frequency):

1. Improved shop equipment (for example, lubrication systems)
2. Increased bus size (length and width)
3. Fare box collection systems (locked fare boxes, exact change, and so on)
4. Bus air conditioning

Only one of the respondents cited application of the computer to scheduling and inventory, while a few indicated specific changes affecting bus operation, for example, air load size levelers, larger transmission.

Technological change can have several potential effects on the jobs of mass transit employees. First, innovations can alter the work patterns of employees—requiring them to alter their work schedules, job duties, or skill levels. None of the union and management respondents maintained that recent technological changes (over the past five years) have materially altered their job characteristics although a few of the respondents indicated that operators and maintenance employees had to undergo some training when new braking and transmission systems were introduced. Also, no job classifications have been seriously altered or eliminated due to recent technological changes. A second, more profound effect of technological change occurs when the number of bargaining unit jobs is either increased or decreased as a result of the innovation.[2] One ATU national official has succinctly placed this possibility in historical perspective:

> The transit industry, over the years, has participated in many innovations and technological changes. We have learned to live with them, sometimes at a great cost to ourselves. Originally, our first fight against innovation and technological change—first and last one, I believe— was our resistance to the changeover from the two-man car to the one-man car. We got soundly defeated at great price to our own inner wealth within our union and in our stature before our own membership. Our own members stated in public testimony that they drove the

one-man car and felt so good after their 8 hours on the
one-man car that they were able to play a round of golf.
Now this sort of testimony defeated us. Since that time
we have accommodated ourselves to the transition from
the street car to the bus, from the small bus to the
large bus, from the gasoline engine to the diesels; which
almost overnight reduced our maintenance department
and therefore our membership by 50 percent.[3]

Our interviews revealed no current impact of technological change
on job loss or gain for the transit properties visited.

Union Involvement in Technological Change

Unions can have an impact on technological change through three
general procedures; namely, suggesting the change to management,
assisting management in planning the change, and implementing the
change on the job.[4] As previously stated, we asked union and management respondents to specify various technological changes occurring

TABLE 7.1

Degree of Influence Exerted by the Union in Technological Changes

Dimension of Union Impact	Union Response[a]	Management Response[b]	t = Statistic[c]
Suggesting the change	4.00	4.57	1.89[d]
Planning the change	4.10	4.63	1.98[d]
Implementing the change	4.43	4.60	1.71

[a] Mean score for 30 specific technological changes cited by
union respondents.

[b] Mean score for 35 specific technological changes cited by
management respondents.

[c] Statistical test applied to differences of means

[d] Significance at $p \leq .05$ level.

Source: Interview responses gathered in the nine-state study
area by the authors.

at their locations within the past five years. We then asked both groups to comment on the union's threefold involvement with each specified change. The scores are presented in Table 7.1 and are based upon a five-point scale: 1—controlling influence, 2—a great deal of influence, 3—some influence, 4—little influence, and 5—the union was not a factor. While the union's perceived involvement in suggesting and planning the changes is significantly higher, from a statistical standpoint, than that indicated by the corresponding management response, it must be noted that both groups perceive the unions as having little influence. The major difference regarding suggesting the change is attributed to some union officials who contend that safety considerations prompted the installation of new fare collection systems.

A second question (using the same five-point scale) concerned the union's overall influence in technological change. Union and management responses confirmed the results of the first question, with management's and union's mean score equaling 4.50 and 4.40, respectively, indicating little influence by the union. Three reasons were given by the union representatives for their lack of influence: "The unions and employees have worked to develop new techniques and tools for which no rewards have been given; in fact, management employees have claimed credit"; "Employer maintains unions have no right to suggest or influence planned technological change"; and "Union doesn't desire that much input but would seek protection if employees were laid off as a result."

This latter reason was echoed by many management officials who contend that most of the changes so far have been for the betterment of the employee's position. However, if employees were adversely affected by the introduction of new equipment, the unions would seek greater involvement in related decisions. Some management officials speculated that the protection provisions in Section 13(c) reduce the possibility of the aforementioned situations.[5] Another indication of little union involvement in technological change emerges from the labor agreement analysis: Only six of the labor agreements contain provisions for joint union-management committees, and none of these agreements specifies technological change as a topic for joint discussion.

A final dimension of union involvement in technological change relates to the union's overall policy position on this issue. One observer of the union movement has noted, "From the viewpoint of history it is notable that outright union obstruction to technological change is conspicuously absent in the contemporary situation."[6] An ATU national official places this observation in the context of the mass transit industry:

It is not my impression, but it may be yours, that
transit labor, more than any other group, has powerful individual and institutional self-interests impelling
it to resist the introduction of advanced systems of
urban transportation. Of course, labor does not look
with favor upon every proposal for change. But it can
generally be counted as friendly to innovation if
public policies and programs for implementation are
sound and collective bargaining is preserved.

Much depends, however, upon the facts and
circumstances of a particular situation. So long as
the workings of these future systems in a real-life
setting can only be imagined, we have only the most
rudimentary knowledge of their likely attributes and
impact. We do not know yet what our attitudes may
ultimately be. [7]

However, this official also suggested that the Dial-A-Bus (computerized bus scheduling system operating on the basis of customers'
telephoned requests) could make transit service more demand
responsive, fill in the gaps left unserved by present services, and
create better service to more people.

Subsequent to this official's comments, the completely auto-
mated Bay Area Rapid Transit System (BART) was implemented.
This same official expressed the national union's concern about a
BART accident that occurred October 2, 1972:

All those responsible for allowing the BART trains
to operate under the control of mechanical gadgets
instead of under the direct control of a motorman, are
guilty of gross negligence. We believe the general
public who ride these automated systems should insist
that safe operation requires a human hand at the controls
of BART trains. [8]

An increased number of rapid transit systems, projected by some
union officials to equal 20 by approximately 1990, would have profound effects on the jobs of mass transit employees. The potential
impact of rapid transit systems on jobs was expressed by the
following statement:

Many of the rapid transit systems that will be developed
over the next decade are expected to be run automatically
through the use of computers. Accounting functions, maintenance operations and scheduling may also be performed
largely through the use of computers. In addition, ticket

sales and collection and analysis of power equipment func-
tioning could be handled by automatic methods. The use of
such equipment will probably limit employment opportunities
in many operating, clerical, and maintenance occupations.[9]

It appears that the national unions have anticipated and have attempted
to mitigate the possibility of technological displacement of employees:

Work and work hard, against any and all attempts to
establish a transit authority in your community until
and unless you receive written assurances or legislative assurances that your membership will be employed
by the proposed transit authority with all your rights
and privileges.[10]

We are accommodating ourselves to that in two ways;
we are asking that the legislation that inaugurated these
systems must bear reference and guarantees of collective
bargaining and protection of the employees who are
affected, not just adversely, who are affected because
we do not want to be in the position of proving the
adverse effect. That is sometimes difficult. They may
argue that the adverse effect came from some other
factor than the rapid transit or the use of federal funds
or whatever they were making. If they are affected we
want to be protected by legislation and we are insistent
insofar as we are able that our local unions in supporting
such legislation attempt and insist that it be placed in
the legislation at the time the systems are being inaugurated in the state legislature at the first level, not at the
level where they first say, "Well, let's put this thing on
the tracks first—let's get the thing off the ground, then
we will take care of you." . . . We are also taking care
of ourselves, to a large extent, by our contracts which
to a greater degree are now insisting that these changes
be accommodated by attrition, that the immediate employee not be affected and that the present employees not be
shouldered with the total cost of innovation and technological
change.[11]

In summary, local mass transit unions currently have little
influence in technological innovations, and appear to be relatively
unconcerned about their role unless technological innovations make
serious inroads into job content or employment positions. National
union concern over this issue appears more pronounced, at present,
than concern found at the local level.

SECTION 13(c) OF THE
URBAN MASS TRANSPORTATION ACT OF 1964

The shift in ownership of transit properties from private to
public could have had substantial effects on the collective bargaining
rights of transit employees. As Barnum noted, when a transit system
is in private hands, its collective bargaining is governed by the
National Labor Relations Act and the ruling court cases.[12] However,
the shift to public ownership causes a change in the collective bargaining relationships, for then this act is no longer the governing
statute. The various local and state laws governing labor relations
with public employees become effective and the result is generally
an inferior set of collective bargaining rights for the worker relative to
those of the private sector worker.[13] But Section 13(c) of the Urban Mass
Transportation Act of 1964 provides for a continuation of the collective
bargaining rights as well as employee protection provisions for
transit employees when their system becomes publicly owned.[14]

The union feels that collective bargaining is a critical right,
regardless of the ownership, and as Dan Maroney, international
president of ATU, stated:

> If there is one thing I would like to impress upon you
> today it is the fact that the right to bargain collectively
> is the single most important—and therefore jealously
> guarded—possession which the transit union member
> has. Unlike many public employees in this state and in
> other parts of the country, who have only recently obtained
> the right to organize and bargain—or as in this state,
> the right merely to "meet and confer" with management
> over the issues of wages, hours and working conditions—
> the transit employee has long had full collective bargaining
> rights, as established by the federal labor laws, which
> includes the right to strike, if warranted, to improve his
> standard of living and working conditions.[15]

In 1962, the ATU lost a long strike in Dade County, Florida,
after which the transit system there became publicly owned and the
employees lost all collective bargaining rights.[16] Fearing the
consequences of losing collective bargaining rights in other public
takeovers of transit systems, the ATU decided to work for the inser-
tion of provisions requiring the protection of collective bargaining,
and employee protection provisions, in the legislation concerning
federally funded transit assistance grants.

Labor argued for a section in the transit assistance legislation that
would require that employee protection provisions be made, including

the prevention of any curtailment of collective bargaining rights to
the extent that such provisions would not be inconsistent with state
or local law, prior to any federal aid. In debates that took place in
both the Senate and House, several amendments were offered modifying
the language of the employee protection provision. Organized labor
argued that past collective bargaining rights must be guaranteed,
regardless of state or local laws, for even with a revised section
that removed the specific language permitting preemption by state
and local policy, the union felt that the opportunity was present for
destruction of bargaining rights. As Maroney stated:

> Those of you who may have read the debates or were
> around at the time, know that certain interests, led
> by Senator Tower of Texas, wanted to phrase Section
> 13(c) (2) to read "continuation of collective bargaining
> rights in accordance with state law." Naturally, for
> those employees in the South and Southwest this would
> have meant the effective end of collective bargaining in
> mass transit. . . . As you know, this position was
> defeated in Congress and the so-called Memphis formula
> was used in areas where there was no legal way under
> state and local law for a public transit employer to com-
> ply with Section 13(c) (2). [17]

The language that was contained in the final draft of the bill
that became the Urban Mass Transportation Act of 1964 mandates
that employees and their unions will not lose any rights as a result
of the conversion from private to public ownership. As the act stated:

> It shall be a condition of any assistance . . . that fair
> and equitable arrangements are made, as determined
> by the Secretary of Labor, to protect the interests of
> employees affected by such assistance. Such protective
> arrangements shall include, without being limited to,
> such provisions as may be necessary for . . . the
> continuation of collective bargaining rights. [18]

Barnum noted that while the act does not specify the exact procedure for protecting collective bargaining and employee rights, the
legislative history indicates that Congress intended employee protections to be negotiated by the parties involved, not imposed by the
government on the parties. [19]

The Urban Mass Transportation Act of 1964 established a program of loans and grants to assist states and localities in the development of improved mass transportation facilities, equipment, techniques,

and methods with the cooperation of mass transit companies, both public and private; to encourage the planning and establishment of areawide urban mass transportation systems needed for economical and desirable urban development with the cooperation of mass transportation companies, both public and private; and to provide assistance to state and local governments and their instrumentalities in financing such systems, to be operated by public or private mass transportation companies as determined by local needs.[20] In order to provide for a continuation of collective bargaining and employee protections, including protection against decreases in transit employment from projects funded under this act, the Congress included several relevant provisions:

> Section 3 (e) of the Urban Mass Transportation Act of 1964 as amended, provides that:
> No financial assistance shall be provided under this Act to any State or local public body or agency thereof for the purpose, directly or indirectly, of acquiring any interest in, or purchasing any facilities or other property of a private mass transportation company, or for the purpose of constructing, improving, or reconstructing any facilities or other property acquired (after the date of the enactment of this Act) from any such company, or for the purpose of providing by contract or otherwise for the operation of mass transportation facilities or equipment in competition with, or supplementary to the service provided by an existing mass transportation company, unless . . . the Secretary of Labor certifies that such assistance complies with the requirements of Section 13 (c) of the Act.[21]

> Section 13 (c) provides as follows:
> It shall be a condition of any assistance under Section 3 of this Act that fair and equitable arrangements are made, as determined by the Secretary of Labor, to protect the interests of employees affected by such assistance. Such protective arrangements shall include without being limited to, such provisions as may be necessary for (1) the preservation of rights, privileges, and benefits (including continuation of pension rights and benefits) under existing collective bargaining agreements or otherwise; (2) the continuation of collective bargaining rights; (3) protection of individual employees against a worsening of their

positions with respect to their employment; (4) assurance of employment to employees of acquired mass transportation systems and priority of reemployment of employees terminated or laid off; and (5) paid training or retraining programs. Such arrangements shall include provisions protecting individual employees against a worsening of their position with respect to their employment which shall in no event provide benefits less than those established pursuant to Section 5(2) (f) of the Act of February 4, 1887 (24 Stat. 379), as amended. The contract for the granting of any such assistance shall specify the terms and conditions of the protective arrangements.[22]

EMPLOYEE PROTECTION

Several national agreements arising from transportation statutes form the precedent for the labor protection provisions in the transit industry. In fact, Section 13(c) relies on the Transportation Act of 1920, which called for a plan to unify the nation's railroads into a limited number of systems. Although employee protection was not actively considered at that point, the procedures for settling railway labor disputes arising from merger activity were present. In 1926, the Railway Labor Act was passed containing five basic purposes, which were the prevention of service interruption; the guarantee of employee rights to organize; the provision of complete independence for organization by both union and management; the prompt settlement of disputes over wages, work rules, or working conditions; and the prompt settlement of disputes over interpretation of existing contracts or grievances.[23]

The procedures for settling disputes in connection with employee protection were established by the Railway Labor Act, and amendments provided added strength to the important protections in such areas as the right of employees to organize for collective bargaining, union shop agreements, and enlargement of the scope of the law to include other transportation modes. With the Emergency Transportation Act of 1933, a greater emphasis was placed on employee protection for transport workers, and the act stated that no employee was to be in a worse position with respect to compensation as a result of a reduction in the work force.[24] The act of 1933 also provided for compensation for losses of property and expenses incurred for employee transfers. The Washington Job Protection Agreement, signed in 1936 between 21 national rail organizations and 85 percent of all railroads, provided for economic protection to those employees affected by the "coordination" of two or more rail carriers. An employee was guaranteed that he would not have a worse position, with respect to compensation and rules covering working conditions, than he occupied at the time of coordination. The period of protection covered five years and, with certain conditions, did provide for a displacement allowance.[25]

It must be noted that all of these laws and agreements covering labor protection were in response to mergers and consolidations of railroads, and the Interstate Commerce Commission (ICC) either accepted the conditions agreed upon between the parties or, in some cases, imposed protective provisions, under the authority of Section 5(2)(f) of the Interstate Commerce Act. Basically, these protections allow employees monetary compensation, which can reflect loss of benefits, loss of earnings, and unusual expenses associated with loss of a particular job position. The New Orleans case, decided by the ICC in 1952, contained the most comprehensive set of agreements that had yet emerged from railroad cases.[26] Involving employees of a rail terminal company, the conditions called for an allowance to be paid to separated or demoted employees based upon the preceding 12 months' earnings. As Robert Lieb notes, "Employees are essentially guaranteed a continuation of the income level realized prior to the displacement or demotion for a specified number of years."[27] It must be pointed out that, for an employee to receive compensation as the result of a railroad coordination, under the provision of Section 5(2)(f) for rail operation, the ICC requires that the effect of the coordination be not only direct, but also adverse to a specific individual. Section 13(c) incorporated Section 5(2)(f) as a minimum and has clearly gone beyond that restrictive interpretation. Under the provision of Section 13(c), the individual employees are protected against a worsening of their positions with respect to their employment. Where such worsening cannot be avoided, affected employees are entitled to compensatory benefits no less than those that have evolved under Section 5(2)(f) of the Interstate Commerce Act for the protection of railroad employees. Section 13(c) specifies that these protections are a minimum and serve only as a floor.[28]

As the act states, utilizing the provisions of Section 5(2)(f), a transit employee who is affected by a federally assisted project will be guaranteed that such a project will not place the employee in a worsened position for a period of four years or the length of his employment with the transit system, whichever is shorter. However, the act guarantees protection to all "employees affected," not just simply affected transit employees. As a matter of practice, the Departments of Transportation and Labor have been interpreting this section to apply only to transit employees. Alan Altshuler notes:

Finally, paratransit has come to be widely recognized
during the past year [1975] as posing the most unsettled
issues in the arena of section 13c labor protection.
Existing transit employers have shown virtually no
interest in providing dial-a-ride or special services.
Demand-responsive transit has been developing therefore, primarily outside the scope of existing transit,
using unpaid labor or labor paid at substantially below
the prevailing transit rates. Union leaders worry that
such competition may undermine existing labor standards,
may drain patronage from existing transit operations,
and may draw public subsidy dollars away from conventional transit.

By contrast, the primary concern of federal officials is what the effect of paratransit development may
be on the scope of section 13c coverage—in particular,
on the issue of taxi employee coverage. To the extent
that UMTA [Urban Mass Transit Administration] funds
are used in support of taxilike operations, or of operations that are clearly competitive with taxi service,
the case for exclusion of taxi employees from section 13c
protection is weakened. The issue goes well beyond
the question of how to draw the boundary between transit and taxi service because the decisive test under
section 13c is simply adverse impact, not definition
as transit. [29]

In 1970, Amtrak was established through the Rail Passenger
Service Act, which contained an employee protection provision that
was to provide for fair and equitable arrangements to protect the
interests of employees of railroads affected by discontinuances of
intercity rail passenger services. Section 2 of that act provided that
the rates of pay, working conditions and all collective bargaining
and other rights, privileges and benefits (including continuation of
pension rights and benefits) of railroad employees under applicable
laws and/or existing collective bargaining agreements or otherwise
shall be preserved unless changed by future collective bargaining
agreements or applicable statutes. [30] The period of coverage for
employee protection was extended to six years under Amtrak and
this coverage appears now to be the minimum level of benefits; and
the typical Section 13(c) agreement specifies a six-year benefit program.

While the above agreements concerning employee protection
deal with rail operations, the Urban Mass Transportation Act sought
to protect employees through similar language; for example, one of

the key provisions of Section 13(c) is the guarantee of a continuation
of collective bargaining rights. However, it is necessary for the
reader to understand that if a strike or binding arbitration is prohibited by state law, then the means for resolving bargaining impasses
need not be included in that guarantee. Larry Yud notes that many
people confuse a specific provision negotiated for a given Section 13(c)
agreement with the wording of Section 13(c) in the Urban Mass Transportation Act. The act does not require continuation of the right to
strike in order to satisfy the requirement of the continuation of
collective bargaining rights or employee protection. If the state law,
by right of operation, does not allow the employee the right to strike
or management the right to lock out their employees, but might at
some future time allow such actions, Section 13(c) will not prohibit
this right in advance.[31]

In dealing with the question of adverse effects on employees
from Section 6 of the Urban Mass Transportation Act, providing
for federally assisted demonstration projects, Yud commented that
with the discontinuance of a project, management did not necessarily
have to bear the employee protection costs because of the discontinuance. He felt that those displaced employees do not necessarily
meet the adverse effect standards under the federal assistance program.[32]

In discussing employee protection requirements, Yud suggested
that he did not believe the protection provisions would produce
excessive, if any, additional costs under the provisions of Section
13(c) agreements negotiated for operating assistance. Although, he
did note:

> One major factor is that maintenance services will
> require some additional funds in order to provide
> continuation or expansion of services under Section
> 5 assistance grants. I see two possible ways that
> adverse effects can come about from operating
> assistance. One is the competitive effect. If federal
> operating assistance given to one system can be
> shown to adversely impact on a competing system,
> the employees of the competing system may be able
> to make a case if they were adversely affected as a
> result of the federal assistance and be entitled to
> protection. The other problem area is in attempting
> to measure the economic efficiency expected or
> obtained through federal assistance. If a particular
> productivity measure is established and employees
> are adversely affected, e.g., displaced, then it is
> possible to envision a claim would be filed under Sec-
> tion 13(c).[33]

Implementation of Protection

Normally, when the Department of Transportation receives a request from a property for financial assistance, it sends a copy to the Department of Labor, which, in turn, notifies the union holding bargaining rights for that property, as well as other unions and transit members that might be affected by the project. If there is difficulty in settling upon terms mutually agreeable to the union and management, the Department of Labor provides advice and mediation services. In practice, the Labor Department has the philosophy of approving any agreement between the parties, as long as there is no outright violation of the law. [34]

The administration of Section 13(c) has changed substantially from its early days when the Department of Labor insisted on little more than a warranty from grant applicants that the condition of employees in an existing system would not be worsened as a result of the granting of federal assistance. In addition to advance notice to the primary labor organization and emphasis on collective bargaining, the department has given increased attention to the provisions of Section 5(2)(f), as modified by the Amtrak provisions, of the Interstate Commerce Act and has carefully followed the mandate of the Supreme Court, which ruled that Section 5(2)(f) of the Interstate Commerce Act includes all of the historic arrangements developed under the provisions of that act. These include arbitral decisions, ICC decisions, and the plethora of job protection agreements worked out in the rail industry.

Actual agreements vary because of the local conditions, which recognize the individual properties and the sets of relationships that have developed between the local unit and management. In the field investigation for this research, we found that union respondents in 12 of the 20 sites visited indicated that the ATU international field representative was always included in the Section 13(c) negotiations and, in fact, with only minor exceptions, established the conditions of protections. As Barnum notes, this is not unusual as the industry is characterized by pattern bargaining.[35] In an examination of the Section 13(c) agreements collected from the visited properties, there were few differences, and then only minor ones, among the various Section 13(c) agreements.

On July 23, 1975, representatives of the American Public Transit Association, the ATU, and the TWU signed a National Employee Protective Agreement, which, under the Urban Mass Transportation Act, is designed for use by individual transit employers and organizations representing employees in the area of proposed operating-assistance projects. Appendix C contains a copy of that model agreement. Yud commented that this agreement was to serve as a model,

not imposed by the Department of Labor, but rather voluntarily
negotiated between the parties. While the model agreement for
operating-assistance grants covers a wide range of conditions, the
parties could not prepare an agreement that would cover all of the
situations that may arise in obtaining operating-assistance grants.
In an accompanying memorandum to the model 13(c) agreement, a
procedure was set out for covering areas in which the model agreement was silent; for instance, a special memorandum to the Secretary
of Labor from Louis M. Gill, dated July 18, 1975, prescribes the
procedure for covering situations dealing with paratransit. The intention of the memorandum accompanying the national agreement
model was to outline a method for agreement to fit particular situations
and therefore is, in fact, an extension of the national agreement.[36]
Reflecting the spirit of labor-management cooperation, one management representative stated:

> Recent developments encourage me to think that we are
> entering a new era of cooperation on the labor-manage-
> ment front in our transit industry. As you know, federal
> operating subsidies can be obtained only if the parties
> agree to protect employees against adverse impact resulting
> from those subsidies. Such employee protection is pro-
> vided in Section 13 (c) of the Urban Mass Transportation
> Act. It had been anticipated that it would be difficult to
> negotiate the thousands of agreements which would have
> been necessary under the new subsidy program. I am
> pleased to report, however, that the American Public
> Transit Association and the unions involved have recently
> gotten together and negotiated a so-called national 13 (c)
> agreement. I would hope that the operating subsidy agree-
> ment might be followed by a similar nation model agree-
> ment applying to capital projects which also require 13 (c)
> protection.[37]

It has been charged that labor unions use Section 13(c) to pre-
vent transit innovation, and some management officials appear to be
distrustful of the procedures adopted by the Labor Department. Based
on the results of in-depth interviews at 20 transit properties with
both union and management respondents, there was no experience
found to ascertain costs under the application of Section 13(c) agreements. The field interviews were conducted in a nonstructured,
informal, confidential manner in order to obtain both positive and
negative comments concerning the advantages and disadvantages,
for both union and management, of Section 13(c) agreements, and also
to obtain some approximation of the performance of the Labor

TABLE 7.2

Union and Management Responses to the Effect of Section 13(c)
Provisions under the Urban Mass Transportation Act,
Based upon 20 Sites Visited, 1975-76

Questions	Management Responses	Union Responses
Advantages to management		
No advantage to management	8	4
Basis for provision of fund for continued operations and service improvements	12	8
Insuring fair agreements for employee protection and improving employee morale	6	5
Disadvantages to management		
Slowness of the negotiations	6	2
Delays in receiving funds	4	0
No knowledge of the cost involved in providing protections	10	0
Excessive labor protection	8	0
Restricts management rights	14	0
Procedures are not clear	3	0
Not related to collective bargaining	10	1
Must negotiate a new 13(c) agreement with each grant	5	0
No disadvantage to management	2	12
Advantages to union		
No advantage to union	5	3
Provides employee protection and job security	13	16
Continuation of collective bargaining rights	8	10
Power lever in bargaining	3	1
Disadvantages to union		
Creates greater aggressiveness in bargaining	1	3
Union is forced to deal with public bodies	0	1
No disadvantage to union	7	12
Role of Department of Labor in 13(c) administration		
No help received from department	0	3
Department is highly labor biased	13	0
Department has provided for fair interpretation and administration of 13 (c)	4	10
Department is slow	2	0
Department was very helpful	2	2
No knowledge of department's role	1	7

Note: Responses may not equal 20 for either category because of actual comments; that is, several respondents listed several answers for the broad question areas. These data represent simple frequencies of response for each category, not necessarily for each property.

Source: Interview responses gathered in nine-state study area by the authors.

Department in administering Section 13(c). Table 7.2 presents the comments obtained from these interviews. While there is not whole-hearted approval of Section 13(c) by management respondents, the decision makers seem to recognize that without Section 13(c) agreements there could be no federal funding assistance. Management objections seem to be basically that Section 13(c) agreements tend to limit management rights and that there is no clear indication of the cost of the employee protection. As the table shows, we found that ten management respondents felt that negotiations concerning 13(c) agreements had no real effect upon normal collective bargaining over the labor contract. These findings seem to support the summary statements issued from a conference hosted by the Urban Mass Transportation Administration (UMTA) in November of 1975, which noted that:

> Of the many factors which affect transit industry labor-management relationships, the provisions and implemen-tation of Section 13 (c) of the Urban Mass Transportation Act appear to be among the least significant, either in arriving at contractual agreements or in the substance of those agreements. Although the perception by those not involved in collective bargaining of the influence of 13 (c) ranges from "no effect" to "blackmail," the per-ception by the parties themselves is that 13 (c) is not a significant issue in negotiations.

The summary also stated:

> It was the judgment of the researchers and most of the participants that if 13 (c) had never been enacted, the problems and issues facing the industry in the area of labor relations would be similar, if not identical in magnitude and composition.
>
> It was generally agreed that the attention and level of importance given to the ramifications of the jurisdic-tional disputes involving 13 (c) is misplaced and unwar-ranted. Such a confrontation takes out of context the overriding concern of the Act as a whole, which must be the Federal interest and the public interest in assuring a viable and a responsive mass transit system. It is in this framework that labor's and management's respon-sibilities, whether on the 13 (c) issue or in the broader context of labor-management relations, should be assessed.[38]

As an internal report prepared for the Labor Department, concerning the administration of Section 13(c), noted:

> Operators of properties, both major and minor, complain
> that they are unaware of the importance or complexity of
> the 13 (c) requirements until they are far down the road
> of acquiring their grants. At this point 13 (c) rises to "hit
> them in the head." They feel they are at a bargaining dis-
> advantage and often only 13 (c) stands in the way of final
> funding approval. [39]

Our field interviews provided for a variety of responses about
the difficulties concerning Section 13(c) negotiations; the main problem appears to be with city and local area governments, and their
representatives, who, first, do not necessarily have the comprehensive skills to understand the complexity of employee protection
provisions and, second, do not have the consummate negotiation
skills to effectively complete a Section 13(c) agreement. Many of the
comments about the problems of Section 13(c) negotiations, which
have been publicized, do not necessarily agree with the comments
from the professional negotiators (management respondents who have
decision-making positions with respect to collective bargaining) that
we interviewed in this research.

In commenting on the difficulties of the individuals' inability
to discern between the specific provisions of an individual Section 13(c)
agreement and the provisions of Section 13 (c) in the act, Yud noted
that these problems were covered in the abovementioned research
report prepared for the Labor Department:[40]

> Some operators feel that 13 (c) is administered in fact
> to protect the institutional rights of the unions rather
> than the rights of individual employees. They claim that
> many of the complex arrangements that have evolved in
> 13 (c) agreements over the years really have no appli-
> cation to their own situations but that the unions, in
> order to protect their institutional rights, ignore the
> merits of individual cases and expand the agreement
> in each new case, using the most favorable recent agree-
> ment as a floor. This, they argue, uses the 13 (c) legis-
> lation for a purpose for which it was never intended, i.e.,
> to insure the continuation of a particular set of institu-
> tional arrangements rather than to protect the rights of
> the individual employees. The Secretary (of Labor), they
> say, could better perform his duties under the statute
> and still protect the employee's rights, including his

right to be represented by a union through collective
bargaining, if he certified applications without forcing
the grant applicant to agree to the most favorable contract yet negotiated.[41]

In spite of the controversy over Section 13(c), the record of
administration is impressive. After approximately 1,500 certifications
and many millions of dollars of federal assistance, there have been
only a very small number of cases in which an individual is being
paid or has been paid either a displacement or dismissal allowance.
The development of a national model 13(c) agreement for operating
financial assistance is viewed as "a definite step in the right direction
for the 13 (c) program."[42] As Yud noted, "We were immediately
confronted by an amazing increase in applications [for federal financial operating assistance] for 279 urbanized areas that were eligible
for formula grant money."[43] The model agreement, it is felt by
many, will speed up the process of certification and reduce some of
the unfavorable comments from recipients about delay.

In administering Section 13(c), the Department of Labor was
not given a series of guidelines, other than to allow for the parties
to negotiate their own individual conditions, given the local situation
with respect to the existing laws. In such negotiations, the unions
appear to have structured their bargaining to reflect the potential
of fewer jobs, reduced earnings, and threatened loss of existing
benefits. Increasing emphasis is now, and in the future will be,
placed on the problems flowing from innovations and changes in
service levels as a result of technology and paratransit.

Transit labor unions have consistently supported UMTA's
activity in the development of demand-responsive transit.[44] As
Altshuler noted, "In 1969 and 1970, when UMTA's interest in dial-
a-ride temporarily flagged, the Amalgamated Transit Union on
several occasions publicly urged the UMTA administrator to move
full speed ahead."[45] The union has viewed dial-a-ride as a rare
transit innovation that was labor intensive and as one that might
greatly improve transit employment opportunities. In several of
the dial-a-ride projects, union labor was protected from intrusion
by part-time or nonunion labor; however, the future of union workers
for dial-a-ride systems seems doubtful and has become of great concern to the international union. As Maroney noted:

. . . while attending the Transportation Research
Board Paratransit Conference in Washington, D.C.,
I once again heard one of the participants advocating
that the employees we represent had overpriced
their services and should return to subsidizing the

industry by eroding their working conditions, and in
particular, by allowing the management to utilize
part-time employees at a lesser rate. This theory
not only would take away from the benefits of the
transit employees, thereby destroying transit as a
long-term, career, occupation. . . .

Thus, we face still another threat from those
who would use the new paratransit modes—dial-a-ride,
van pools, shared-ride taxis, etc., to destroy transit
jobs by using volunteer para operators, or part-time
employees at the minimum wage, and no other benefits, to siphon off peak hour ridership and fares from
the mainline system. . . . The Amalgamated Transit
Union will not support paratransit if it is used as a
weapon to destroy our members' jobs, or to reduce
their wages, or to worsen their working conditions.[46]

Additionally, our field interviews found that a related concern in
implementing Section 13(c) agreements was a lack of understanding
on the part of all management respondents of the complete background
of Section 13(c). This confusion might lead to fears by public officials
that Section 13(c) would cause the extension of collective bargaining
to all public employees:

Of course, Section 13 (c) requires that only past
collective bargaining rights must be continued.
Legislation applying to other public employees
would have to go further and establish a uniform
set of rights for all covered workers. This is so
because almost all of the nation's transit employees
had already bargained under the NLRA [National
Labor Relations Act] when Section 13 (c) was passed,
so 13 (c) needed only to extend to public sector transit the uniform and comprehensive rights granted by
the NLRA. Since other public employees do not have
a common legal history of collective bargaining,
legislation applying to them would have to include a
uniform set of guidelines that would apply to all,
regardless of past activity.[47]

Perhaps some dispute between the two federal agencies (DOT and
DOL) handling federal assistance to transit has added some fuel to
the fire of misunderstanding. The professional management negotiator in our survey seemed much less concerned about Section 13(c)
agreements than did the resident managers, public officials, and

trade association representatives, and even some union officers at
the local level in the Southeast.

It appears that the Department of Labor has attempted to
provide for voluntary settlements; however, two union and two management respondents indicated that the union has occasionally utilized
certain provisions of 13(c) agreements as a lever or threat in collective bargaining. It should be emphasized that the attitude is shared
only by a few of the total respondents. In the main, our survey
results reflected the attitude of Louis Gambaccini:

> On the subject of 13 (c), I certainly accept the premise that
> employees who are adversely affected as a result of federal
> aid are entitled to some protection against the impact of
> that assistance. In fact, 13 (c) negotiations, to the extent
> that they involve labor at the outset in the planning, policy
> and decision-making process, may even be helpful in ob-
> taining union acceptance of needed improvements. I am
> also satisfied that the Department of Labor would not acqui-
> esce in any attempt to use 13 (c) as a vehicle to improperly
> "blackmail" management in an effort to force it to accept
> substantive contractual terms having no relation to 13 (c).
> Nor, so far, have 13 (c) agreements resulted in anything
> like the catastrophic charges to the industry which were
> feared.[48]

MINORITIES AND TRANSIT

Employment and Promotion of Minorities

Despite continued decline in the transit industry, minority
employment now comprises an even larger proportion of total employment than 25 years ago. Several individuals have explained the relative increase of minority employment as a function of the location
of the industry in the cities, the crime problem in the cities, and
the industry's loss of status, which induced whites to seek other
employment. However, in the Southeast, federal legislation and the
actions of local managements and local units of the ATU and TWU
appear to have been important factors accounting for the increase
in minority employment.

With minor exceptions, employment in the transit industry
generally remained closed to minorities except in certain few
classifications, mainly in the unskilled maintenance jobs, until after
1945; however, mass transit was not unique in its exclusion of minorities from key jobs prior to the 1940s.[49] Railroad operations and
rules have had significant impact on the urban transit systems and

the organizations representing employees. The "railroad philosophy," as described by Herbert Northrup, carried over into the transit industry through union influence, company policy, and employee attitudes:

> The Negro is in an anomalous position. He is denied a voice in the affairs of nearly all railway labor organizations; yet collective bargaining on the railroads has received wider acceptance than in almost any other American industry. He is for the most part, ineligible for promotion although promotion in the industry is based almost exclusively upon seniority. [50]

P. W. Jeffress attributes the increase of minority employment in transit through 1945 to three basic factors: the nature of the work: the conversion of some companies from private to public ownership; and the efforts of the federal government through such agencies as the President's Committee on Fair Employment Practice. [51] Because of the relative attractiveness of transit work, including both pay and status, many minority employees sought positions doing platform work. Although vehicle operation does not require excessive amounts of skills, the status and responsibility made platform service attractive. However, these same reasons often hindered the minority individuals from gaining employment as operators and it was not until after 1945 that minority employment reached a proportional representativeness in the North. The conversion from private to public ownership, particularly where public authorities acquired and operated the transit system, allowed for civil service rules to take effect governing hiring and upgrading policies. Even where transit employees were not brought under civil service, public ownership caused changes because generally the state legislatures wrote nondiscrimination clauses into the transit authorities' charters. In tracing union and management policies concerning hiring and promoting, as well as acceptance into the bargaining unit, the record shows several indications that either management or local units used threats or presumption of acts in maintaining low levels of minority employment prior to 1950. Several studies reported that the attempts of minorities to obtain platform jobs were thwarted by the threat of the local division to strike if minority employees were hired for these positions. [52] There has been the charge that locals of ATU restricted membership to whites or otherwise catered to pressure or prejudice of whites in some cities. [53] The ATU seems to have allowed its local unit more autonomy in racial matters than did the TWU, but, of course, TWU did not represent as many properties as did the ATU; this is especially true in the Southeast. [54]

Minority employment practices varied greatly from one city to another; however, a very important trend in the post-World War II era has been the change of the racial mix of transit employees. The proportion of black and other minorities has risen from 3.0 percent in 1940 to 6.4 percent in 1950, 10.9 percent in 1960, and approximately 35 percent in 1976. In one study of minority employment for the 1950-60 era, it was noted that even with a declining total transit employment, the rate of decline was slower for minority employees than for whites. Therefore, the percentage of minority employees has been increasing and minorities have been gaining in the proportion of jobs they fill.

Jeffress feels that the rise of minority employment in transit operations has occurred without any clear-cut, commonly accepted method of formulating manpower policy among organizations in the transit industry. [55] In only two of our on-site interviews were there any indications of formalizing a program of manpower planning. In light of this lack of formal programs to fill manpower needs, it is not surprising to find that most transit firms have only informal, nondiscriminatory manpower programs. For the publicly owned and/ or operated systems, the statements of nondiscrimination are in the form of catchall phrases included in the charter as drawn up by the legislature or municipal government. Private systems also have statements concerning nondiscrimination and upgrading of minority employees. An examination of all labor agreements for the nine-state southeastern study area showed that only eight contracts contain a clause that specifically prohibits racial discrimination in employment. In many cases, statements prohibiting discrimination are somewhat superficial in that there does not appear to be formal communication of the policy or an adequate method of implementation, including follow-up procedures.

Recruiting practices have a direct effect on employment, and the past practices of several firms have restricted the opportunities for minorities to be included in the transit work force on an equal basis. [56] With the majority of transit jobs at the entry level, that is, operator positions, there has been a relatively high degree of turnover of operators, especially during the first months of employment when seniority affords little or no priority in picking runs. The fact that minorities are hired for entry-level jobs does not dismiss the subject of job discrimination, since there have been clear indications that these are jobs that have generally been given to minorities and from which the minority member could not readily move. Seniority rules influence the upgrading procedures in many transit operations, except in the few cases where a civil service merit system governs promotions. In the review of the seniority systems in transit operations in the nine-state study area, the seniority systems seemed to be

similar among firms in the industry, particularly where seniority
was a prime factor in promotions. Separate seniority lists for
minority and white employees, which used to exist in many southern
cities, have now been combined into a single seniority list. However,
a simple combined seniority list does not necessarily remove de
facto racial discrimination, but may only perpetuate past employment
practices. More specifically, blacks who were unable to obtain
employment because of racial discrimination prior to the passage of
the Civil Rights Act of 1964 found themselves grouped at the bottom
of the seniority list and effectively prevented from promotion opportunities. This issue was dealt with in a 1974 consent decree signed
by New Orleans Public Service, Inc., in which the public utility-
owned transit operation agreed to a significant revision in seniority
and promotion questions for employees.[57] While not admitting any
violation of law or any racial discrimination in employment, a
settlement of a 1970 lawsuit was reached through a consent order
calling for no discrimination against black employees in all terms
and conditions of employment. The order established steps for
advancement from the operator classification and from the lower-
rated jobs in the maintenance division to upper-level and supervisory
jobs in all divisions in the transit department. In general, the order
provided that "the next vacancies (at each station, where appropriate)
in each such job, would be filled by black employees and that every
second vacancy thereafter would be filled by black employees, if
black employees with the usual qualifications for the job were available in the next lower-rated job classification."[58] In addition, special
rights for black maintenance division employees were established.
The settlement also provided that black employees in the transit
department would be notified in writing as to the potential job opportunities for which they may be qualified with New Orleans Public Service outside the transit department, and the order also established
procedures by which such employees could be placed on transfer
rosters for jobs for which they are qualified. The next vacancy in
each such non-transit-department job would be filled by a black
employee on the transfer roster, until the roster had been exhausted.
The settlement also established a new procedure for pick lists.
White and black operators employed on or before a given date,
(November 29, 1971) were listed on a master pick list on an alternating basis, so that the most-senior white was first, the most-senior
black was second, and alternating whites and blacks followed. Operators hired after that date were listed without regard to race, in
descending order of operator seniority. The position of an operator on
stationwide pick lists was determined by the operator's relative
position on the master pick list. The order also established a pick
of vacations as well as setting up the length of vacations.

With the disappearance of segregated seniority rosters, seniority rules have not generally worked against upgrading of minority employees. Northrup states that generally a broad seniority area works to the advantage of minority employees in upgrading, but to their disadvantage in times when employment is falling.[59] The argument is that in times of decreasing employment, reduction in force has taken its effect on the minority employees since they have been concentrated in the lower-level jobs. This has not been the case in several cities where sudden waves of retirement have occurred. In several instances where advancement requiring seniority has come more slowly than might have been expected, the types of settlements or arrangements such as in New Orleans have provided minority employees with almost instant upgrading.

Unions and Minorities

In relative terms, unions have had only minor influences over racial employment policies in mass transit in the Southeast, for there have been no union hiring halls and the unions that have had the most power in the transit industry have not flagrantly barred minority membership. Correspondingly, the union and management officials interviewed in the field indicated that hiring of all bargaining unit employees and the supervision and implementation of affirmative action programs are unilateral management rights. While there have been some segregated local units in the South until recently and existing black caucuses in large northern cities, it is not evident that the unions prevented transit systems from hiring minorities when otherwise the management might have done so.[60] The increasing proportion of black transit workers, combined with the national policy of equal employment opportunity, has had an important impact on the organization and bargaining of both union and management. As a matter of practical consideration in collective bargaining, the impact of racial composition of the bargaining unit seems to make itself felt more directly through differences in age and seniority of employees. As several respondents noted, older employees are more concerned with issues such as seniority and pensions, while younger, and for the most part, less-senior employees, are more concerned with issues such as wages and vacations. Management respondents indicated, in the nine-state study area, that most of the older employees tend to be white and have more seniority, while most of the newer employees with less seniority tend to be nonwhite, and the differences in priorities connected with different issues tend to take on racial overtones at some properties.[61]

Jeffress and W. B. Gould note that although civil rights has often been stressed by the dissidents who have formed black caucuses, it appears that the real issue is that the ethnic composition of the membership is changing faster than that of the union leadership. Gould feels that "black participation in union decision making is an integral part of the establishment of fair employment patterns."[62] It would appear that the local units in the Southeast are adjusting to having minority members in leadership positions, although the statistical counts are biased in favor of heavy minority representation in the leadership of some locals and almost none in other units. In fact, in five of the 20 sites in the Southeast selected for on-site visits, there was no minority member in the local division's leadership, and in three other instances, one black was on the bargaining committee (not as an elected member) for those three units, with the remainder of the leadership being white. Therefore, in these eight properties employing a total of approximately 2,500 union members, with 40 percent of employees being of a minority, there are no elected minority members in the leadership and only three minority individuals in an appointed capacity on bargaining committees. As one minority respondent, a bargaining committee member in a unit with all white union leadership, commented: "I act as the go-between for the union leadership and the black rank-and-file member and believe that the white union leadership can best act as our spokesmen with the white leadership in our city." Interestingly, for the 20 cities visited, our research found that where union local leadership contained few minority individuals, there were also few minority employees working in the maintenance or garage classification (mechanics and craftsmen); and the higher the percent of minority individuals in the union leadership, the greater the proportion of minority workers in the garage or maintenance classifications. This finding appears to be valid regardless of the union organization representing the workers. It was also interesting to note that of all the management officials interviewed at the 20 sites, only one management respondent in a decision-making capacity for collective bargaining purposes was black.

Barnum notes that in spite of policy statements affirming the nondiscrimination position of transit unions, neither the ATU nor the TWU has been free from discrimination in the past. There is some reason to believe that there is a feeling by black union members that their interests and concerns are not being adequately dealt with, and this feeling has brought about a number of racially separate groups or racial caucuses within national and local unions, even extending to the few employee associations in the transit industry. As of 1970, approximately 22 percent of the transit industry's craftsmen were black,[63] a figure that compares most favorably with other industries. Most of the large-city transit systems are in the public sector and, in 1970, Equal Employment Opportunity Commission statistics collected for selected cities indicated that approximately

34 percent of all employees and 38 percent of the transit workers were black. This has been a significant improvement as black craftsmen were scarce in the transit industry as of 1966. One of the reasons was the absence of company apprenticeship programs combined with the recruiting of the craftsmen from other industries instead of the upgrading of lower-level transit employees, but the shortage of craftsmen forced transit operations to train and upgrade minorities.

TABLE 7.3

Minority Employment at Transit Operations in a Nine-State
Southeastern Area, Based upon 20 Interview Sites, 1975-76
(percent of total)

City Size	Minority Union Members			Minority Union Leadership[*]
	Operators	Craft Employees	Total	
Under 250,000	40	27	38	23
250,000-500,000	48	27	45	39
Over 500,000	59	47	56	20
Total	55	43	52	27

[*] Includes not only elected officers of local divisions, but also minority individuals serving appointed terms on the bargaining committees.

Source: Interview responses gathered in nine-state study area by the authors.

Based on the field research conducted in the nine-state study area, 52 percent of the union members in those 20 cities were minority employees, with 55 percent of operators being minority workers and 43 percent of the garage employees being minority workers (see Table 7.3). As noted earlier, it was found that 92 percent of all employees at the transit properties visited were part of the bargaining unit. As found in earlier studies, the percentage of minority workers for both the operator and garage employee classifications was higher in the larger cities, accounting for 50 percent and 47 percent, respectively, at the sites visited in 1975-76. Approximately 27 percent of local union leadership are minority employees, with an interesting phenomenon noted: that in cities of from 250,000 to 500,000 population, 39 percent of union leadership are minority employees. The reader must be aware that the term union leadership, for the purposes of this research, included not only elected union officers, but also minority employees appointed to bargaining committees. However, the indication is that substantial integration both in the work force and local leadership positions in the union has been achieved in the nine-state Southeastern study area. Again, these results are based upon 20 cities in the Southeast and it is not the intention to utilize the findings to generalize about minority employment or union leadership in the entire transit industry.

THE PUBLIC INTEREST

Bernard M. Baruch once placed public interest in perspective: "While the rights and interests of labor and of business must be respected, the rights of the public deserve at least equal consideration."[64] These "rights of the public," or the public interests, receive considerable discussion among business and labor leaders as well as public officials. At one extreme, some would argue, as Milton Friedman has, that "there is one and only one social responsibility of business—to use its resources and engage in activities designed to increase its profits so long as it stays within the rules of the game. . . . Similarly, the social responsibility of labor leaders is to serve the interests of the members of their union."[65] However, others argue with equal enthusiasm that businessmen and labor leaders must accept new and enlarged responsibilities today because prosperity has enormously augmented the power these groups possess.[66]

When a firm, such as a mass transit operation, supplies an important public service and in most cases is publicly owned or heavily subsidized with public funds, the importance of directly serving the public interests becomes heightened. Consequently, the need increases for a better understanding of the concept of public interest. Unfortunately, public interest is a generic term and is difficult to define and, especially, to operationalize. These difficulties should not serve to discourage our efforts, for as one practitioner put it, "The public manager's obligation to be responsive to the public interest or social equity is not lessened by the difficulty of definition or implementation."[67]

The purposes of this discussion are to examine closely the concept of the public interest as viewed by both labor and management in the transit industry; and to determine managerial power to serve the public interest in a unionized setting. In nonunion firms, managerial discretion in this area appears to be constrained only by the stockholders (or by the political framework, if a public agency) and to a slight degree by the legal framework. However, in unionized

firms, labor organizations have the legally protected right to negotiate work rules and other conditions of employment. Hence, management officials might legitimately contend that, at best, their authority
to act in the public interest is shared by the union, and, at worst,
their authority in this matter is overruled by collective bargaining
and subsequent employee grievances.

This discussion begins with a brief description of the data
sought, and the methodology used, in connection with some general
and specific dimensions of the public interest. Later, the extent
to which these public interest dimensions are included in the labor
agreement is examined and the respective degrees of union and
management involvement in these issues are determined. It is hoped
the discussion will be beneficial both to policymakers and to industry
practitioners by providing a better understanding of the concept of
public interest, as viewed by union and management practitioners,
and a fuller knowledge of the extent to which these two groups agree
on the dimensions of the public interest. Furthermore, insight is
provided into the relative amount of managerial discretionary power
to act on public interest issues.

The Concept of Public Interest in Mass Transit

The data on public interest were derived from the interviews
with union and management officials at 20 mass transit properties
and from the labor agreements of the organized properties in the
nine-state study area. The interview data approached the public
interest from two perspectives. First, union and management respondents were asked open-ended questions that required them to give
their definitions of the public interest as well as indicate how the
other party would define this concept. Secondly, the respondents
were asked to quantify the following nine dimensions of the public
interest:

Item 1. Improved safety of the vehicle

Item 2. Reduced fares for disadvantaged groups

Item 3. Guaranteeing uninterrupted service by binding arbitration for every unresolved negotiation item and
grievance

Item 4. Training programs for upgrading and promoting

Item 5. Improved efficiency of operations (for example,
computerized run scheduling)

Item 6. Guarantees protecting employees' jobs in case of
technological change or layoffs

Item 7. Improved environmental impact of buses (for example,
less noise and air pollution)

Item 8. Insuring that your transit employees' wages are
equal to, or better than, those in other agencies
having similar working conditions and cost of living

Item 9. Increased services

In quantifying these public interest measures, each respondent
was asked the following two questions:

Given your knowledge of these factors, the needs of
your own property, and your awareness that each dollar
spent on each factor does not yield equal benefit, suppose
that you have an additional amount of funds to spend in
a typical year. Assume that these funds equal 100 units;
how would you distribute these units across the following
items?

How would you rank these items in terms of how you
feel they contribute to the public interest (1 being most
important, 9 being least important)?

It should be noted that these dimensions were formulated by the
authors' discussions with union, management, and government
officials prior to the on-site interviews. These measures represent
not just nine areas that have an impact on the public interest, but more
specifically, they are public interest factors that compete for
limited transit funds. Allocation of available revenue among these
items is a function of both management discretion and union power.

Public Interest Definitions

Generally speaking, the responses to the open-ended questions
indicate that union and management have a great deal in common in
their definitions of the public interest in mass transit. Roughly 75
percent of the respondents referred to the agency's obligation to
provide service to citizens, particularly to those who cannot use
other means of transportation. Frequently cited dimensions of this
service include safe and comfortable vehicles; courtesy toward
passengers; convenient and promptly-adhered-to schedules servicing
the greatest number of customers; and reasonable fares, particularly
with regard to senior citizens. It should be mentioned, however,
that management representatives frequently cite the problem of
balancing these dimensions against often severe cost constraints.
The second major public interest category, reflecting comments by
20 percent of the respondents, pertains to alleged low wages and
poor working conditions for mass transit employees. Management
and union respondents suggesting this category indicated that it is

very much related to better customer service in that beneficial working conditions will maintain, and in some cases, attract adequate personnel necessary for service obligations.

The general agreement between union and management respondents regarding the public interest is not completely supported when each is asked how they think the other defines the concept. Less than half of the management and union respondents (48 percent) believe the other would define public interest in a similar manner. At 45 percent of the properties where interviews were held, management representatives suggested that unions qualify the public interest in terms of contractual provisions and working conditions, with less attention given to cost considerations. Likewise, 30 percent of the union representatives stressed that management's emphasis on cost savings might deter from the service dimension of public interest.

It is difficult to suggest reasons behind the differing perceptions that labor and management have regarding each other's definition of public interest. Quite possibly this is due to the lack of communication on this issue in collective bargaining; particularly since the concept is vague and difficult to operationalize in terms that would facilitate the collective bargaining process. Again, it is important to note that when asked for a definition of public interest on an individual basis, management and union representatives have more in common than they perceive.

Additionally, union and management tend to agree that strikes by mass transit employees significantly affect the public interest. About one-third of the respondents indicated that strikes adversely affect customers, many of whom are "transit captive" and would not be able to get to work without mass transit. A similar number of respondents contended that the affected customers either lose their job or permanently find alternative means of transportation; the result being a permanent loss of ridership. However, one management and one union official countered that mass transit only accounts for 5 percent of travelers; therefore, a strike by mass transit employees would not be detrimental to the overall public interest.

Quantifying Public Interest Measures

Quantification of the public interest dimensions noted earlier provides a somewhat specific view of the opinions of labor and management. The results exhibit several areas of common agreement between labor and management as well as some public interest factors on which there is substantial disagreement. The graphs in Figures 7.1 and 7.2 provide an overview of the findings, showing the average rank and average amount of priority allocated to each of the nine public

FIGURE 7.1

Relationship between Mean Priority Ranks and Mean
Allocation of Priority to Nine Public Interest
Items—Management Respondents

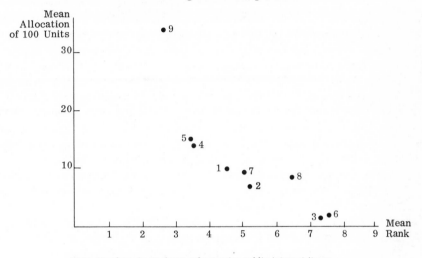

Note: Numbers in quadrant refer to nine public interest items.
Source: Interview responses gathered in nine-state study area by the authors.

FIGURE 7.2

Relationship between Mean   Priority Ranks and Mean
Allocation of Priority to Nine Public Interest
Items—Labor Respondents

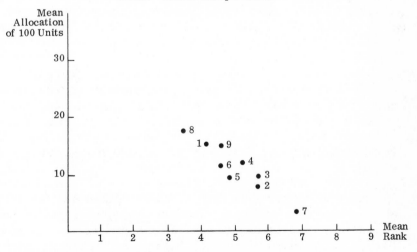

Note: Numbers in quadrant refer to nine public interest items.
Source: Interview responses gathered in nine-state study area by the authors.

153

interest factors by each group. For each item, management and labor assigned a rank of one to nine, one indicating the highest priority, nine the lowest. For example, in Figure 7.1, item 9 (increased services) has an average rank of 2.4091 and, consequently, is considered by management as the highest priority of the nine items. This average rank is calculated simply by summing all of the ranks assigned to item 9 by management and dividing this total by the number of management respondents (22). Items to the right of item 9 have numerically larger mean ranks and, thus, lower priorities. The average allocation indicates the mean number of units allocated to each of the nine public interest dimensions from the 100 units each respondent was asked to allocate. To illustrate, item 9, which is assigned the highest priority by management, receives 860 total units from all management respondents or an average allocation of 34.5 units out of the total of 100 units. In general, as you move from the upper left of the graph to the lower right, the items are assigned lower priorities and receive smaller amounts from the 100 units allocated.

As mentioned above, management attaches the highest priority and allocates the largest number of units to increased services (item 9). Improved efficiency of operation (item 5) and training programs for upgrading and promoting (item 4) receive the second highest ranking and amount of units. Guaranteeing uninterrupted service by binding arbitration (item 3) and employee protection guarantees (item 6) receive the lowest rank and number of units.

Figure 7.2 displays the same information for labor. As shown in the graph, labor attached highest priority and allocated the largest number of its 100 units to insuring that transit employees' wages are adequate (item 8), and the lowest priority and the smallest amount of its 100 units to improved environmental impact of buses (item 7). The remaining items are too evenly clustered to permit any further meaningful generalizations.

The greater the dispersion from left to right in the graphs, the greater the degree of agreement within groups with regard to the ranking of each item. Greater dispersion along the vertical axis indicates a strong desire by the group to allocate relatively large numbers of the 100 units among a few public interest dimensions and relatively few units to others. According to the graphs, it appears that management respondents tended to vote more as a group and were willing to allocate relatively large amounts of their 100 units for high-priority items. To illustrate, management is in almost total agreement on the need for increased services (item 9) and the lack of need for binding arbitration and employee protection guarantees (items 3 and 6, respectively). Additionally, the need for training programs (item 4) and improved efficiency of operations (item 5) is fairly well distinguished from the remaining items. Labor's views, on the other hand, are not so clearly defined. The horizontal and vertical dispersion between labor's highest-ranking item (adequate wages) and the lowest (improved environmental impact) is much less than the dispersion between management's highest and lowest rankings. In fact, Figure 7.2 shows most of the items to be fairly closely bunched together with little difference within the labor respondents as to relative ranking or average number of units allocated to each item.

TABLE 7.4

Observed and Expected Relative Priority Rankings for
Public Interest Item 1 (Improved Safety)

| Relative | Number in Group Assigning Rank | |
Rank	Management	Union
High priority (1, 2, 3)		
Observed	7	15
Expected	9.49	12.51
Medium priority (4, 5, 6)		
Observed	13	6
Expected	8.50	10.80
Low priority (7, 8, 9)		
Observed	2	8
Expected	4.31	5.69

Note: Chi-square = 8.2833, significant at .05 level, two degrees of freedom. In this table and in Tables 7.5 through 7.12, the expected frequency enables the reader to make comparisons between the frequency one would expect to find if the two groups were alike and the actual, observed frequency. The expected frequency is calculated as follows. In the above table, for example, ten respondents (two management plus eight union) assigned a low priority to improved safety. Since there were 22 management and 29 union respondents (51 total respondents), we would expect, in the absence of any group differences, that of the ten assigning this item a low priority, 22/51 x 10, or 4.31, would be management frequency, and 29/51 x 10, or 5.69, would be union frequency. Where the observed frequency differs substantially from the expected frequency, this indicates group differences and the chi-square will rise.

Source: Interview responses gathered in nine-state study area by the authors.

TABLE 7.5

Observed and Expected Relative Priority Rankings
for Public Interest Item 2 (Reduced Fares)

Relative Rank	Number in Group Assigning Rank	
	Management	Union
High priority (1, 2, 3)		
Observed	4	8
Expected	5.18	6.82
Medium priority (4, 5, 6)		
Observed	13	8
Expected	9.06	11.94
Low priority (7, 8, 9)		
Observed	5	13
Expected	7.76	10.24

Note: Chi-square = 5.21686, two degrees of freedom.

Source: Interview responses gathered in nine-state study area by the authors.

To facilitate a meaningful statistical comparison of the relative rankings assigned by management and union respondents to the nine public interest items, the rank scores are collapsed as follows: rank scores of 1, 2, and 3 are classified as high priority; rank scores of 4, 5, and 6 are classified as medium-range priority; and rank scores of 7, 8, and 9 are classified as low priority. Chi-square analysis is used to test for significant differences in rankings between the two groups. The results are presented in Tables 7.4 through 7.12, which show observed and expected frequencies of relative rankings for each of the nine public interest items suggested to the 22 management and 29 union respondents. As the tables indicate, management and union respondents give significantly different degrees of priority to improved safety (item 1), guaranteeing uninterrupted service by means of binding arbitration (item 3), employee job protection guarantees (item 6), improved environmental impact of buses (item 7), insuring comparable transit employee wages (item 8), and increased services (item 9).

In assigning a relative priority to improved safety of the vehicle, management respondents tended most frequently to assign a medium-range rank score (4, 5, or 6) while union respondents most frequently assigned a high priority (1, 2, or 3) to this item. However, a sizable number of union respondents (8) assigned improved safety a low priority.

Guaranteeing uninterrupted service by binding arbitration for every unresolved negotiation item and grievance (item 3) overwhelmingly received a low priority from management respondents, with 18 out of 22 assigning it a low priority. The opinions of union respondents on this item were much more evenly distributed among the three priority categories; however, the largest single group of respondents (12) gave the item low priority. It appears that management is strongly opposed to guaranteed binding arbitration, and local union leaders are somewhat cool to the idea as well. Perhaps this is due to the lack of experience with this technique among many union and management officials.

Management opinion of guarantees protesting employees' jobs in case of technological change or layoffs (item 6) is again consensual, with 17 out of 22 assigning item 6 a low priority and none assigning it a high priority. Most of the union respondents (23) assigned item 6 a high (10 respondents) or medium-range (13) priority, indicating much more concern for this issue than management respondents.

One public interest issue that union respondents care little about is improved environmental impact of buses (item 7), with 17 out of 29 assigning this item a low priority and only one assigning it a high

TABLE 7.6

Observed and Expected Relative Priority Rankings for
Public Interest Item 3 (Uninterrupted Service—Arbitration)

Relative Rank	Number in Group Assigning Rank	
	Management	Union
High priority (1, 2, 3)		
Observed	2	8
Expected	4.31	5.69
Medium priority (4, 5, 6)		
Observed	2	9
Expected	4.75	6.25
Low priority (7, 8, 9)		
Observed	18	12
Expected	12.94	17.06

Note: Chi-square = 8.4530, significant at .05 level, two degrees of freedom.

Source: Interview responses gathered in nine-state study area by the authors.

TABLE 7.7

Observed and Expected Relative Priority Rankings for
Public Interest Item 4 (Training Programs)

Relative	Number in Group Assigning Rank	
Rank	Management	Union
High priority (1, 2, 3)		
Observed	12	9
Expected	9.06	11.94
Medium priority (4, 5, 6)		
Observed	8	11
Expected	8.20	10.80
Low priority (7, 8, 9)		
Observed	2	9
Expected	4.75	6.25

Note: Chi-square = 4.48042, two degrees of freedom.
Source: Interview responses gathered in nine-state study area by the authors.

TABLE 7.8

Observed and Expected Relative Priority Rankings for
Public Interest Item 5 (Improved Efficiency)

Relative	Number in Group Assigning Rank	
Rank	Management	Union
High priority (1, 2, 3)		
Observed	12	10
Expected	9.49	12.51
Medium priority (4, 5, 6)		
Observed	8	9
Expected	7.33	9.67
Low priority (7, 8, 9)		
Observed	2	10
Expected	5.18	6.82

Note: Chi-square = 4.70177, two degrees of freedom.
Source: Interview responses gathered in nine-state study area by the authors.

TABLE 7.9

Observed and Expected Relative Priority Rankings for
Public Interest Item 6 (Employee Job Protection Guarantees)

| Relative | Number in Group Assigning Rank | |
Rank	Management	Union
High priority (1, 2, 3)		
Observed	0	10
Expected	4.31	5.69
Medium priority (4, 5, 6)		
Observed	5	13
Expected	7.76	10.24
Low priority (7, 8, 9)		
Observed	17	6
Expected	9.92	13.08

Note: Chi-square = 18.19848, significant at .01 level, two
degrees of freedom.

Source: Interview responses gathered in nine-state study area
by the authors.

TABLE 7.10

Observed and Expected Relative Priority Rankings for
Public Interest Item 7 (Improved Environmental Impact of Buses)

| Relative | Number in Group Assigning Rank | |
Rank	Management	Union
High priority (1, 2, 3)		
Observed	7	1
Expected	3.45	4.55
Medium priority (4, 5, 6)		
Observed	10	11
Expected	9.06	11.94
Low priority (7, 8, 9)		
Observed	5	17
Expected	9.49	12.51

Note: Chi-square = 10.32684, significant at .01 level, two
degrees of freedom.

Source: Interview responses gathered in nine-state study area
by the authors.

TABLE 7.11

Observed and Expected Relative Priority Rankings for
Public Interest Item 8 (Insuring Comparable Transit Wages)

| Relative | Number in Group Assigning Rank | |
Rank	Management	Union
High priority (1, 2, 3)		
Observed	5	18
Expected	9.92	13.08
Medium priority (4, 5, 6)		
Observed	4	7
Expected	4.75	6.25
Low priority (7, 8, 9)		
Observed	13	4
Expected	7.33	9.67

Note: Chi-square = 12.19976, significant at .01 level, two
degrees of freedom.

Source: Interview responses gathered in nine-state study area
by the authors.

TABLE 7.12

Observed and Expected Relative Priority Rankings for
Public Interest Item 9 (Increased Services)

| Relative | Number in Group Assigning Rank | |
Rank	Management	Union
High priority (1, 2, 3)		
Observed	17	8
Expected	10.78	14.22
Medium priority (4, 5, 6)		
Observed	3	13
Expected	6.90	9.10
Low priority (7, 8, 9)		
Observed	2	8
Expected	4.31	5.69

Note: Chi-square = 12.36210, significant at .01 level, two
degrees of freedom.

Source: Interview responses gathered in nine-state study area
by the authors.

priority. Management opinion appears to be more mixed, with the largest number of respondents (10) assigning item 7 a medium-range priority.

Priorities assigned by union and management respondents to insuring that the transit employees' wages are equal to, or better than, those in other agencies having similar working conditions and cost of living (item 8) are in general directly opposed. Most management respondents (13) assigned this item a low priority, while most union respondents (18) felt item 8 deserved a high priority.

The public interest item receiving the strongest management support was increased services (item 9), with 17 out of 22 assigning this item a high priority. Union respondents, on the other hand, varied in their relative rankings, with the largest number (13) assigning item 9 a medium-range priority.

In addition to the relative ranking, each respondent was asked to allocate 100 units over the nine dimensions. As mentioned earlier, each union and management official was asked to allocate 100 units to the nine dimensions based upon his knowledge of the dimensions and needs of his property. The allocation of these units reflects not only the respondent's priorities, but to some extent also provides insight into the relative strength of his priorities. Table 7.13 contains a comparison of unit amounts allocated to each of the nine public interest factors by labor and management. A multivariate analysis of variance test reveals, F-value = 7.3710, significant at the .001 level, indicating a significant difference in the allocations of the two groups. Testing to determine the relative effect of each of the nine factors in distinguishing or discriminating between the two groups reveals the rankings shown in the right-hand column of Table 7.13. Of the nine items, the most powerful discriminator between labor and management is employee protection guarantees (item 6), with increased services (item 9) being the second most powerful discriminator. Interestingly, although labor allocated considerably more of its 100 units to comparable wages (item 8) than management, this factor is not a particularly useful discriminator between the two groups. Also of interest is the finding that allocation for binding arbitration (item 3) is the third most powerful discriminator between the two groups. As noted earlier, management respondents assigned a low priority to binding arbitration and union respondents were mixed in their opinions of the need for binding arbitration. Apparently, although labor did not rank binding arbitration very high, they are willing to spend substantially more funds for it than management.

Because there appear to be substantial differences between labor and management in the unit amounts each allocates to the various public interest factors, discriminant analysis using generalized

TABLE 7.13

Comparison of Mean Allocations of Priority by Group
(Based on Allocation of 100 Units)

Item Number and Topic	Allocation		Ranking of Discriminatory Power
	Management	Labor	
1. Improved safety	8.0454	15.2069	7
2. Reduced fares	4.5000	7.5862	8
3. Uninterrupted service—arbitration	1.5909	8.6897	3
4. Training programs	15.9095	11.8275	9
5. Improved efficiency	17.0454	8.8621	4
6. Employee job protection guarantees	1.8181	11.6207	1
7. Improved environmental impact of buses	7.9090	3.6207	5
8. Insuring transit wages are comparable	8.6363	17.6552	6
9. Increased services	34.5454	14.9310	2

Note: F = 7.37100, significant at the .001 level.
Sample: 22 management and 29 union respondents.
Source: Interview responses gathered in nine-state study area by the authors.

162

squared differences is performed to see how effectively one can predict a respondent's position, that is, labor or management, from his allocations. In essence, after generating the discriminant function, the individual allocations are put in to the discriminate function to test the ability to predict correctly the position of each respondent by his response. The results, given in Table 7.14, show the respondent's position to be almost perfectly predictable; that is, the allocations of individuals in each group are sufficiently different to permit predicting the group to which an individual belongs simply by looking at his allocation.

TABLE 7.14

Classification of Respondents on the Basis of
Allocations Using Discriminant Analysis

| Number of Observations | Classified into Group | |
From Group	Management	Union
22 Management	21	1
29 Union	2	27

Source: Interview responses gathered in nine-state study area by the authors.

To summarize, the responses to the unstructured questions dealing with the definition of public interest indicate substantial agreement between labor and management. Seventy-five percent of the union and management respondents agree that the agency has an obligation to provide service to citizens, with many commonly cited dimensions of this obligation from both groups. However, when asked their perceptions of their counterpart's definition, both groups believe that management and union definitions have much less in common. Union respondents at about one-third of the properties believe management is overly concerned with cost savings, sometimes to the detriment of providing adequate service. Almost one-half of the management respondents, on the other hand, feel that unions are more concerned with contractual provisions and working conditions, with insufficient concern for cost consideration.

The priorities attached to the nine public interest factors presented to management and union officials tend to support somewhat these perceptions of the two groups. Management tends to be most concerned with increased services, training programs, and improving efficiency of operations. Obviously, two of the items stress productivity improvements and concern for costs. Labor attaches highest priorities to comparable wages, improved safety, employee job protection guarantees, and increased services. Again, two of the items, comparable wages and job protection, could be very applicable to the labor agreement. Thus, it appears that management and union leaders are acting in a responsible manner, at least within the framework of responsibilities (noted earlier) provided by Friedman. Each group tends to define and operationalize the public interest primarily in terms of the needs and desires of the group it directly represents, although there were some occasions where union and management respondents transcended narrow constituent interests. While this inevitably results in some conflict, it is our opinion that such a relationship between union and management is not only healthy, but vital to mass transit.

MANAGERIAL DISCRETIONARY POWER TO SERVE
THE PUBLIC INTEREST

Contract Language Covering Public Interest Issues

One potential constraint on management's power to serve the public interest is applicable contract language. For this reason, we have examined labor agreements to determine the extent to which the contract includes dimensions of the public interest as well as other related dimensions. Although the term "public interest" is not specifically referred to in over 75 percent of the contracts, many contracts contained clauses that reflect the significance of the public interest.

Over 85 percent of the contracts contained provisions that specify the employees' obligation to operate the vehicles in a safe manner. Sixty percent of the contracts contained specific reference to the provision of uninterrupted service. And, more than two-thirds of the contracts specified the employees' obligation to treat customers in a courteous and respectful manner. The wording of such provisions is exemplified in these contract statements:

> The parties recognize that the best interest of the community and the job security of the employees depend upon the firm's success in establishing and maintaining safe, effective, and courteous service to the community.
>
> Whereas, the company is engaged in rendering transportation service to the city of _____ , and to

> the public generally, and it is the desire of both
> parties hereto that such service may be rendered in
> a manner that will best serve the public convenience
> and necessity without interruption; . . .

While one might assume that inclusion of public interest language in
the contract represents union intrusion, it should be noted that these
provisions do not involve any cost either to management or to the
union, and their relatively vague terminology appears to have little
effect on related managerial discretion. We are more interested in
ascertaining the extent to which contract provisions limit the scope
of managerial discretion in this regard.

With respect to the somewhat cost-oriented dimensions of the
public interest specified earlier, there are few directly related provisions in the labor agreements. Even though the union and management are in general agreement on the need for improved safety of
the vehicles, fewer than 20 percent of the contracts provided for
joint committees to deal with safety issues. Less than 40 percent
contained provisions for safety meetings, and of those that did, more
than half made attendance voluntary. While the union did not allocate,
on the average, as many of its 100 units to increased services as
did management, both groups attached a relatively high priority to
the need for increased services. When viewed in terms of contract
language, there were no provisions that either require joint involvement by the union and management to increase services or limit
management's ability to curtail services during the contract period.

The two issues that labor ranked significantly higher than did
management, comparable wages (item 8) and employee job protection
guarantees (item 6) are not translated into labor agreement provisions.
With the exception of cost-of-living adjustments, which are contained
in most contracts, there were no provisions for defining a basis of
comparability for wage determination. With respect to employee job
protection guarantees, none of the contracts contained restrictions
on the determination of when layoffs are needed or how many employees are to be laid off. Only 20 percent of the contracts required
advance notice of layoffs and none provided any severance pay for
layoffs. It should be mentioned, however, that employees receive
some job protection if the company receives either capital or operating
assistance from the UMTA; perhaps labor and management officials
believe the related legal protections of Section 13(c) of the 1964 Urban
Mass Transportation Act are sufficient.

The same pattern is true for other issues examined; for example,
few contracts provided for apprenticeship programs or formalized
training programs, joint committees aimed at improving efficiency
of operations, or policies that limit or prohibit fare increases or even

TABLE 7.15

Extent of Union Influence in Administrative
Aspects of Public Interest Issues
(number of responses)

Public Interest Issue	Management and Union Involvement				
	Unilateral Management Right	Contract Provision Pertaining to Issue	Union Can Grieve or Management Has Obligation to Confer	Management Must Receive Union Approval for Issue	Union Has Right to Negotiate Issue
Employee protection					
Layoffs of employees—determination					
Union respondents	16	1	2	0	1
Management respondents	17	1	2	0	0
Layoffs of employees—procedures					
Union respondents	6	12	2	0	0
Management respondents	5	12	3	0	0
Increased and/or efficient service					
Length of runs					
Union respondents	11	6	2	1	0
Management respondents	11	9	0	0	0
Application for capital grants					
Union respondents	17	0	1	2	0
Management respondents	20	0	0	0	0
Scheduling changes (routes)					
Union respondents	13	3	3	0	1
Management respondents	14	3	3	0	0
Scheduling changes (times)					
Union respondents	13	5	2	0	0
Management respondents	15	4	0	1	0
Technological change (for example, bus design)					
Union respondents	16	0	3	0	1
Management respondents	20	0	0	0	0
Time standards (run times of routes)					
Union respondents	11	0	6	0	3
Management respondents	7	3	10	0	0
Training programs for upgrading and promoting					
Training and apprenticeship					
Union respondents	11	3	5	0	1
Management respondents	16	3	1	0	0

Source: Interview responses gathered in nine-state study areas by the authors.

provide for union input into decisions on fare changes. This is of particular interest since the major union in the mass transit industry, the ATU, has for many years urged a no-fare policy to accommodate the public interest; for example, resultant attraction of additional customers to mass transit would ease traffic and pollution problems.

Union Influence in Administrative
Aspects of Public Interest Issues

Thus far, we have indicated that in open-ended questions union and management officials tend to agree that service is the most important dimension of the public interest in mass transit. Contract language dealing with public interest issues tends to be restricted to phrases such as "the employee and the union have an obligation to promote uninterrupted service," phrases which involve little or no cost either to the union or management. Additionally, contractual silence appears to reflect either lack of agreement or concern by labor and management over other public interest issues, for example, comparable wages, improved efficiency of operations, and increased services.

The results of our contract analysis are further confirmed in interviews with management and union respondents. More specifically, each of the interview respondents was asked to assess the degree of management and union involvement in each of nine administrative aspects of public interest issues. With each issue, the respondent was asked to indicate if he perceived the issue to be a unilateral management right or one which (1) was presently covered by a contract provision; (2) the union has the right to grieve over; (3) management must receive union approval on before enactment; or (4) the union has the right to negotiate. The results are shown in Table 7.15. (This table is a partial replication of Table 3.6; however, because the degree of union involvement in these issues is pertinent to the public interest, the data are insightful and warrant repeating.)

An analysis of the responses pertaining to employee protection issues reveals that management is limited by the labor agreement in terms of the particular employees that can be laid off; however, both management and union respondents agree that management has the unilateral right to determine the timing and extent of employee layoffs. Similarly, management has a somewhat contractually free hand in their efforts to make services more efficient through application for grants to finance new equipment or technological change in existing equipment, as well as in instituting scheduling changes. Unions do have significant involvement in one related administrative aspect, length of runs; more specifically, many labor agreements specify the proportion of straight runs (those runs which are continuous, containing no time intervals between pieces of work). Finally, management typically has the unilateral right to determine the need for and content of training and apprenticeship programs.

Several overall conclusions result from the data in Table 7.15. First, union and management respondents are in relative agreement on their respective involvements in administrative aspects of public interest issues. Secondly, the responses confirm the results of our contract analysis—management often has power to act on public interest issues. These conclusions, coupled with the observation reported in Chapter 3—that union and management respondents attach some degree of permanence to the unilateral management rights—indicate a relatively unconstrained atmosphere for management in serving the public interest through transit operations.

NOTES

1. Walter Fogel and Archie Kleingartner, Contemporary Labor Issues (Belmont, Calif.: Wadsworth, 1968), p. 335.

2. Gardner Ackley, "Automation: Threat and Promise," New York Times Magazine, March 22, 1964, pp. 16, 52, 54, and 57.

3. W. Bierwagon, "Labor's Response to Innovation in the Transit Industry," in Proceedings of A Series of Conferences on Organized Labor, Transportation Technology and Urban Mass Transit in the Chicago Metropolitan Area, ed. Stanley Rosen and Scott Schiave, (Chicago: University of Illinois at Chicago Circle, 1973), pp. 236-37.

4. This classification roughly parallels that of Martin Wachs, "Fostering Technological Innovation in Urban Transportation," Traffic Quarterly, January 1971, p. 41.

5. At least one observer of mass transit operations suggests that management's lack of influence in technological innovations matches that of the union—management officials are often given the technology "as is," with little involvement in the development or planning process. Stanley Rose, "Organized Labor, Technology and Innovation in Mass Transit" (Speech delivered at the Conference on Unions, Management Rights and the Public Interest in Mass Transit, Jacksonville, March 22, 1976.) Our investigation did not attempt to verify empirically this contention although it appears to be a most appropriate dimension for future research.

6. Jack Barbash, "The Impact of Technology on Labor-Management Relations," in Contemporary Labor, ed. Fogel and Kleingartner, p. 340.

7. Bierwagon, "Labor's Response," pp. 236-37.

8. Ibid., pp. 6 and 7. See also In Transit, August-September 1972, p. 13, and November 1972, p. 11.

9. National Commission on Technology, The Outlook for Technological Change and Employment, app. 1, "Technology and American Society" (Washington, D.C.: National Commission on Technology, 1966), p. 83.

10. "The President's Desk," In Transit, May 1971.

11. Bierwagon, "Labor's Response," p. 237.

12. Darold T. Barnum, "National Public Labor Relations Legislation: The Case of Urban Mass Transit," Labor Law Journal 27 (March 1976): 168.

13. Ibid. See also, J. J. McGinley, Labor Relations in the New York Rapid Transit System 1904-1944 (New York: King's Crown Press, Columbia University, 1949); A. W. MacMahon, "The New York City Transit System: Public Ownership, Civil Service, and Collective Bargaining," Political Science Quarterly 56 (June 1941); P. Freund, "Labor Relations in the New York Rapid Transit Industry, 1945-1960," (Ph.D. diss., New York University, 1964); Dallas M. Young, "Fifty Years of Labor Arbitration in Cleveland Transit," Monthly Labor Review 83 (May 1960); and U.S. Department of Labor, Division of Public Employee Labor Relations, Labor-Management Services Administration, Summary of State Policy Regulations for Public Sector Labor Relations (Washington, D.C.: U.S. Government Printing Office, 1975).

14. Section 13(c) has been a major factor in protecting collective bargaining, as a former international president of ATU noted:

> So far as our membership is concerned, Section 13(c)
> has made a tremendous contribution in the protection of
> collective bargaining and arbitration in the public sector
> of the transit industry. I am pleased to note that we have
> been almost entirely successful in our efforts to require
> municipalities involved in assuming public control and
> ownership of a formerly private system to preserve and
> continue existing collective bargaining arrangements,
> even in cases of abandonments, in order to qualify for
> federal transit assistance.

15. D.V. Maroney, Jr., "Collective Bargaining in Mass Transit" (Speech delivered at the conference on Unions, Management Rights, and the Public Interest in Mass Transit, Jacksonville, March 22, 1976).

16. After a strike of nine months, Dade County floated municipal bonds, bought the privately owned Miami Transit System, and simultaneously extinguished union recognition and collective bargaining

rights by operation of law. See Dade County v. Motor Coach Employees, 157 So.2d 176.

17. Maroney, "Collective Bargaining."

18. Barnum, "National Public Labor," p. 171. For a detailed analysis of the history of Section 13(c), see Jefferson Associates, "Administration of Section 13(c)—Urban Mass Transportation Act," Report to the U.S. Department of Labor, Contract #L-72-32 (January 1972), pp. 5-19; and "A Study of the Administration of Section 13(c)" (Unpublished U.S. Department of Labor study conducted in 1971 by W.L. Horvitz).

19. Ibid.

20. Jefferson Associates, "Administration," p. 5. See also, G. M. Smerk, "Development of Federal Mass Transportation Policy," Indiana Law Journal 47 (1972): 249-92.

21. Urban Mass Transportation Act of 1964, as amended, SS 3(e), 49 U.S.C.A., SS 1609 (1971).

22. Ibid., SS 13(c). As provided by the Transportation Act of 1940, as amended, 549 J.S.C. 45(2)(f) (1971), the protective arrangement reads as follows:

> As a condition of its approval, under this paragraph
> (2), of any transaction involving a carrier or carriers
> by railroad subject to the provisions of this part, the
> Commission [Interstate Commerce Commission] shall
> require a fair and equitable arrangement to protect the
> interests of the railroad employees affected. In its
> order of approval the Commission shall include terms
> and conditions providing that during the period of four
> years from the effective date of such order such trans-
> action will not result in employees of the carrier or
> carriers by railroad affected by such order being in a
> worse position with respect to their employment, except
> that the protection afforded to any employee pursuant to
> this sentence shall not be required to continue for a longer
> period, following the effective date of such order, than
> the period during which such employee was in the employ
> of such carrier or carriers prior to the effective date
> of such order. Such arrangement shall contain provisions
> no less protective of the interests of employees than those
> heretofore imposed pursuant to this subdivision and those
> established pursuant to section 405 of the Rail Passenger
> Service Act (45 U.S.C. 565). Notwithstanding any other
> provisions of this Act, an agreement pertaining to the
> protection of the interests of said employees may here-
> after be entered into by any carrier or carriers by railroad

and the duly authorized representative or representatives of its or their employees.

23. H.M. Levinson et al., Collective Bargaining and Technological Change in American Transportation (Evanston: Northwestern University Press,1971), pp. 128-29.

24. H.W. Risher, The Crises in Railroad Collective Bargaining, A Study of the Institutional Impediments to Change in the Industrial Relation System (Springfield, Va.: National Technical Information Service, U.S. Department of Commerce, 1972).

25. J.E. Burke, "Protective Agreements and Unified Mass Transit," in Proceedings, ed. Rosen and Schiave, pp. 121-28.

26. See Order of the Interstate Commerce Commission in Finance Docket No. 15920, New Orleans Union Passenger Terminal Case, 282 ICC 271 (January 16, 1952).

27. Robert C. Lieb, Labor in the Transit Industry (Washington, D.C.: Office of Transportation Systems Analysis and Information, U.S. Department of Transportation, 1976), p.33.

28. An interesting comment is in Alan Altshuler, "The Federal Government and Paratransit," in Paratransit, Special Report 164, ed. Sandra Rosenbloom (Washington, D.C.: Transportation Research Board, 1976), p. 97:

> The provisions of section 13c have been applied by Congress in the High Speed Ground Transportation Act of 1965, the Rail Passenger Act of 1974, the Juvenile Justice and Delinquency Prevention Act of 1974, and the Nurse Training Act of 1975. In both of the latter "human service" acts, the issue was fear on the part of organized labor that government might support efforts at de-institutionalization. The point to note here is that congressional support for the principle of section 13c— that government money should not be used to harm employees—appears today to be more deeply embedded in the governmental fabric than ever.

29. Ibid., p. 99.

30. U.S. Department of Labor, News Release, USDL 71-217 (Washington, D.C., April 16, 1971), pp. 2-3.

31. Yud is special assistant for mass transit in the Office of the Undersecretary, U.S. Department of Labor, and is in charge of employee protection for the department. His comments were answers to audience questions concerning employee protection at the Conference on Union, Management Rights, and the Public Interest in Mass Transit, Jacksonville, March 23, 1976.

32. Ibid.

33. Ibid.

34. Larry F. Yud, "Employee Protection" (Speech delivered at the Conference on Unions, Management Rights, and the Public Interest in Mass Transit), Jacksonville, March 23, 1976. As Yud notes:

> In line with the Congressional intent that, wherever appropriate, the protective language should be developed as a result of collective bargaining, the Department of Labor refers copies of the application to any labor organization representing employees in the service area of the project and solicits their views with respect to appropriate terms and conditions of employee protection. The individual parties involved are then encouraged to reach agreement on employee protective terms and conditions. The Department of Labor gives applicants for Federal assistance and/or the operating company on one hand, and the union representatives of the employees on the other, the greatest possible latitude and encouragement to develop their own mutually acceptable arrangements to protect the interests of employees who may be actually or potentially affected. The Department of Labor stands ready and is frequently called upon to furnish technical and mediatory assistance to the parties in their efforts to reach agreement.

35. Barnum, "National Public Labor," p. 171.

36. Yud, "Employee Protection."

37. Louis J. Gambaccini, "A Common Purpose: Labor and Management in the Future of Public Transportation" (Speech delivered at the Conference on Unions, Management Rights, and the Public Interest in Mass Transit, Jacksonville, March 22, 1976).

38. Urban Mass Transportation, "The Summary, Conclusions and Recommendations of the Transit Industry Labor-Management Relations Research Conference and Symposium," mimeographed (Washington, D.C., November 20, 1975), p. 3.

39. Jefferson Associates, "Administration," p. 26.

40. Yud, "Employee Protection."

41. Jefferson Associates, "Administration," pp. 27-28.

42. Gambaccini, "Common Purpose."

43. Yud, "Employee Protection."

44. Altshuler, "The Federal Government."

45. Ibid.

46. D. V. Maroney, Jr., "Collective Bargaining."

47. Barnum, "National Public Labor," p. 176.

48. Gambaccini, "Common Purpose."

49. P.W. Jeffress, "The Negro in the Urban Transit Industry," in Herbert R. Northrup, et al., Negro Employment in Land and Air Transport, Studies of Negro Employment, vol. 5 (Philadelphia: Industrial Research Unit, Wharton School of Finance and Commerce, University of Pennsylvania, 1971), part 4, p. 1.

50. Herbert R. Northrup, Organized Labor and the Negro (New York: Harper and Brothers, 1944), p. 48.

51. Jeffress, "Negro" p. 24.

52. M. Ross, All Manner of Men (New York: Reynal and Hitchcock, 1948); R. Marshall, The Negro Worker (New York: Random House, 1967); P. Foner, Organized Labor and the Black Worker, 1919-1973 (New York: Praeger, 1973); W.B. Gould, "Labor Relations and Race Relations," in Public Workers and Public Unions, ed. S. Zagoria (Englewood Cliffs, N.J.: Prentice-Hall, 1972); and J. A. Davis, "Employment of Negroes in Local Transit Industry," Opportunity 22 (April-June 1944): 63-65.

53. Jeffress, "Negro," pp. 67-75.

54. Barnum, "National Public Labor," pp. 80-82.

55. Jeffress, "Negro," pp. 68-70.

56. Herbert R. Northrup et al., Negro Employment in Basic Industry, Studies of Negro Employment, vol. 1 (Philadelphia: Industrial Research Unit, Wharton School of Finance and Commerce, University of Pennsylvania, 1970), pp. 318-23.

57. Consent Order in Civil Action No. 70-2946, Section D., Henry Faggen v. New Orleans Public Service Inc., et al., U.S. District Court, Eastern District of Louisiana, March 8, 1974.

58. Ibid.

59. Northrup, et al., Employment, pp. 182-85.

60. Gould, "Labor Relations," pp. 151-55.

61. Based upon field interviews with management respondents representing 12 of the 20 sites visited.

62. Gould, "Labor Relations," p. 155.

63. Ibid., p. 153.

64. Willard W. Wirtz, Labor and the Public Interest (New York: Harper & Row, 1964), p. 46.

65. Milton Friedman, Capitalism and Freedom (Chicago: University of Chicago Press, 1963), pp. 133-35.

66. For example, see Paul T. Heyne, Private Keepers of the Public Interest (New York: McGraw-Hill, 1968).

67. Jay F. Atwood, "Collective Bargaining's Challenge: Five Imperatives for Public Managers," Public Personnel Management 5 (January-February 1976): 29-30.

8

SUMMARY

Results of the collective bargaining process are of central interest in the fields of industrial relations and mass transit. In most bargaining models, outcomes serve as one of the principal dependent variables, yet there has been a lack of empirically based research on labor-management relations in urban mass transit. One of the problems encountered with the use of formal bargaining models is that these models are normative, rather than descriptive or explanatory; that is, instead of incorporating propositions that explain or describe the behavior of labor-management relationships, or the factors that shape the results of the process, the models are directed to predicting how the parties should behave, given certain assumptions about such factors as their rationality, information, preferences, and risk-taking abilities.

Through the analysis of all labor agreements for transit systems in a nine-state southeastern area and extensive field research, which included visits to 20 properties to administer an in-depth, confidential series of questions, this study aims to allow the reader a better understanding of the issues, the behavior of parties to the bargaining process, and some insight into the formulation of solutions to the problems of labor-management relations in mass transit. To accomplish this task, the research was designed to allow for a description of the bargaining process and identification of significant parameters included in negotiations. The research results also provide a concept of union involvement in mass transit issues, sufficiently developed to include the underlying complexity of forces affecting union involvement; this has been measured in quantitative terms and associated with the following independent variables: city size, type of ownership, size of the bargaining unit, and number of buses. The results were grouped according to administrative issues, economic issues, impasse resolution issues, and institutional issues.

The framework utilized in the research, namely, a list of 249 transit-specific variables, to analyze all labor agreements in the study area on a provision-by-provision basis is, perhaps, one of the major results of the research project.

Chapter 2 presents a descriptive overview of the collective bargaining process at the 20 interview sites. Perhaps our most pervasive observation pertains to the established relationship between labor and management representatives—collective bargaining at these properties has spanned an average of four decades, resulting in an average of 20 labor agreements for each property. Our interviews revealed that the length of the labor-management relationship, coupled with extensive, related experience of the management and union negotiators, has fostered a general atmosphere of mutual respect. Additionally, the established relationship has resulted in flexible contract negotiations in which the length of negotiations appears adequate to resolve the issues; negotiation sessions are scheduled to meet the preferences and other commitments of the management and union representatives; and few formalized ground rules, other than there being no press coverage of sessions, are needed to regulate negotiation conduct.

Because of this relationship, management and union respondents perceive little need to involve in collective bargaining individuals outside their respective organizations. All of the union respondents indicated that there are mechanisms for direct membership input in the formulation and/or approval of negotiation proposals, the most common procedures being the following: members initiate proposals in a union meeting; the obtained proposals are refined by the union negotiation committee; the membership votes on the committee's proposals before they are presented to management; and the membership votes on accepting the negotiated labor agreement. Another common practice is for the union to have an international representative present during contract negotiations. Similarly, the management negotiator may include other management representatives, for example, superintendent of maintenance, attorneys, nonresident management service officials, in negotiations depending on the particular issue to be resolved. However, with the exception of the services of the Federal Mediation and Conciliation Service, none of the management and union respondents perceived any benefit to be derived from direct involvement by government officials—local, state, or federal—in the collective bargaining process. The primary objections to this involvement are that government officials do not understand the many complexities of mass transit operations, and that the political environment compels these officials to be buddies with everybody. Also, a somewhat large proportion of the respondents believe that some federal agencies, for example, the Department of Transportation, have "no real concern one way or the other regarding collective bargaining," an attitude possibly derived from the lack of agency communication on labor-management issues. Finally, management and union respondents have been reluctant to enlist the involvement of outsiders, including the general public and the press, in collective bargaining; this tactical reluctance is due to the perceived antilabor attitudes of the local community.

A related objective of Chapter 2 was to uncover the extent and nature of several potential influences on the collective bargaining process. In examining the organizational scope or structure of collective bargaining, we found decentralization in publicly owned agencies, that is, mass transit employees' concerns are negotiated and included in a labor agreement separate from that of other municipal employees. This procedure probably stems from the unique work rules appropriate for mass transit employees as well as from the possible fear by some local government officials that certain employee protection provisions inherent in the mass transit operation would be extended to other public employees. For those facilities having more than one bargaining unit, there appears to be little subsequent influence in collective bargaining; for example, there were no reported instances of coordinated bargaining at these facilities. However, an exception to this observation occurs at a few privately owned facilities where the settlement attained by the numerically dominant industrial union tends to be passed on to the mass transit union at the same facility. The vast majority of the interviewed sites have bargaining units composed of both craft and operating employees. Operating employees, averaging 80 percent of the bargaining unit membership, appear to dominate the selection and resolution of issues and benefits negotiated. Another structural element—competitive services in the community—appears to have no perceived impact on the collective bargaining process. Although some national union leaders have voiced concern over potential employee displacement resulting from paratransit development, none of the local management and union officials volunteered the belief that this concern would affect their particular facility in terms of job loss or reduced governmental assistance.

Organizational characteristics of the particular agency were examined to determine their potential effect on the collective bargaining process. While some studies have found a positive relationship between public ownership and employee wage gains, only one-third of management and union respondents believed that employee wage gains are greater under public ownership of the transit system. The

overall impression was that the public-versus-private-ownership
distinction is not particularly useful to understanding collective
bargaining as related results depend upon the particular capabilities
of the individual negotiators. Many of the properties in our study
relied on management service companies, which appear to have two
major advantages: they facilitate financial assistance in terms of the
"Memphis formula"; and they provide labor relations expertise derived
from labor-management experiences at several properties.

Somewhat surprising was the lack of influence exerted by the
budget-making process on collective bargaining; for example, almost
no relationship between contract starting and expiration dates and
the agency's fiscal year was observed. Perhaps a more significant
observation is that most agencies can revise their budgets even after
the final-approval date to account for labor contract settlements.
The relationship between budget making and collective bargaining
poses an almost unsolvable dilemma. If the budget is held sacred,
then collective bargaining, as envisioned through national labor
relations policy, does not exist. On the other hand, if collective
bargaining is entirely removed from budgetary constraints, fiscal
responsibilities are abated at taxpayer expense.

Most of the mass transit properties appear relatively unaffected
by state or federal labor laws, particularly since many of these agencies retain their previously negotiated impasse resolution machinery
under the Memphis formula. One notable exception pertains to the
1974 amendments to the Fair Labor Standards Act, placing mass
transit operations under some of the act's provisions. All of the
labor respondents expressed pleasure over these amendments because
fewer work hours per operator would perhaps reduce a safety hazard;
and work rescheduling to comply with the amendments might result
in the hiring of additional employees. However, a few of the union
representatives also believed that employees' take-home pay might
be reduced if the rescheduling and/or addition of employees diminished
the total weekly work hours per employee. The majority of management
respondents expressed concern over the implementation of these
amendments during existing contract periods, indicating implementation added a substantial and unanticipated cost to their operations.

Institutional issues, covered in Chapter 3, concern the preser-
vation of union security and managerial prerogatives. One dimension
of union security refers to union membership as a condition of
employment. While only one-fifth of the analyzed labor agreements
have explicit union shop provisions, requiring union membership as
a condition of employment, the proportion of employees who are
union members appears quite high; over 90 percent of the bargaining
unit employees at the 20 interviewed sites are union members. A
related contractual provision, found in all but one of the labor

agreements, is dues checkoff. However, most of the analyzed labor agreements were silent on topics dealing with certain managerial actions, for example, subcontracting and supervisors' performing bargaining unit work, which can also affect union security. We are not certain that contractual silence equals the presence of a unilateral management right, particularly since none of the union respondents indicated problems with these issues. An open-ended interview question asked management and union respondents to define the union's unilateral right. Most respondents indicated this right is that of insuring the enforcement of contract provisions through contract negotiations and the grievance procedure.

Management rights, in part, relate to the extent to which management can unilaterally decide where people work and what type of work is performed. Several issues were analyzed pertaining to management's operation of the facility: only two of these issues, bidding of runs and administration of layoffs, were found in the vast majority of the analyzed labor agreements. Our interviews confirmed the contractual silence over these issues; also, many of the union respondents indicated that several of these issues were not proper subjects for contract negotiation. It should be mentioned that these two exceptions, bidding of runs and administration of layoffs, do not fundamentally usurp management's discretionary capability to run the operation; thus, the results suggest that management has a relatively unencumbered hand in operating the facility. An open-ended interview question asked the respondents to define management's unilateral rights. The majority of union respondents stated management's unilateral rights are limited to the management prerogative provision in the labor agreement, whereas a smaller portion of management respondents stated their unilateral rights pertain to any item not stated in the labor agreement.

All of the 33 variables in the contract analysis that deal with institutional issues were analyzed by organizational structure, city size, unit size, and number of buses. The overall degree of union involvement in these issues is relatively low, confirming the results of on-site responses. However, the degree of union involvement in these issues tends to be positively associated (.05 level of statistical significance) with size, that is, unit size, number of buses, and population.

Chapter 4 contains a discussion of the major issues in recent contract negotiations that were primarily economic issues. Although a few union and management respondents indicated concern over such issues as grievance procedures and the scope of management's rights, the vast majority of those interviewed emphasized wages, cost-of-living adjustments, health benefits and pension plans, and vacation provisions as the major issues in recent negotiations. The emphasis on economic issues is probably due to the fact that collective bargaining in the mass transit industry has a long history, and many, if not most, noneconomic issues have already been settled.

A major economic issue indicated by all respondents is wages. Theoretically, the determination of an economically appropriate wage rate for transit employees based on productivity is difficult, if not impossible, because of the public nature of transit services and the mixture of revenue sources. Consequently, many transit employers and union leaders must rely on wage comparisons as the basis for wage demands during collective bargaining. We found that comparability is used fairly extensively in wage determination, particularly with respect to geographical comparisons and size of company. However, union and management seldom agree on a common definition of wage comparisons.

Negotiated wage rates for operators on January 1, 1976, ranged from $3.00 per hour to $5.96 per hour, while the range for craft employees was $3.35 per hour to $6.77 per hour; the hourly mean wage rates for operators and craft employees were $4.40 and $4.90, respectively. Approximately 60 percent of the labor agreements contain provisions for cost-of-living adjustments. All the cost-of-living provisions use the Consumer Price Index and, for the most part, make adjustments on a quarterly basis.

When wage rates are examined by organization type, no significant differences are found between privately and publicly owned transit operations. In fact, the most revealing breakdown of wage rates appears to be by city size, with operators and craft employees in cities of less than 500,000 population earning substantially lower wages than their counterparts in cities with more than 500,000 population.

In addition to wages, indirect forms of compensation, such as vacation, sick leave, and funeral leave, are important economic issues. Most of the labor agreements also contain provisions for contingent benefits, that is, insurance protection. However, aside from basic hospital-medical-surgical insurance for employees, contract language is generally vague. Insurance coverage such as major medical, accident insurance, or life insurance, for the employee and/ or his family is most often not specified. Instead, many labor agreements contain a reference to a general insurance plan, not specifying types of coverage, extension to family, or insurance cost responsibility. This same vagueness in contract language applies equally to pension plans.

When all of the 87 variables in the contract analysis dealing with economic issues (excluding wage rates) were analyzed by organization structure, city size, unit size, and number of buses, it was found that city and company size are better indicators of the relative degree of union involvement in economic issues than is public or private ownership.

In Chapter 5, administrative issues are examined. Resolutions to administrative issues tend to be fairly uniform, probably reflecting the lengthy collective bargaining relationships of most southeastern transit properties (mentioned earlier). In fact, a comparison of issues and resolutions by organizational structure, city size, unit size, and number of buses revealed no significant differences in the degree of union involvement with respect to administrative issues.

Chapter 6 focuses on issues relating to impasse resolution. Impasses can occur over two forms of industrial disputes: disputes of right, that is, grievances that appeal alleged contract violations; and disputes of interest, that is, labor contract negotiations where one party seeks to have a permanent change included in the labor agreement.

All but one of the properties in our study have a contractual provision for a grievance procedure. However, there is a great deal of variation among the properties with regard to the definition of a grievance, the number of steps in the grievance procedure, the date of grievance initiation (date of incident or date of discovery), the extent to which union appeal and management decision time limits are specified in the contract, and the total contractually specified length of time for a grievance to go through the entire procedure. Although many mass transit properties are publicly owned, the heritage of private ownership accounts for the use of binding arbitration as the final grievance step in almost all the labor agreements. The vast majority of the arbitrary provisions do not specifically exclude any grievance issues from this process; however, some labor agreements prohibit arbitration over some adverse actions, contract negotiations, and jurisdictional questions covered under statutes or civil service laws. All but one of the properties using arbitration allow, either expressly or through contractual silence, the arbitrator to resolve questions of arbitrability, and all labor agreements stipulate that the final arbitration is binding. The vast majority of the labor agreements place no time limit on the final arbitration decisions; thus, it can potentially take a very long time to arrive at the final grievance disposition.

None of the privately owned mass transit properties expressly allows the employee to continue the grievance after the union aborts. Also, none of the investigated contracts expressly prohibits the union's screening of employee grievances to determine whether the grievance is justified.

The ATU has consistently encouraged arbitration as an impasse resolution technique for interest disputes. However, it appears that the use of arbitration as an impasse resolution technique for interest disputes has declined over the years. Only two of our interviewed properties had recently experienced this procedure, with affected management and union respondents being apprehensive over its eventual outcome. The most common impasse resolution technique in interest disputes is mediation. The interview respondents had mixed reactions concerning the effectiveness of this technique, indicating that the effectiveness depends upon the individual personality and capability of the mediator. The most often cited handicap of the mediator is his unfamiliarity with the complexities inherent in mass transit operations.

Another impasse resolution technique is the strike. The vast majority of the labor agreements prohibit strikes during the term of the labor agreement; presumably, this contractual provision at least implicitly recognizes the strike option during a negotiation impasse after the agreement expires. Contractual silence, coupled with few legal constraints on strike activity, would suggest a frequent usage of this impasse resolution technique. However, there has been little recent strike activity at the properties studied. This finding might be attributed to two factors: the antistrike philosophy of the ATU; and a belief by some management and union respondents that strikes result in a permanent loss of wages and revenues as well as in adverse public opinion.

All of the 58 variables in the contract analysis dealing with impasse resolution issues were analyzed by organizational structure, city size, unit size, and number of buses. There were no statistically significant relationships between these variables and the degree of union involvement in impasse resolution issues.

IMPRESSIONS

The following issues do not represent definitive conclusions based on our findings; however, they do represent rather important discussion areas that have been suggested by our interviews with mass transit practitioners and by our analysis of labor agreements. It is our contention that while these issues currently have no immediate resolution, their subsequent discussion and research by interested parties is crucial before any related policies can be formulated and implemented.

Collective Bargaining and Public Policy

Labor legislation formalizes public policy while, at the same time, it establishes conditions for the effectiveness and scope of collective bargaining. For example, the commencement and formulation of labor-management relationships at many of the mass transit facilities were greatly influenced by the Wagner Act. A crucial justification for this act was that the employment relationship should mirror the democratic society as a whole; therefore, determination of working conditions should

be entitled to the same democratic process. Thus, a major purpose
of the Wagner Act was to encourage collective bargaining between
employee and management representatives; indeed, negative sanctions
(unfair labor practices) could be applied if management officials
failed to live up to their statutory obligation. Implicit in this act was
the concept of good faith—a sincere effort by employee and management
representatives to meet with the intention of reaching a mutually
acceptable labor agreement. With very few exceptions, it appears that
the public policy reflected in the Wagner Act, including good faith
bargaining, is in effect at the transit properties studied, particularly at
those properties where labor and management representatives have
had long experience with each other in a collective bargaining atmosphere.

However, the shift from private to public ownership may
eventually subject mass transit operations to proposed federal public-
employee bargaining legislation. It is, of course, difficult to specu-
late on how this legislation will affect mass transit's labor relations
since there are so many different legislative alternatives now being
considered. One of these alternatives, the extension of the National
Labor Relations Act to all public employees, would presumably have
little effect on mass transit's labor relations. However, other types
of public employee legislation could have some potentially devastating
effects on this relationship. For example, legislation requiring that
mass transit employees be represented in a more inclusive bargaining
unit could retard the heretofore established collective bargaining
relationship. A labor agreement that covered many public employee
classifications would probably not include the multitude of rather
complex work scheduling provisions necessary for efficient operation
of the mass transit system. This would particularly be the case if
the unique work concerns and community of interests of mass
transit employees were not in accord with the other numerically
dominant public employee classifications. Perhaps an inclusive public
employee bargaining unit is appropriate where none of the involved
classifications has had a prior collective bargaining relationship.
However, to force mass transit employees into a larger bargaining
unit would deprive these employees of their history of negotiation
results under the National Labor Relations Act.

Another area for proposed public employee labor legislation
is impasse resolution. Using Executive Orders 10988 and 11491 as
guides, it is quite conceivable that eventual public employee legislation may disregard arbitration and/or the use of the strike as an
impasse resolution technique. Based on our interviews, these techniques have been used quite sparingly in mass transit labor negotiations in the Southeast; to date, there have been no instances where
their use has resulted in a significant, permanent crippling of either

labor-management relationships or mass transit operations. Some noted labor authorities have suggested that certain public employee groups be given the right to strike if they are performing a nonessential service. This dimension, if applied to public employee bargaining legislation, could have some implications for mass transit operations. It will not be easy for legislators to distinguish between essential and nonessential services, particularly since these terms carry emotional connotations of worth or importance to the community. To be sure, a strike inconveniences all of the mass transit customers; however, some of our interview respondents suggested that mass transit serves a small portion of the commuters; and the permanent loss of ridership incurred after a strike suggests that some passengers have adjusted to alternative forms of transportation. Yet, there is a certain segment of the population that is transit captive, and a mass transit strike could permanently affect their employment with a particular firm. If legislation includes the dimension of essential service, it is conceivable that a mass transit property could have some of its services declared essential, with other services not falling into this category.

Perhaps a more pervasive element of public employee legislation is sovereignty—the notion that government administrates the sovereignty of the public and, therefore, cannot relinquish this right to another organization. None of the interviewed management and union respondents suggested the potential applicability and effects of this concept in their labor relations activities. However, based on existing public employee legislation (local, state, and executive orders), sovereignty can have serious implications for the scope of collective bargaining. It appears that the established labor-management relationship in mass transit could be jeopardized if this relationship is altered by federal public employee bargaining legislation patterned on the sovereignty principle.

A related policy issue concerns the degree of involvement by government officials in the collective bargaining process. None of the interviewed management and union respondents indicated any direct experience with state, local, and federal government officials (excluding Federal Mediation and Conciliation Service); perhaps more important is the conviction expressed by the respondents that government officials (Federal Mediation and Conciliation Service excepted) should not be involved in the collective bargaining process.

Under the provisions of several statutes, there is the basis for development of directions by the U.S. Department of Transportation concerning labor policies. It seems apparent that Congress intended that the Department of Transportation should contribute to the public interest through the encouragement of cooperation between various levels of government, carriers, labor, and other interested parties toward the achievement of national transportation objectives; stimulation of technological advances in transportation; provision of general leadership in the identification and solution of transport problems; and development, and recommendation to the president and Congress for approval, of national transportation policies and programs to accomplish these objectives, with full and appropriate consideration of the needs of the public, users, carriers, industry, labor, and the national interest. One of the important responsibilities of the secretary of transportation is to consult and cooperate with the secretary of labor in gathering information regarding the status of labor-management contracts and other labor-management problems as well as promoting industrial harmony and stable employment conditions in all modes of transportation. Perhaps in formulating this policy government officials should consider the following questions before becoming directly involved in the collective bargaining process: What is the related agency or governmental policy regarding collective bargaining? If there is no appropriate policy, what guidelines can be established that will preserve the collective bargaining relationship and, at the same time, accommodate agency and/or constituent concerns? Perhaps an initial step would be to obtain input from mass transit practitioners. A general understanding of labor relations principles and practices is a necessary but not sufficient condition for policy formulation and implementation. Since the focal points of collective bargaining are work rules, related policy questions can only be approached with a thorough understanding of mass transit's work environment.

Wage Determination

Although wages of transit employees have increased substantially over the past ten years, future increases are likely to meet heavy resistance from management. Unless ridership and fare revenue increase dramatically, and there is no reason to think they will, mass transit operations will become even more dependent on federal subsidies for survival. This scenario raises several crucial questions for both labor and management and government.

First, if government, whether local, state, or federal, provides subsidies to mass transit, what role should it play in the resolution of economic issues? As discussed previously, it does not appear beneficial for the government to become directly involved in the determination of wages, vacation pay, and so on. However, it is our opinion that where subsidies are provided, the government has the right and the obligation to demand responsible and accountable interaction between labor and management.

A closely related question concerns wage determination, namely, what factors should be used to determine wage rates? Management has frequently indicated that the productivity of labor has declined in recent years. Labor has zealously denied these claims. Despite these references to productivity, it is fairly evident that definitional problems and the declining nature of the mass transit industry have caused practitioners, both labor and management, to disregard productivity measures as a wage-determining factor. It appears research is badly needed in the area of labor productivity because, in the absence of productivity measures, it is difficult to evaluate or justify collectively bargained wage settlements.

While the need for productivity measures is apparent, extreme caution must be taken in the development of such measures. In addition to the substantial definitional problems associated with productivity, care must be taken to insure that any productivity standards applied to labor may be influenced by labor. Current industry practices call for management to decide on bus design and size, routes and schedules, marketing issues, and fare levels. Our research confirms unions' contention that the operator and union have no input into these decisions, have little-to-no influence over the results, and yet are often held accountable for the results. At present, productivity measures such as revenue-passenger miles or simply passenger miles may be applied to management but should not be extended to labor, as labor has little input into the decision-making process and cannot directly influence the outcome. Out contention is that any attempts at productivity-based bargaining must include labor input and agreement. This will be difficult to put into practice since productivity reflects a myriad of influences, for example, marketing decisions, political constraints on service levels. The difficulties arise because many of the factors affecting productivity are closely guarded management rights and because of the problems encountered in integrating these influences into an overall productivity model.

In the absence of any adequate productivity measures, it would seem desirable to rely on meaningful comparisons in establishing wage levels. We found management and union respondents quite willing to compare various aspects of their location with other locations in the determination of economic issues. Unfortunately, there was little agreement over which comparisons would be mutually acceptable. Part of this difficulty rests on the observation that the economic package is multifaceted; that is, rates of pay, contingent benefits, payment for time not worked, and premium pay provisions may all vary. While we found no sentiment among management and union respondents for seeking to establish mutually agreed-upon bases for comparisons, we feel the topic should be seriously addressed in collective bargaining before it can be dismissed out of hand.

Technological Changes and Employee Protection

Related to work rules, but much broader in scope is the entire question of the response to technological change. The issue is whether unions and labor relations act in such a manner as to deter management from adopting technological changes that may be desirable. This is perhaps one of the most basic issues in labor relations. All transit labor unions publicly state that they are not opposed to technological changes. Generally three broad conditions are given with that statement: that the changes can be demonstrated to improve the efficiencies and competitive positions of the particular service; that employees are adequately protected; and that labor shares in the gains of resulting productivity improvements.

In practice these conditions can be translated into a labor policy on technological changes. It is interesting to note that, on the basis of our findings, neither union nor management respondents felt that unions play any role in technological change in the transit industry in the Southeast. However, since employees can be adversely affected by certain technological changes, the unions seek some method of protecting employees, for example, severance pay, natural or controlled attrition, or assurance of job or employment maintenance. The development of such programs and contract clauses represents the acceptance of the philosophy that labor has the right to protection; that is, it has developed equity in the jobs involved that must be recognized by management, and any related cost must be included in the proposed change. Our research revealed a distinction between the local unit interviewed and the international with regard to the degree of concern over the philosophy. Perhaps this difference is due to the lack of substantive technological changes that result in employee attrition. However, both local and national union officials are in accord over a prominent employee protection provision, namely, Section 13(c).

Section 13(c) issues have generated a great deal of concern among management, labor, and government officials. The major criticisms of this provision of the Urban Mass Transportation Act are that it impedes system efficiency; it can add potentially undefined costs to the provision of transit service; it can lock communities into greater levels of service than the market level can reasonably support; it can be used to enhance unions' bargaining power or as an instrument of blackmail; and it may discourage public authorities from seeking federal assistance. Our research revealed that the last criticism is the only operational problem of Section 13(c). While management and union officials are very much attuned to 13(c), it does appear that some public officials are reluctant to endorse grant applications because of fears associated with the negotiations for

Section 13(c) agreements. A possible way to mitigate this problem
is to educate the local public officials as to the purpose and actual
results to date of implementing Section 13(c) agreements. While
this appears concurrently to be the main concern with Section 13(c),
there are other potentially substantive problems that must be addressed,
such as paratransit operation, including the definition of "affected
employees."

Variable Number	Variable and Response Code
1	**Recognition**

0   No reference
1   Some form of recognition for the specific local indicated
2   1 + definition of unit in terms of job titles, work location, or department

2	**Bargaining Unit**

0   No reference
1   Members only
2   All employees in unit
3   Those employees who have authorized union to represent them

3	**Exclusivity**

0   No reference
1   Employees explicitly retain right to self-representation
2   Union explicitly represents members only
3   Union is "exclusive" or "sole" representative
4   Union is designated formal representative and/or "no other agreements" clause
5   1 + 2

4	**Union Security—Members**

0   No reference
1   Maintenance of membership (with escape period)
2   Modified agency shop (may contribute to charity instead of union)
3   Agency shop
4   Union shop with grandfather clause
5   Union shop

6   Union shop clause accompanied by
    explicit waiver if in conflict with
    applicable state and/or federal law
7   Provision for union shop if applicable
    federal and/or state law changes
8   Open shop

5   Checkoff—Provision

0   No reference
1   Contract allows checkoff (with authori-
    zation card)
2   Contract allows checkoff but with speci-
    fic provision for revocation by employee
    prior to contract expiration
3   Contract provision relating to dues
    changes and checkoff procedures
4   2 + 3
5   Contract does not allow checkoff
    procedure

6   Checkoff—Administration

0   No reference to checkoff procedure
1   Provision for checkoff procedure but
    no reference to checkoff administration
2   Contract provision relating to exclusion
    of specific employee categories for
    checkoff
3   Waiver of management liability
4   2 + 3
5   Provision for checkoff procedure and
    administration
6   Contract does not allow checkoff pro-
    cedure

7   Cost of Checkoff

0   No reference
1   Union required to pay cost of checkoff
2   Management required to pay cost of
    checkoff
3   Union, management share cost of
    checkoff
4   Contract does not allow checkoff pro-
    cedure

Variable Number	Variable and Response Code

8   Discrimination

0   No reference
1   Clause prohibits discrimination and/or other acts that would discourage union membership

9   Paid Time Off for Stewards and for Investigation of Grievances

0   No reference
1   Provision allowing paid time off for stewards
2   Provision allowing paid time off for stewards (or other officials) to investigate grievances with some time limits, for example, reasonable or specific
3   Provision allowing for time off without pay for stewards to investigate grievances
4   Specific prohibition against handling grievances on company time

10   Method of Steward Representation

0   No reference
1   Contract limits number of stewards, areas represented, or provides other specific restrictions on their activities
2   Contract outlines specific duties of stewards
3   1 + 2

11   Paid Time Off for Employees Involved in Grievance Procedure

0   No reference
1   Employees involved in grievance procedure receive paid time off
2   1 with some time limits, for example, reasonable or specific
3   Paid time off specifically prohibited

12   Paid Time Off for Union Officials for Negotiation or Meetings

0   No reference
1   Paid time off for negotiation or meetings
    (if during working hours, or with other
    other minor restrictions)
2   Provision allowing time off without pay
    for negotiation or meetings
3   Time off—contract silent regarding pay

13   Paid Time Off for Delegates or Officers
     for Union Business

0   No reference
1   Paid time off (with restrictions)
2   Time off without pay
3   Time off—contract silent regarding pay

14   Paid Time Off for Anyone for Other Union
     Activity

0   No reference
1   Some provided
2   Some provided without pay
3   Time off—contract silent regarding pay

15   Superseniority—Stewards

0   No reference
1   Provided

16   Superseniority—Other Officers

0   No reference
1   Provided

17   Use of Bulletin Boards

0   No reference
1   Provided with management restrictions
    of use
2   Provided without management restric-
    tions of use (or contract silent on
    restrictions)

18   Premises Provided on the Property for
     Union Meetings

Variable Number	Variable and Response Code

0   No reference
1   Provided with restrictions, for example, advance notice
2   Provided without management restrictions (or contract silent)
3   Prohibited

19   **Access to Premises for International Representatives**

0   No reference
1   Provided with management restrictions (for example, advance notice)
2   Provided without management restrictions of use (or contract silent on restrictions)
3   Prohibited

20   **Management Aid to Other Unions**

0   No reference
1   Prohibited

21   **Bargaining Unit Integrity—Contracting Out**

0   No reference
1   Contracting out prohibited
2   Contracting out restricted (for example, regular employees not to be laid off or discharged)
3   Contracting out restricted (according to motive of management: for example, economy, efficiency are OK; elimination of union or discrimination are prohibited motives)
4   Specific management prerogative to contract out
5   Other specific provision on contracting out (for example, specific function to be contracted out, only union labor to be used)
6   Other provision restricting management's right to move work out of bargaining unit (for example, must

observe union jurisdiction; restrict
work by supervisors, temporary employees, welfare recipients, students,
prisoners; avoid overtime)

7   2 + 6

22   ## Supervisor Performing Bargaining Unit Work

0   No reference
1   Prohibited or restricted
2   1 + provision for penalty payment

23   ## Wage Rate Ranges—Drivers

0   No reference
1   No rate ranges
2   Contract specifies: steps _____
     time _____ (months)
9   Not appropriate—bargaining unit not
     covered by this contract

24   ## Wage Rate Ranges—Craft Employees

0   No reference
1   No rate ranges
2   Contract specifies: steps _____
     time _____ (months)
9   Not appropriate—bargaining unit not
     covered by this contract

25   ## Wage Rate Ranges—Apprentices

0   No reference
1   No rate ranges
2   Contract specifies: steps _____
     time _____ (months)
9   No appropriate—bargaining unit not
     covered by this contract

26   ## Progression through the Ranges—Drivers

0   No reference (no range)
1   Automatic—function of time
2   Automatic unless employer initiated
     withholding for cause

Variable Number	Variable and Response Code

3   Merit, subject to grievance procedure
4   Merit, on management prerogative
5   No reference but range does exist (for example, schedule specifies wages are "minimums")
6   Substantial proportion are automatic and a substantial proportion are merit
9   Not appropriate—bargaining unit not covered by this contract

27   <u>Progression Through the Ranges—Craft Employees</u>

0   No reference (no range)
1   Automatic—function of time
2   Automatic unless employer initiated withholding for cause
3   Merit, subject to grievance procedure
4   Merit, on management prerogative
5   No reference but range does exist (for example, schedule specifies wages are "minimums")
6   Substantial proportion are automatic and a substantial proportion are merit
9   Not appropriate—bargaining unit not covered by this contract

28   <u>Progression through the Ranges—Apprentices</u>

0   No reference (no range)
1   Automatic—function of time
2   Automatic unless employer initiated withholding for cause
3   Merit, subject to grievance procedure
4   Merit, on management prerogative
5   No reference but range does exist (for example, schedule specifies wages are "minimums")
6   Substantial proportion are automatic and a substantial proportion are merit
7   1 + 4
9   Not appropriate—bargaining unit not covered by this contract

29   **Wage-Setting Practices (Jointly Agreed-upon Wage Comparability Definition That Will Be Used in Contract Negotiations)**

0   No reference
1   Survey to be done or prevailing rate to be part of formula or considered in establishing wages
2   Survey to be done or prevailing rate to be followed in establishing wages
3   Cost of living only specified determinant
4   2 + 3

30   **Cost of Living: Index Used**

0   No reference
1   Consumer Price Index
2   Other (specify)

31   **Cost of Living: Base Year and Conversion Ratio**

0   No reference
1   1957–59, .2
2   1957–59, .3
3   1957–59, .4
4   1957–59, .5
5   1957–59, .6
6   1957–59, .7
7   1967, .2
8   1967, .3
9   1967, .4
10   1967, .5
11   1967, .6
12   1967, .7
13   (other, specify)

32   **Cost of Living: Number of Cost-of-Living Adjustments per Year**

0   No reference
1   4
2   2
3   1
4   7 in 2 years

Variable Number   Variable and Response Code

33   Cost of Living: Minimum Guarantees

0   No reference
1   Minimum guaranteed increase per adjustment period
2   Guaranteed no decrease in negotiated wage rate if index declines below base index
3   Provision for reducing negotiated wage rate if index declines below base index
4   No guarantee (that is, contract silence) preventing reduction in negotiated wage rate if index declines below base index
5   1 + 2

34   Overtime Allowance (Premium)

0   No reference
1   Compensatory time off at straight time
2   Compensatory time off at premium rate
3   Extra pay at straight time rate
4   Extra pay at premium rate
5   Combination of above
6   Employee option (straight time)
7   Employee option (premium time)
8   Employer option (straight time)
9   Employer option (premium time)
10   Other provision

35   Report Pay for Extra Board (Required Reports Only)

0   No reference
1   Exempt from overtime computation
2   Contract specifies same but silent with regard to overtime payment
3   Included in computation for overtime pay
9   Not appropriate—bargaining unit not covered by this contract

36   Preparatory Time

0   No reference
1   Exempt from overtime computation
2   Contract specifies same but silent with
     regard to overtime payment
3   Included in computation for overtime pay
9   Not appropriate—bargaining unit not
     covered by this contract

37   Time Spent Completing Accident Reports

0   No reference
1   Exempt from overtime computation
2   Contract specifies same but silent with
     regard to overtime payment
3   Included in computation for overtime pay

38   Intervals Between Pieces of Runs

0   No reference
1   Exempt from overtime computation
2   Contract specifies same but silent with
     regard to overtime payment
3   Included in computation for overtime pay
9   Not appropriate—bargaining unit not
     covered by this contract

39   Court Appearances

0   No reference
1   Exempt from overtime computation
2   Contract specifies same but silent with
     regard to overtime payment
3   Included in computation for overtime pay

40   Safety Meetings

0   No reference
1   Exempt from overtime computation
2   Contract specifies same but silent with
     regard to overtime payment
3   Included in computation for overtime pay

41   Meal Relief

0   No reference

Variable Number | Variable and Response Code

1 Exempt from overtime computation
2 Contract specifies same but silent with regard to overtime payment
3 Included in computation for overtime pay
4 2 for maintenance only

42 Relief Time

0 No reference
1 Exempt from overtime computation
2 Contract specifies same but silent with regard to overtime payment
3 Included in computation for overtime pay
9 Not appropriate—bargaining unit not covered by this contract

43 Check-in Time

0 No reference
1 Exempt from overtime computation
2 Contract specifies same but silent with regard to overtime payment
3 Included in computation for overtime pay
9 Not appropriate—bargaining unit not covered by this contract

44 Call-in Time

0 No reference
1 Exempt from overtime computation
2 Contract specifies same but silent with regard to overtime payment
3 Included in computation for overtime pay

45 Traffic Problems

0 No reference
1 Exempt from overtime computation
2 Contract specifies same but silent with regard to overtime payment
3 Included in computation for overtime pay
9 Not appropriate—bargaining unit not covered by this contract

46   Delivery of Mail

0   No reference
1   Exempt from overtime computation
2   Contract specifies same but silent with
     regard to overtime payment
3   Included in computation for overtime pay
9   Not appropriate—bargaining unit not
     covered by this contract

47   Time Needed for Medical Attention Not
                          Charged to Sick Leave

0   No reference
1   Exempt from overtime computation
2   Contract specifies same but silent with
     regard to overtime payment
3   Included in computation for overtime pay

48   Remainder of Shift After Robbery

0   No reference
1   Exempt from overtime computation
2   Contract specifies same but silent with
     regard to overtime payment
3   Included in computation for overtime pay
9   Not appropriate—bargaining unit not
     covered by this contract

49   Holiday Allowance (Premium) for Time Worked

0   No reference
1   Compensatory time off
2   Compensatory time off at premium rate
3   Extra pay at straight time rate
4   Extra pay at premium rate
5   Other provision
6   Straight time for 8 hours and premium
     for all time over 8 hours

50   Call-in Pay

0   No reference
1   1 hour (minimum) guaranteed at straight
     time

Variable Number

Variable and Response Code

2   2 hours (minimum) guaranteed at straight time

3   3 hours (minimum) guaranteed at straight time

4   4 hours (minimum) guaranteed at straight time

5   5 hours (minimum) guaranteed at straight time

6   6 hours (minimum) guaranteed at straight time

7   7 hours (minimum) guaranteed at straight time

8   8 hours (minimum) guaranteed at straight time

9   Other (specify)

51   Report Periods for Extra Board

0   No reference
1   Required number of daily show-ups (specify exact number) _____
9   Not appropriate—bargaining unit not covered by this contract

52   Report Pay for Extra Board—Amount

0   No reference
1   Guarantee (specify)
9   Not appropriate—bargaining unit not covered by this contract

53   Report Pay for Extra Board—Premium

0   No reference
1   Provision for premium for show-ups in excess of required minimum
9   Not appropriate—bargaining unit not covered by this contract

54   Shift Premium—Drivers

0   No reference
1   Specify premium amount and time
   _____   _____

9   Not appropriate—bargaining unit not
     covered by this contract

55   Shift Premium—Craft and Other Employees

0   No reference
1   Specify premium amount and time

          _____   _____

9   Not appropriate—bargaining unit not
     covered by this contract

56   Other Premium—Drivers

0   No reference
1   Training allowance
2   Other (specify)
9   Not appropriate—bargaining unit not
     covered by this contract

57   Other Premium—Craft and Other Employees

0   No reference
1   Training allowance
2   Other (specify)
9   Not appropriate—bargaining unit not
     covered by this contract

58   Job Evaluation

0   No reference
1   Citation of job evaluation silent with
     regard to union participation
2   Provision requiring union participation
     or specific subject of grievance procedure
3   Provision requiring advance notice only
     to union of proposed changes
4   Unilateral management right

59   Longevity Pay

0   No reference
1   Maximum, less than $100 annually
2   Maximum, $100–$500 annually
3   Maximum, exceeds $500
4   Other provision for longevity

Variable Number   Variable and Response Code

60   Paid Holidays

                               0   No reference
                               1   4 days
                               2   5 days
                               3   6 days
                               4   7 days
                               5   8 days
                               6   9 days
                               7   10 days
                               8   11 days
                               9   12 days
                               10   8 days—drivers, 9 days—garage

61   Paid Vacation (after 1 year)

                               0   No reference
                               1   1 week or less
                               2   1 to 2 weeks
                               3   2 weeks or more
                               4   Other provision (specify)

62   Paid Vacation (after 2 years)

                               0   No reference
                               1   1 week or less
                               2   1 to 2 weeks
                               3   2 weeks or more
                               4   Other provision (specify)

63   Paid Vacation (after 3 years)

                               0   No reference
                               1   1 week or less
                               2   1 to 2 weeks
                               3   2 weeks or more
                               4   Other provision (specify)

64   Paid Vacation (after 5 years)

                               0   No reference
                               1   1 week or less
                               2   1 to 2 weeks

3   2 to 3 weeks
4   3 to 4 weeks
5   4 to 5 weeks
6   5 or more weeks

65   Paid Vacation (Maximum)

0   No reference
1   1 week or less
2   1 to 2 weeks
3   2 to 3 weeks
4   3 to 4 weeks
5   4 to 5 weeks
6   5 to 6 weeks
7   6 or more weeks

66   Paid Vacation Use

0   No reference
1   Severance (death benefit)
2   Retirement
3   Pay in lieu of vacation (may be restricted)
4   Vacation only
5   1 + 2
6   1 + 3
7   1 + 2 + 3
8   Other purpose (specify)

67   Eligibility for Vacation Days

0   No reference
1   Other (specify minimum eligibility)
     Days _____ percent _____

68   Vacation Scheduling

0   No reference
1   Bid by seniority
2   Unilateral management right
3   Bid by seniority with restrictions
4   Management will give full consideration
     to seniority but at discretion of depart-
     ment head

69   Vacation Pay—Amount—Regular Drivers

Variable Number	Variable and Response Code

0   No reference
1   Based on contractually defined workweek
2   Based on regular scheduled run time prior to vacation
9   Not appropriate—bargaining unit not covered by this contract

70 Vacation Pay—Amount—Extra Operators

0   No reference
1   Based on minimum hour guarantee
2   Based on some calculation of average weekly earnings for specified period prior to vacation with some minimum guarantee
3   Based on contractually defined workday or workweek
9   Not appropriate—bargaining unit not covered by this contract

71 Vacation Pay— Amount—Craft and Other Employees

0   No reference
1   Based on contractually defined work week
2   Other (specify)
9   Not appropriate—bargaining unit not covered by this contract

72 Paid Sick Leave (Minimum Eligibility)

0   No reference
1   Other (specify days) _____

73 Paid Sick Leave—Days Deductible

0   No reference
1   First day—unconditional
2   First day—conditional (doctor's certificate or employee out for specified minimum number of days eliminates deductible days)
3   First 2 days—unconditional

4   First 2 days—conditional
5   First 3 days—unconditional
6   First 3 days—conditional
7   First 4 days—unconditional
8   First 4 days—conditional
9   More than 4 days

74   Paid Sick Leave (Maximum Rate of Cumulation)

0   No reference
1   1/2 day per month or less
2   1/2 to 1 day per month
3   1 to 1 1/2 days per month
4   Over 1 1/2 days per month
5   Other (specify)

75   Paid Sick Leave (Maximum Cumulation)

0   No reference
1   30 days or less
2   31-60 days
3   61-90 days
4   91-120 days
5   121 days or more (unlimited)
6   Other provision—no unilateral change
7   Other provision

76   Paid Sick Leave (Uses— family illness,
personal business, vacation)

0   None of the following
1   Family illness
2   Personal business
3   Vacation
4   1 + 2
5   1 + 3
6   2 + 3
7   1 + 2 + 3

77   Paid Sick Leave (Uses—retirement, severance, other)

0   None of the following
1   Retirement (including death benefit)
2   Severance (including death benefit)

Variable Number   Variable and Response Code

3   Other (including funeral)
4   1 + 2
5   1 + 3
6   2 + 3
7   1 + 2 + 3

78   Military Services—Reserves

0   No reference
1   Time off—no pay or contract silence
      or may use vacation
2   Time off with residual pay (in addition
      to regular vacation)
3   Time off with full pay

79   Jury Duty (Other Legal Duties Excluding
                      Company Business)

0   No reference
1   Time off—no pay or provision for pay
2   Time off—no pay or provision for pay
      but with report in requirements
3   Time off with residual pay
4   Time off with residual pay but with
      report in requirements
5   Time off with full pay
6   Time off with full pay but with report
      in requirements
7   Time off with partial residual pay with
      report in requirements

80   Legal Duties Involving Company Business

0   No reference
1   Time off—no pay or provision for pay
2   Time off—no pay or provision for pay
      but with report in requirements
3   Time off with residual pay
4   Time off with residual pay but with
      report in requirements
5   Time off with full pay
6   Time off with full pay but with report
      in requirements

81   Leave for Union Business

0   No reference
1   Leave without loss of seniority or benefits
2   Leave with resumption of seniority and benefits upon return
3   1 plus restrictions on number on leave at any one time
4   2 plus restrictions on number on leave at any one time
5   Leave for union business with contract silence with respect to seniority or benefits

82   Leave of Absence Excluding Union Officers

0   No reference
1   Leave for management-approved purpose
2   Reference to leave of absence; silence with regard to management-approved purpose
3   Leave of absence only cited for promotion to supervision

83   Training Leave, Exams (Excluding Chauffeur's License), Professional Meetings, with or without Allowance or Pay

0   No reference
1   Job advancement leave provided
9   Not appropriate—bargaining unit not covered by this contract

84   Chauffeur's License Provision

0   No reference
1   Paid time off for exam
2   1 + some provision for payment for license renewal
3   1 + some provision for payment for initial license fee and renewal
4   1 + some provision for payment for initial license fee
5   Contract silent with regard to paid time off for exams

Variable Number	Variable and Response Code

6   5 + some provision for payment for license renewal

7   5 + some provision for payment for initial license fee and renewal

8   5 + some provision for payment for initial license fee

9   Not appropriate—bargaining unit not covered by this contract

85

Paid Funeral Leave—Eligibility and Amount in Death of Parents or Legal Guaradian

0   No reference to paid funeral leave

1   Reference to paid funeral leave but no reference regarding eligibility in death of parents

2   1 day

3   2 days

4   3 days

5   4 days

6   5 days

7   6 days

8   7 days

86

Paid Funeral Leave—Eligibility and Amount in Death of Spouse

0   No reference to paid funeral leave

1   Reference to paid funeral leave but no reference regarding eligibility in death of spouse

2   1 day

3   2 days

4   3 days

5   4 days

6   5 days

7   6 days

8   7 days

87

Paid Funeral Leave—Eligibility and Amount in Death of Children

0   No reference to paid funeral leave

1   Reference to paid funeral leave but no
     reference regarding eligibility in death
     of children
2   1 day
3   2 days
4   3 days
5   4 days
6   5 days
7   6 days
8   7 days

88   Paid Funeral Leave—Eligibility in Death of
          Siblings (May Be Restricted to Full Blood)

0   No reference to paid funeral leave
1   Reference to paid funeral leave but no
     reference regarding eligibility in death
     of full-blood siblings
2   1 day
3   2 days
4   3 days
5   4 days
6   5 days
7   6 days
8   7 days

89   Paid Funeral Leave—Eligibility and Amount
          in Death of Grandparents

0   No reference to paid funeral leave
1   Reference to paid funeral leave but no
     reference regarding eligibility in death
     of grandparents
2   1 day
3   2 days
4   3 days
5   4 days
6   5 days
7   6 days
8   7 days

90   Paid Funeral Leave—Eligibility and Amount
          in Death of Parents-in-law or Relatives-in-
          law

Variable Number	Variable and Response Code

0	No reference to paid funeral leave
1	Reference to paid funeral leave but no reference regarding eligibility in death of parents-in-law or relatives-in-law
2	1 day
3	2 days
4	3 days
5	4 days
6	5 days
7	6 days
8	7 days
9	2 days—parents-in-law, 1 day—other relatives-in-law

91   Paid Funeral Leave—Eligibility and Amount in Death of Aunts, Uncles, Cousins, or Other Relatives

0	No reference to paid funeral leave
1	Reference to paid funeral leave but no reference regarding eligibility in death of aunts, uncles, cousins, or other relatives
2	1 day
3	2 days
4	3 days
5	4 days
6	5 days
7	6 days
8	7 days

92   Number of Preceding Categories Relatives' Deaths Making Employees Eligible for Funeral Leave

0	No reference to paid funeral leave
1	1
2	2
3	3
4	4
5	5
6	6
7	7
8	8

93   <u>Split Shift—Assignment</u>

0   No reference
1   Management has unilateral right to
     assign split shift
2   Management right to assign split shifts
     is limited

94   <u>Split Shift - Maximum Spread Time Before
                        Overtime Paid</u>

0   No reference
1   Spread time not to exceed 11 hours
2   Spread time not to exceed 12 hours
3   Spread time not to exceed 13 hours
4   Spread time not to exceed 14 hours

95   <u>Scheduled Days Off—Regular Drivers</u>

0   No reference
1   Workweek must provide 2 consecutive
     days off or consist of five consecutive
     days
2   Workweek consists of 5 days
3   Workweek consists of 6 days
4   Other scheduling arrangement
9   Not appropriate—bargaining unit not
     covered by this contract

96   <u>Scheduled Days Off—Extra Operators</u>

0   No reference
1   Workweek must provide 2 consecutive
     days off or consist of five consecutive
     days
2   Workweek consists of 5 days
3   Workweek consists of 6 days
9   Not appropriate—bargaining unit not
     covered by this contract

<u>Scheduled Days Off—Craft and Other Employees</u>

0   No reference
1   Workweek must provide 2 consecutive
     days off or consist of 5 consecutive days

Variable Number   Variable and Response Code

2   Workweek consists of 5 days
3   Workweek consists of 6 days
9   Not appropriate—bargaining unit not
     covered by this contract

98   Work Performed on Holiday—Drivers (Total
      Amount of Money for Working Holiday)

0   No reference
1   Twice the base hourly rate
2   2 1/2 times the base hourly rate
3   3 times the base hourly rate
4   Other (specify)
9   Not appropriate—bargaining unit not
     covered by this contract

99   Work Performed on Holiday When Same
      Falls on Scheduled Day Off—Drivers (Total
      Amount of Money For Working Holiday)

0   No reference
1   Twice the base hourly rate
2   2 1/2 times the base hourly rate
3   3 times the base hourly rate
4   3 1/2 times the base hourly rate
5   4 times the base hourly rate
6   Other (specify)
9   Not appropriate—bargaining unit not
     covered by this contract

100   Work Performed on Scheduled Day Off
       Provided Full Workweek Has Been Worked—
       Drivers

0   No reference
1   The base hourly rate
2   1 1/2 times the base hourly rate
3   2 times the base hourly rate
4   Other (specify)
9   Not appropriate—bargaining unit not
     covered by this contract

101   Work Performed in Excess of 8 Hours or
       Defined Day in Any One Day (Drivers)

0   No reference
1   1 1/2 times the base hourly rate
2   2 times the base hourly rate
3   Other (specify)
9   Not appropriate—bargaining unit not
     not covered by this contract

102   **Work Performed in Excess of the Regularly**
           Scheduled Workweek— Drivers

0   No reference
1   1 1/2 times the base hourly rate
2   2 times the base hourly rate
3   Other (specify)
9   Not appropriate—bargaining unit not
     covered by this contract

103   **Spread Time—Drivers**

0   No reference
1   Work in excess of 10 hours spread time
     paid at 1 1/2 times base hourly rate
2   Work in excess of 11 hours spread time
     paid at 1 1/2 times base hourly rate
3   Work in excess of 12 hours spread time
     paid at 1 1/2 times base hourly rate
4   Work in excess of 13 hours spread time
     paid at 1 1/2 times base hourly rate
5   Other (specify)
6   Not appropriate—bargaining unit not
     covered by this contract

104   **Work Performed on Holiday—Craft and Other**
           Employees (Total Amount of Money for
           Working Holiday)

0   No reference
1   Twice the base hourly rate
2   2 1/2 times the base hourly rate
3   3 times the base hourly rate
4   Other (specify)
9   Not appropriate—bargaining unit not
     covered by this contract

Variable Number	Variable and Response Code

105

Work Performed on Holiday When Same Falls on Scheduled Day Off—Craft and Other Employees (Total Amount of Money for Working Holiday)

0   No reference
1   Twice the base hourly rate
2   2 1/2 times the base hourly rate
3   3 times the base hourly rate
4   3 1/2 times the base hourly rate
5   4 times the base hourly rate
6   Other (specify)
9   Not appropriate—bargaining unit not covered by this contract

106

Work Performed on Scheduled Day Off Provided Full Workweek Has been Worked—Craft and Other Employees

0   No reference
1   The base hourly rate
2   1 1/2 times the base hourly rate
3   2 times the base hourly rate
4   Other (specify)
9   Not appropriate—bargaining unit not covered by this contract

107

Work Performed in Excess of 8 Hours in Any One Day—Craft and Other Employees

0   No reference
1   1 1/2 times the base hourly rate
2   2 times the base hourly rate
3   Other (specify)
9   Not appropriate—bargaining unit not covered by this contract

108

Work Performed in Excess of the Regularly Scheduled Workweek—Craft and Other Employees

0   No reference
1   1 1/2 times the base hourly rate

2   2 times the base hourly rate
3   Other (specify)
9   Not appropriate—bargaining unit not
     covered by this contract

109   Spread Time—Craft and Other Employees

0   No reference
1   Work in excess of 12 hours spread time
     paid at 1 1/2 times base hourly rate
2   Work in excess of 12 hours spread time
     paid at 2 times base hourly rate
3   Work in excess of 13 hours spread time
     paid at 1 1/2 times base hourly rate
4   Work in excess of 13 hours spread time
     paid at 2 times base hourly rate
5   Other (specify)
9   Not appropriate—bargaining unit not
     covered by this contract

110   Minimum Guaranteed Straight Time Hours
             Paid for Work Performed on Holiday

0   No reference
1   8 hours
2   7 hours—extra operators only
3   8 hours—extra operators only
4   Other (specify)

111   Minimum Guaranteed Hours for a Regularly
             Scheduled Run

0   No reference
1   Less than 8 hours
2   8 hours or more, but less than 8 1/2
3   8 1/2 hours or more, but less than 9
4   9 hours or more, but less than 9 1/2
5   Guarantee specifically excluded
6   42 hours minimum; 52 hours maximum
7   7 1/2 - 8 1/2
8   8 - 10 hours
9   Not appropriate—bargaining unit not
     covered by this contract

112   Determination of Pay for Intervals Between
             Pieces of Regularly Scheduled Runs

Variable Number | Variable and Response Code

0   No reference
1   Intervals of less than 61 minutes paid
2   First interval not paid, second interval—
     company pays shorter of two, all inter-
     vals in excess of two shall be paid
3   All intervals between 6 P.M. and 4 A.M.
     paid
4   Other (specify)
9   Not appropriate—bargaining unit not
     covered by this contract

113

Drivers' Uniforms—Provision

0   No reference
1   Company provides uniforms or uniform
     allowance
2   Employee required to purchase uniforms
     (company may provide assistance in
     obtaining supplier and/or purchase
     discounts
3   Company provides initial uniform,
     employee required to replace as worn
     out
4   Company provides initial uniform, and
     provides uniform allowance for replace-
     ment
5   Employee required to purchase initial
     uniform, company provides uniform
     allowance for replacement
9   Not appropriate—bargaining unit not
     covered by this contract

114

Drivers' Uniforms—Specifications

0   No reference
1   Company sets specifications for uniforms
2   Contract requires purchase of uniform
     from unionized manufacturer
3   1 + 2
4   Other (specify)
9   Not appropriate—bargaining unit not
     covered by this contract

115   <u>Garage Employees' Uniforms—Provision</u>

0   No reference
1   Company provides uniforms or uniform allowance
2   Employee required to provide uniforms
9   Not appropriate—bargaining unit not covered by this contract

116   <u>Tool Allowance</u>

0   No reference
1   Company provides all tools
2   Employee required to provide all small tools
3   2 + provision for company replacement of worn or broken tools
4   Company provides tool allowance
5   Company provides tools at cost
6   All worn-out or condemned tools replaced by authority or employee as applicable
9   Not appropriate—bargaining unit not covered by this contract

117   <u>Job Titles and Duties—Drivers</u>

0   No reference
1   Contract lists titles
2   1 + qualifications or duties
3   Other provisions
9   Not appropriate—bargaining unit not covered by this contract

118   <u>Job Titles and Duties—Garage Employees</u>

0   No reference
1   Contract lists titles
2   1 + qualifications or duties
3   Other provisions
9   Not appropriate—bargaining unit not covered by this contract

119   <u>Physical Exam—Preemployment</u>

0   No reference

Variable Number   Variable and Response Code

1   Company pays
2   Employee pays
3   Cost shared
4   Employee pays and is reimbursed by
     employer upon satisfactory completion
     of probationary period

120   Physical Exam—Fitness Determination

0   No reference
1   Company pays
2   Employee pays
3   Company and employee share cost if
     more than one opinion and/or exam
     involved
4   Company and unions share cost if more
     than one opinion and/or exam involved
5   Three contract exams; silent as to pay-
     ment

121   Probationary Period—Length—Drivers

0   No reference
1   30 days or less
2   31–60 days
3   61–90 days
4   More than 90 days
5   1 + provision for extension
6   2 + provision for extension
7   3 + provision for extension
8   4 + provision for extension
9   Not appropriate—bargaining unit not
     covered by this contract

122   Probationary Period - Length—Craft and
                       Others

0   No reference
1   60 days or less
2   61–90 days
3   91–120 days
4   More than 120 days
5   1 + provision for extension

6   Probationary period cited, yet no true
     limits given
9   Not appropriate—bargaining unit not
     covered by this contract

123   Probationary Period—Discipline

0   No reference
1   Company right to discharge is unilateral
2   Periods can be used for discipline when
     mutually agreed upon by company and
     union
3   1 + 2

124   Promotion to Salaried Level

0   No reference
1   Not required to relinquish union mem-
     bership for a specified period of time
2   Contract silent with regard to seniority
     retention or accumulation upon return
     to bargaining unit
3   Seniority retention and/or accumulation
     prohibited
4   Seniority retention and/or accumulation
     applicable upon return to the unit
5   1 + 2
6   1 + 3
7   1 + 4

125   Hospital–Medical–Surgical (Employee)

0   No reference
1   Full contribution by employee
2   Employer contribution less than 100
     percent, specifically cited
3   Employer contribution (contract does
     not specify employer share of contri-
     bution)
4   Fully paid by employer, specifically
     cited
5   No unilateral change
6   Employee contribution (contract does
     not specify employee share of contribu-
     tion)

Variable Number   Variable and Response Code

7   Contract refers to general insurance
plan; nonspecific reference to this item

126   <u>Hospital-Medical-Surgical (Family)</u>

0   No reference
1   Full contribution by employee
2   Employer contribution less than 100
percent, specifically cited
3   Employer contribution (contract does
not specify employer share of contribution)
4   Fully paid by employer, specifically cited
5   No unilateral change
6   Employee contribution (contract does
not specify employee share of contribution)
7   Contract refers to general insurance
plan; nonspecific reference to this item

127   <u>Major Medical (Employee)</u>

0   No reference
1   Full contribution by employee
2   Employer contribution less than 100
percent, specifically cited
3   Employer contribution (contract does not
specify employer share of contribution)
4   Fully paid by employer, specifically
cited
5   No unilateral change
6   Employee contribution (contract does
not specify employee share of contribution)
7   Contract refers to general insurance
plan; nonspecific reference to this item

128   <u>Major Medical (Family)</u>

0   No reference
1   Full contribution by employee
2   Employer contribution less than 100 percent, specifically cited
3   Employer contribution (contract does not
specify employer share of contribution)

4   Fully paid by employer, specifically
    cited
5   No unilateral change
6   Employee contribution (contract does not
    specify employee share of contribution)
7   Contract refers to general insurance
    plan; nonspecific reference to this item

129   Life Insurance

0   No reference
1   Full contribution by employee
2   Employer contribution less than 100
    percent, specifically cited
3   Employer contribution (contract does
    not specify employer share of contribu-
    tion)
4   Fully paid by employer, specifically
    cited
5   No unilateral change
6   Employee contribution (contract does not
    specify employee share of contribution)
7   Contract refers to general insurance
    plan; nonspecific reference to this item

130   Accident Insurance

0   No reference
1   Full contribution by employee
2   Subsidized by employer at less than 100
    percent, specifically cited
3   Subsidized by employer (contract does
    not specify employer share of contri-
    bution)
4   Fully paid by employer, specifically
    cited
5   No unilateral change
6   Employee contribution (contract does not
    specify employee share of contribution)
7   Contract refers to general insurance
    plan; nonspecific reference to this item

131   Pension, Retirement Plan

0   No reference

Variable Number	Variable and Response Code

1   Participation in legally established plan, no reference to contributions, or benefits; or no "unilateral change" in present plan

2   Refers specifically to contributions by employer

3   Refers specifically to contributions by employee

4   2 + 3

5   Refers specifically to benefits

6   2 + 5

7   3 + 5

8   4 + 5

9   Other references

132 — Retirement Age—Drivers

0   No reference

1   Mandatory at age under 65

2   Mandatory at 65

3   Mandatory at age over 65

4   Optional at age under 65

5   Optional at 65

6   Optional at age over 65

7   Employer options at specified age

8   Employee and employer have options at 65

9   Not appropriate—bargaining unit not covered by this contract

133 — Retirement Age—Craft and other Employees

0   No reference

1   Mandatory at age under 65

2   Mandatory at 65

3   Mandatory at age over 65

4   Optional at age under 65

5   Optional at age 65

6   Optional at age over 65

7   Employer options at specified age

8   Employee and employer have options at 65

9   Not appropriate—bargaining unit not covered by this contract

134 — Seniority Uses— Drivers

0   No reference

1   Layoff

2   Regular run selection

3   Vacation selection (may be restricted)

4   1 + 2

5   1 + 3
6   2 + 3
7   1 + 2 + 3
9   Not appropriate—bargaining unit not
     covered by this contract

135   ## Seniority Uses—Garage Employees

0   No reference
1   Layoff
2   Layoff and vacation
3   Promotion and vacation
4   Layoff and promotion and vacation
5   Layoff, promotion, vacation and transfer
9   Not appropriate—bargaining unit not
     covered by this contract

136   ## Distribution of Overtime Opportunity—Drivers (Excluding Extra Board)

0   No reference
1   Company attempts to equalize but no
     penalties for management error
2   Company attempts to equalize, with
     penalties for management error
3   Other provision (specify, for example,
     seniority emphasized more than equalizing
     overtime hours)
9   Not appropriate—bargaining unit not
     covered by this contract

137   ## Distribution of Overtime Opportunity—Garage Employees

0   No reference
1   Company attempts to equalize but no
     penalties for management error
2   Company attempts to equalize, with
     penalties for management error
3   Other provision (specify, for example,
     seniority emphasized more than equalizing
     overtime hours)
9   Not appropriate—bargaining unit not
     covered by this contract

138   ## Job Posting/Bidding—Garage Employees

0   No reference
1   Bid put on to eligibility list
2   Job posting
3   Other provision to advertise job
4   Provision for management discretion
     with regard to hiring from the outside

Variable Number   Variable and Response Code

                      9   Not appropriate—bargaining unit not covered by this contract

139   **Bidding for Holiday Work—Garage Employees**

                      0   No reference
1   Senior employee in classification and on shift required
2   Strict seniority
3   Employee regularly scheduled to work may bid
4   Miscellaneous bidding arrangements
9   Not appropriate—bargaining unit not covered by this contract

140   **Bidding on Regular Runs—Required Yearly Number of Postings**

                      0   No reference
1   At least one time, management has discretion for more
2   At least two times, management has discretion for more
3   At least three times, management has discretion for more
4   At least four times, management has discretion for more
5   Other provision (specify)
9   Not appropriate—bargaining unit not covered by this contract

141   **Bidding on Regular Runs—Advance Posting**

                      0   No reference
1   Specified advance notice with no reference to amount
2   Specified advance notice with required amount
9   Not appropriate—bargaining unit not covered by this contract

142   **Bidding on Regular Runs—Basis for Selection**

                      0   No reference

1   Seniority sole determinant
2   Seniority sole determinant, if driver
     bids in person (specific contract prohi-
     bition of in absentia bidding or bumping)
3   Seniority sole determinant, if driver
     bids in person (contract silent with
     regard to in absentia bidding or bumping)
4   Other provision (specify)
9   Not appropriate—bargaining unit not
     covered by this contract

143   Changes, Additions, Deletions of Regular
       Runs

0   No reference
1   Open to general bidding procedure any-
     time change occurs
2   Open to general bidding procedure only
     if change occurs specified number of
     days prior to scheduled rebidding of
     regular runs
3   Management can change or discontinue
     run without general pick occurring
4   General bidding if requested by affected
     employee
5   General bidding if in excess of specified
     minimum
9   Not appropriate—bargaining unit not
     covered by this contract

144   Charter Runs and/or Special-Service—Posting

0   No reference
1   Provision specifying minimum advance
     notice
2   Provision specifying advance notice if
     charter cannot be filled off extra board
3   1 + 2
4   Other (specify)
9   Not appropriate—bargaining unit not
     covered by this contract

145   Charter Runs (Extra Work) and/or Special
       Service—Basis for Selection

0   No reference

Variable Number   Variable and Response Code

    1   Extra operators given preference or
         provision stating charter work (extra
         work) performed by extra operators when
         available
    2   Procedure specifying how assignment of
         charter work (extra work) is to be made
    3   Provision restricting probationary
         employees from all or some extra work
         (for example, out-of-town runs)
    4   1 + 2
    5   1 + 3
    6   2 + 3
    7   1 + 2 + 3
    8   Other (specify)
    9   Not appropriate—bargaining unit not
         covered by this contract

146   Charter Runs and/or Special Service—
                           Minimum Guarantee

    0   No reference
    1   8-hour guarantee for stipulated mileage
    2   Minimum hour guarantee for all charters
    3   Minimum hour guarantee for night
         charters only (night being defined by the
         contract)
    4   Other (specify)
    9   Not appropriate—bargaining unit not
         covered by this contract

147   Extra Board—Scope

    0   No reference
    1   Restricted solely to extra operators
         (including probationary employees)
    2   Regular operator temporarily displaced
         from regular run , for example by doc-
         tor appointment, personal business or
         illness, jury duty, is eligible for extra
         board
    3   Regular operator required to report for
         extra board for certain circumstances,
         for example, lose-out, personal illness,
         jury duty

4   2 + 3

5   Regular operators eligible for extra
     board on off time (after run or day off)
     (preference given to regular extra
     operators or contract silent)

6   2 + 5

7   3 + 5

8   2 + 3 + 5

9   Not appropriate—bargaining unit not
     covered by this contract

148   Extra Board—Provision for Rotation

0   No reference—rotation procedure not
     specified

1   Automatic daily rotation of extra operators,
     number in rotation specified, no reference
     to equalizing hours of work assigned

2   Extra board assignment based on first
     in, first out at scheduled reporting time,
     no reference to hours worked

3   Daily rotation of extra operators, speci-
     fies minimum hours required for rotation

4   Daily rotation of extra operators on
     basis of assignment, no reference to
     minimum hours required

5   1 + provision for certain employees
     being differentiated with respect to
     regular rotation procedure, for example,
     late extra operators rotated to bottom

6   Rotation on basis of seniority and provi-
     sion for certain employees being differ-
     entiated with respect to regular rotation
     procedure, for example, late operators
     rotated to bottom

7   3 + provision for certain employees being
     differentiated with respect to regular
     rotation procedure, for example, late
     extra operators rotated to bottom

8   4 + provision for certain employees being
     differentiated with respect to regular
     rotation procedure, for example, late
     extra operators rotated to bottom

9   Not appropriate—bargaining unit not
     covered by this contract

Variable Number	Variable and Response Code

149   Extra Board—Payment for Administrative Error (for example, Runaround)

0   No reference
1   Provision for full payment or credit (in hours) for the amount of the run-around
2   Provision for differential payment or credit for the amount of the runaround
3   Contract silent with respect to payment but provision for attempting to equalize hours
4   Other (specify)
9   Not appropriate—bargaining unit not covered by this contract

150   Extra Board—Penalty for Refusal of Work

0   No reference
1   Rotation to bottom of the extra board
2   Forfeiture of minimum hour guarantee—may be conditional (for example, conditional on all others' refusing the same piece of work)
3   Provision disallowing refusal of assigned work
4   Other
9   Not appropriate—bargaining unit not covered by this contract

151   Promotion Procedure—Garage Employees

0   No reference
1   Refers to merit, management prerogative, or other process in which seniority is not a factor
2   Seniority if other factors are equal, for example, test scores, ability
3   Seniority is one of several factors
4   Other than above or ambiguous
9   Not appropriate—bargaining unit not covered by this contract

152   **Promotion Procedure—Definition of Seniority**

0   No reference (seniority a factor but not defined)
1   Not applicable—seniority not a factor
2   Job classification or line
3   Maintenance department only (for example, excluding drivers)
4   Propertywide
9   Not appropriate—bargaining unit not covered by this contract

153   **Trial Period to Qualify on Promoted Job— Garage Employees**

0   No reference
1   For promotions—mandatory
2   For promotions—optional (management discretion or ability in dispute)
3   1 + provision for extension
4   2 + provision for extension
9   Not appropriate—bargaining unit not covered by this contract

154   **Layoff Procedure—Drivers**

0   No reference
1   Seniority not a factor
2   Seniority one of several factors
3   Seniority subject to exceptions, for example, can perform work, competence
4   Seniority sole determinant
9   Not appropriate—bargaining unit not covered by this contract

155   **Bumping Rights—Drivers**

0   No reference
1   Any job on property (if capable)
2   Any job within job line
3   Bumping and seniority relationship ambiguous
9   Not appropriate—bargaining unit not covered by this contract

Variable Number	Variable and Response Code

156   <u>Layoff Procedure—Garage Employees</u>

0   No reference
1   Seniority not a factor
2   Seniority one of several factors
3   Seniority subject to exceptions, for example, can perform work, competence
4   Seniority sole determinant
9   Not appropriate—bargaining unit not covered by this contract

157   <u>Bumping Rights—Garage Employees</u>

0   No reference
1   Any job on property (if capable)
2   Any job within job line
3   Department
4   Bumping and seniority relationship ambiguous
9   Not appropriate—bargaining unit not covered by this contract

158   <u>Advance Notice—Layoff—Permanent Job Vacancy</u>

0   No reference
1   Permanent layoff only
2   Job vacancies
3   1 + 2
9   Not appropriate—bargaining unit not covered by this contract

159   <u>Severance Notice or Pay</u>

0   No reference
1   Advance notice required, no days specified
2   Three days' to two weeks' notice required for layoff
3   More than two weeks' notice required for layoff
4   Provision for severance benefit longer than above

5   Other provision for severance or layoff
      benefit

160   <u>Military Service</u>

0   No reference
1   Retention of job rights or reference
      to law
2   Accumulation of seniority and benefits
      based on seniority

161   <u>Politics in the Public Service</u>

0   No reference
1   Provision explicitly or implicitly elimi-
      nating political considerations from work
      conditions
2   Provision allowing employee to run for
      political office, including leave of
      absence
3   Provision prohibiting employee from
      running for political office (resign to
      run)

162   <u>Job Protection after Loss of License on
Points (Drivers)</u>

0   No reference
1   Provision for leave of absence
2   Retention in the bargaining unit with
      downgrade
3   Other (specify)
9   Not appropriate—bargaining unit not
      covered by this contract

163   <u>Provision for Negotiated Grievance Procedure
(NGP)</u>

0   No NGP
1   Provision for complete NGP

164   <u>Civil Service (CS) Appeals Procedure</u>

0   No CS procedures, contract silent, or
      not applicable—employees are private

Variable Number	Variable and Response Code

1   Provision for CS procedures which cover topics excluded from NGP

2   Provision for CS procedures which act as dual procedures with NGP, for example, cover same topics

3   Provision for CS procedures which have elements of both 1 and 2

4   Relationship of CS procedures to NGP not stipulated, or no NGP

5   CS procedures act as step in NGP, for example, final appeal

6   Other—CS laws mentioned in contract but not in context of appeals procedures

165   Final Decision in NGP

0   No NGP
1   Official of mass transit agency
2   Authority or governing body of agency
3   Political officers (mayor, city council, other than 2)
4   Binding arbitration
5   Other (specify) (for example, CS on some grievances)
6   Decision level cannot be determined

166   Maximum Number of Steps in NGP (All Steps in Contract Including Arbitration)

0   No NGP
1   Number of steps (specify maximum number of steps in NGP) _____

167   Extent to Which Grievance Procedure Includes Time Limits

0   No NGP
1   No time limits stipulated
2   Includes some appeal limits
3   All appeal limits
4   Some decision limits
5   All decision limits
6   All appeal and decision limits

7 All appeal and some decision limits
8 Some appeal and all decision limits
9 Some appeal and some decision limits

168   Point of Initiation of Grievance Procedure

0 No NGP
1 No reference
2 Date of incident
3 Date of discovery
4 2 or 3

169   Time Limit for Initiation of Grievances
          (Either from Date of Incident or Date of
          Discovery)

0 No NGP
1 No time limit stipulated
2 5 days or less
3 6-10 days
4 11-20 days
5 21-30 days
6 31 or more days
7 Reasonable time
8 No time limits stipulated except for
   discharge and suspension (5 days or
   less)

170   Total Time Limits Stipulated for Manage-
          ment's Last Decision (Before Arbitration
          or Other External Procedure)

0 No NGP
1 Total time limits not stipulated
2 5 days or less
3 6-10 days
4 11-20 days
5 21-30 days
6 31 or more days
7 Reasonable time

171   Special Grievance Procedures

0 No special grievance procedures
1 Special time limits for discipline

Variable Number	Variable and Response Code
	2 Special time limits for selected other issues
	3 Special time limits (1 + 2)
	4 Different steps for discipline
	5 Different steps for selected other issues
	6 Different steps (4 + 5)
	7 1 + 4
	8 3 + 4
	9 2 + 4
	10 1 + 5
	11 2 + 5
	12 3 + 5
	13 1 + 6
	14 2 + 6
	15 3 + 6
	16 No NGP
172	Discipline—Just Cause for Discipline
	0 No reference
	1 Reference
173	Discipline—Statute of Limitations (Maximum Time in Which Employee Accountable for Actions)
	0 No reference
	1 Reference
174	Discipline—Provisions for Definite Disciplinary Status of Employee after Specified Time (Restrictions on Indefinite Suspensions)
	0 No reference
	1 Reference
175	Discipline—Union Representative Present at Disciplinary Meetings and/or given Copy of Disciplinary Notice
	0 No reference
	1 Reference
	2 Reference for discharge only

3   Reference—union representative need not
be present at disciplinary meeting

176   Time Limits of Grievance Procedure May
Be Extended by Mutual Agreement

0   No NGP
1   No provision
2   Yes
3   Time limits of arbitration can be extended;
contract silent with regard to grievance
procedure

177   Grievance Definition

0   No NGP
1   No definition
2   General definition, for example, matter
of concern, complaint, working conditions
3   Definition stating interpretation, application, or violation of agreement

178   Exclusions from NGP

0   No NGP
1   No definition
2   No specific exclusions

179   Topics Included under CS Procedures

0   No CS procedures or contract silent
1   Scope of CS procedures not stipulated
2   Adverse actions
3   Wages, wage adjustments, position
classification
4   Plant administration
5   Changes in employment status
6   2 + 3 + 4
7   2 + 3 + 4 + 5
8   Same as NGP topics (a step in NGP)

180   Presence of Union in NGP

0   No NGP
1   Not stipulated

Variable Number	Variable and Response Code

2   Can be present at some steps
3   Can be present at all steps

181

Union Official Has Right To Initiate Grievance (Even If Not the Aggrieved)

0   No NGP
1   Not stipulated
2   No
3   Yes, unqualified
4   Yes, with majority vote
5   Yes (qualify)

182

Union Has Right to Continue Appeal after Employee Aborts Appeal

0   No NGP
1   Not stipulated
2   No
3   Yes

183

Union Can Refuse to Represent Employee

0   No NGP
1   Not stipulated
2   No
3   Yes

184

Union Can Screen Employee Appeals (for example, Union Decides Whether Employee Grievance Is Justified)

0   No NGP
1   Not stipulated
2   No
3   Yes

185

Union Receives Copy of Final Decision

0   No NGP
1   Not stipulated
2   Yes

186   Involvement of the Union Grievance Committee
                in the NGP

                0   No NGP
                1   Not stipulated
                2   Includes grievance committee at some
                    point

187   Number of Stewards That Are Specified

                0   No NGP
                1   Not stipulated
                2   "Reasonable number"
                3   Number specified (actual number or
                    ratio per shift or department, etc.)

188   Limitations on Movement on Property by
                Stewards and Representatives

                0   No NGP
                1   Not stipulated
                2   Permission of supervisors or other
                    management representative required

189   Time Limitations (on General Handling of
                Grievances) for Stewards and Representatives

                0   No NGP
                1   Not stipulated
                2   "Reasonable"
                3   Specific hours per period listed
                4   Grievances not handled on company time

190   Special Privileges for Stewards and Repre-
                sentatives

                0   No NGP
                1   Not stipulated
                2   Superseniority—layoffs only
                3   No transfers, except in emergency
                4   Notice, if transfers are necessary
                5   No transfers without union permission
                6   2 + 3
                7   2 + 4
                8   2 + 5

Variable Number	Variable and Response Code

191   **Compensation for Stewards and Representatives for Time Lost in Grievance Duties during Working Hours**

0   No NGP
1   Not stipulated
2   No loss of pay during duty hours
3   No pay
4   Prohibited

192   **Use of Outside Union Officials in Appeals Procedure and/or Other Union Business**

0   No NGP
1   Not stipulated
2   Not permitted
3   Permitted

193   **Union Rights in CS Procedures**

0   No CS procedures or contract silent
1   Not stipulated
2   Union prohibited from CS procedures
3   If employee desires, union can be representative
4   Union has right to be present and state views if not chosen by employee as representative
5   3 + 4

194   **Employee Right to Initiate and/or Process Appeal without Union as Representative**

0   No NGP
1   Not stipulated
2   Initiate only afterwards, must have union representation
3   Initiate and process without union representation, although union may be present
4   Initiate and union need not be present at first step
5   Cannot initiate without union

195   Employee Choice of Procedures

                       0   No NGP
                       1   Not stipulated
                       2   No choice since there is no dual proce-
                            dure
                       3   Employee has option between CS and
                            NGP, but decision is binding (cannot
                            abort one and choose the other)
                       4   Employee has option between CS and NGP,
                            but no indication as to whether or not
                            decision is reversible
                       5   Employee must first use NGP and then
                            the CS Procedure
                       6   NGP is used for the informal steps, and
                            the CS procedure for the formal steps

196   Employee Has the Right to Continue after
                       Union Aborts

                       0   No NGP
                       1   Not stipulated
                       2   No
                       3   Yes

197   Type of Hearing or Fact-finding Procedures
                       in NGP

                       0   No NGP
                       1   No provision for fact finding
                       2   No provision for type of hearing board
                       3   Hearing office or board appointed by
                            management
                       4   Tripartite panel
                       5   Equal number of union and management
                            representatives
                       6   Unequal number of union and manage-
                            ment representatives
                       7   CS impartial fact finder selected by
                            American Arbitration Association rules
                       8   Fact finding under state act

198   Hearings or Fact-finding Procedures in CS
                       Grievance Procedures

Variable Number	Variable and Response Code

0   No agency grievance procedure stipulated or contract silent
1   No provision for fact finding or hearing
2   No provision for type of board
3   Hearing officer appointed by management
4   Tripartite panel
5   Equal number of union and management representatives
6   Unequal number of union and management representatives
7   CS board

199   Provision for Mediation as Step in NGP

0   No NGP
1   No reference to mediation
2   Provision

200   Provision for Arbitration

0   No NGP
1   No arbitration provision
2   Provision for arbitration

201   Scope of Arbitration

0   No NGP
1   No arbitration
2   All issues allowed in the NGP
3   Adverse actions only
4   All grievances except discharge cases

202   Exclusions: Definition of Specific Matters Not Subject to Arbitration

0   No NGP
1   No arbitration
2   No specific exclusions
3   Some adverse actions
4   All adverse actions
5   New job classifications or wage rates or any matter subject to negotiation (pensions, job elimination, scheduling)

6   Seniority, promotions
7   Contract negotiations
8   Questions of legality under statutes,
    conflicts with Civil Service laws or
    regulations, or IAV of rules and policies
    of agency
9   Matters where employee has other
    statutory appeal rights

203   Arbitrator Has No Power to Add or Subtract
        From the Contract

0   No provision for NGP
1   No provision for arbitration
2   This statement is in contract
3   This statement is not in contract

204   Method of Arbitration Selection —First Level
        (If Only One Level Specified, It Will Be
        Considered as Second Level)

0   No NGP
1   No provision for arbitration
2   Only one arbitration step
3   Union and management choose their
    respective arbitrators

205   Method of Selection of Arbitrator(s)—Second
        Level

0   No provision for NGP
1   No provision for arbitration
2   No provision for selection of arbitrator(s)
3   Management and union select with no
    outside participation
4   Arbitrators at first level select impartial
    arbitrator
5   Management and union choose their
    respective arbitrator and jointly select
    impartial arbitrator
6   Management and union choose their
    respective arbitrator and the arbitrators
    jointly select the impartial arbitrator
7   Management and union select impartial
    arbitrator (impartial arbitrator is only
    member of arbitration panel)

Variable Number   Variable and Response Code

8   Arbitrators at first level select if can't
     agree; management and union select
     arbitrator

206   Authority of Arbitrator's Award—First Level

0   No NGP
1   No arbitration
2   Advisory
3   Binding if agreement is reached
4   Only one level of arbitrator, which is
     treated as second level

207   Authority of Arbitrator's Award—Second Level

0   No NGP
1   No arbitration
2   Advisory
3   Binding

208   Provision for Expense of Arbitration

0   No provision for NGP
1   No provision for arbitration procedure
2   No provision for expense of arbitration
3   Management pays expense
4   Parties share expense equally
5   Expense shared equally except for own board
     member(s) if it is a tripartite board or if
     it is first-level arbitration
6   Expense shared equally with maximum limit
7   Union pays expenses
8   Other, i.e., loser pays, employees pay
     some portion, state pays

209   Provision for Referral to Arbitration

0   No provision for NGP
1   No provision for arbitration procedure
2   No provision for referral to arbitration
3   Referral at request of union
4   Referral at request of grievant, but union
     must agree to pay half of costs first

5   Referral at request of union and/or
grievant
6   Referral at request of grievant
7   Referral at request of either party
8   Referral by mutual consent of both parties
9   Referral by request of management
10   Automatic referral if grievance not
settled in NGP

210   Question of Arbitrability

0   No provision for NGP
1   No provision for arbitration procedure
2   No provision for deciding questions of
arbitrability
3   Provision relating to arbitrability

211   Time Limit for Appeal of Grievance to
Arbitration

0   No NGP
1   No time limits stipulated
2   5 days or less
3   6-10 days
4   11 to 20 days
5   21 to 30 days
6   31 or more days
7   Reasonable time
8   No arbitration

212   Time Limits for Selection of Arbitrator(s)—
First Level

0   No NGP
1   No time limits stipulated
2   5 days or less
3   6-10 days
4   11-20 days
5   21-30 days
6   31 or more days
7   Reasonable time
8   Only one level, therefore being considered
as second level
9   No provision for arbitration

Variable Number   Variable and Response Code

213   Time Limits for Selection of Arbitrator(s)—
                       Second Level

                       0   No NGP
                       1   No time limits stipulated
                       2   5 days or less
                       3   6–10 days
                       4   11–20 days
                       5   21–30 days
                       6   31 or more days
                       7   Reasonable time
                       8   No provisions for arbitration

214   Time Limits for Arbitrator's Decision—
                       First Level

                       0   No NGP
                       1   No time limits stipulated
                       2   5 days or less
                       3   6–10 days
                       4   11–20 days
                       5   21–30 days
                       6   31 or more days
                       7   Reasonable time
                       8   Only one level, therefore being considered
                            as second level
                       9   No provisions for arbitration

215   Time Limits for Arbitrator's Decision—
                       Second Level

                       0   No NGP
                       1   No time limits stipulated
                       2   5 days or less
                       3   6–10 days
                       4   11–20 days
                       5   21–30 days
                       6   31 or more days
                       7   Reasonable time
                       8   No provisions for arbitration

216   Time Limits for Compliance with Arbitrator's
                       Decision

0   No NGP
1   No time limits stipulated
2   5 days or less
3   6-10 days
4   11-20 days
5   21-30 days
6   31 or more days
7   No provisions for arbitration

217   Employer-Employee Efficiency

0   No reference
1   Refers to greater efficiency or better
     performance of service; adequate ser-
     vice to community
2   Refers to union obligation to promote
     efficiency and other aims listed above

218   Public Interest

0   No reference
1   Specifically referred to
2   1 + reference to union obligation with
     regard to the public interest

219   Public Interest—Uninterrupted Service

0   No reference
1   Specifically referred to
2   1 + reference to union obligation with
     regard to the public interest

220   Public Interest—Safe Operation of Vehicles

0   No reference
1   Specifically referred to
2   1 + reference to union obligation with
     regard to the public interest

221   Public Interest—Courteous and Respectful
       Treatment

0   No reference
1   Specifically referred to
2   1 + reference to union obligation with
     regard to the public interest

Variable Number	Variable and Response Code

222

Public Interest—Customer Relations—
Passenger Illness

0   No reference
1   Specifically referred to
2   1 + reference to union obligation with
    regard to the public interest
9   Not appropriate—bargaining unit not
    covered by this contract

223

Public Interest—First Aid Training

0   No reference
1   General reference
2   Company provides first aid training
9   Not appropriate—bargaining unit not
    covered by this contract

224

Public Interest—Customer Relations—
Handicapped Passengers

0   No reference
1   Specifically referred to
2   1 + reference to union obligation with
    regard to the public interest
9   Not appropriate—bargaining unit not
    covered by this contract

225

Public Interest—Promptness in Meeting
Scheduled Stops

0   No reference
1   Specifically referred to
2   1 + reference to union obligation with
    regard to the public interest
9   Not appropriate—bargaining unit not
    covered by this contract

226

Public Interest—Mission of Organization—
Customer Satisfaction

0   No reference
1   Specifically referred to

2   1 + reference to union obligation with
regard to the public interest

227   Safety Meetings

0   No reference
1   Provision specifying minimum number
of meetings held
2   Attendance required
3   Attendance voluntary (may require union
encouragement)
4   Attendance voluntary but minimum number required
5   1 + 2
6   1 + 3
7   1 + 4

228   Management Prerogatives Clause

0   No reference
1   Reference

229   Selection of Employees

0   No reference or contract silent
1   Contract specifies procedures only
2   Contract specifies unilateral management
right

230   Layoffs of Employees—Determination of
When Needed

0   No reference or contract silent
1   Contract specifies procedures only
2   Contract specifies unilateral management
right

231   Layoffs of Employees—Scheduling

0   No reference or contract silent
1   Contract specifies procedures only
2   Contract specifies unilateral management
right

232   Length of Runs

Variable Number	Variable and Response Code

0   No reference or contract silent
1   Contract specifies procedures only
2   Contract specifies unilateral management right
9   Not appropriate—bargaining unit not covered by this contract

233   Scheduling Changes— Routes

0   No reference or contract silent
1   Contract specifies procedures only
2   Contract specifies unilateral management right
9   Not appropriate—bargaining unit not covered by this contract

234   Scheduling Changes—Times

0   No reference or contract silent
1   Contract specifies procedures only
2   Contract specifies unilateral management right
9   Not appropriate—bargaining unit not covered by this contract

235   Technological Changes

0   No reference or contract silent
1   Contract specifies procedures only
2   Contract specifies unilateral management right

236   Time Standards—Run Times

0   No reference or contract silent
1   Contract specifies procedures only
2   Contract specifies unilateral management right
9   Not appropriate—bargaining unit not covered by this contract

237   Apprenticeships

0   No reference or contract silent
1   Contract specifies procedures only
2   Contract specifies unilateral management
    right

238   Bidding of Runs

0   No reference or contract silent
1   Contract specifies procedures only
2   Contract specifies unilateral management
    right
9   Not appropriate—bargaining unit not
    covered by this contract

239   Joint Committees

0   No reference
1   Safety only
2   Issues other than or in addition to safety

240   Contract Length

0   No reference
1   1 year or less
2   2 years or less (over 1 year)
3   3 years or less (over 2 years)
4   4 years or less (over 3 years) etc.
5   Clause regarding length but not explicit

241   Sanctions

0   No reference
1   No-strike clause—general prohibition
2   No-strike clause—contract term only
3   1 + no job actions, for example, slow-
    downs, sickouts
4   2 + no job actions
5   1 + no lockout
6   2 + no lockout
7   1 + no job action + no lockout
8   2 + no job action + no lockout
9   1 + penalties
10   2 + penalties
11   3 + penalties
12   4 + penalties

Variable Number   Variable and Response Code

13   5 + penalties
14   6 + penalties
15   7 + penalties
16   8 + penalties

242   Impasse Procedures—New Contract

0   No reference
1   Old contract to remain in force during negotiations
2   Old contract to remain in force during negotiations involving third party
3   Mediation
4   Fact finding
5   Advisory arbitration
6   Binding arbitration
7   3 + 2
8   4 + 2
9   5 + 2
10   6 + 2
11   3 + 5

243   Exclusions from Impasse Procedures

0   No reference
1   Certain issues are excluded

244   Procedure for Reopening or Terminating Contract

0   No reference
1   Contract termination automatic; advance notice must be given to begin negotiation
2   Contract termination automatic; contract silent regarding advance notice
3   Contract termination only by parties giving specified notice; contract continues indefinitely otherwise
4   Procedure—no specific schedule; no mention of budget; 30 days' notice by either party of intent to modify
5   Procedure—schedule; for example, steps to initiate and proceed with negotiations,

or dates by which certain steps will be
taken; no mention of budget
6   Same as 4 except budget specifically
mentioned
7   Other termination procedure; no mention
of budget
8   Same as 7 mentioned except budget
specifically

245   Past-Practice Clause

0   No reference
1   Past practices shall not be unilaterally
changed
2   Past practices superseded by this
agreement
3   Other reference to past practices or
rates

246   Prohibition of Discrimination

0   No reference
1   Reference

247   Free Transportation

0   No reference
1   Employee only
2   Employee plus family (some or all
members)
3   1 + other special provisions, for example,
retired employees, surviving family
4   2 + other special provisions
5   Retired employees only

248   Accident Report

0   No reference
1   Must be completed within specified
period of time
2   Provision specifying company assistance
in completing accident report
3   1 + 2
4   Must be completed; no time limit specified

Variable Number   Variable and Response Code

249   <u>Fare Integrity</u>

0   No reference
1   General provision, for example, duty
     of bus driver to maintain fare integrity
2   Procedures indicating method of fare
     accountability
9   Not appropriate—bargaining unit not
     covered by this contract

Study Site (company name)_____

Time/Date of Interview_____

Address of Place of Interview_____

Names and Titles of Persons Interviewed_____

1. Brief history of the respondent's background including amount and type of experience in collective bargaining and contract administration, as well as the present organizational position (or union office) of the respondent.

2 What is the size of your transit operation in terms of: (Most recent fiscal year—get date)

total vehicles miles	_____
fixed (round trip) route miles	_____
charter miles	_____
fare box revenues	_____
charter revenues	_____
operating expenses	_____
number of buses	_____
number of passengers	_____
size of population served	_____

3. Are there any facilities producing competitive services or adjacent services? Yes _____ No _____ If the answer is Yes, what is the extent of these services?

   How does this situation affect the bargaining process?

4. A. What were the number of bargaining unit employees (or equivalent) at your facility ten years ago? _____ Five years ago? _____

   B. What is your future (five years from now) employment projection for your facility? Increased_____Decreased _____ Stabilized _____

5. A. How many employees are currently covered under the labor agreement(s)? _____

B. What is the current proportion of nonmanagerial employees who are organized? _____

C. What is the approximate number of bargaining unit employees that are dues-paying union members? _____

D. What is the current ratio of labor costs to total mass transit costs? _____

E. What are the current operating costs per mile? _____

F. What are the current labor costs per mile? _____

G. How are labor costs per mile and ratio of labor to total mass transit cost used in labor negotiations?

6. A. Is there more than one bargaining unit at your facility?
Yes _____ No _____ If answer is Yes, how many? _____ The local unions involved? _____

B. How does this affect bargaining at your facility (e.g., coordinated bargaining)?

7. A. What is the actual number of bargaining unit employees by classification? Total _____ Break out the classifications.

operators _____
craft   _____
clerical   _____ (including apprentices and helpers)
other bargaining unit employees _____

B. How does this distribution typically affect the collective bargaining process? e.g., Do presented and obtained proposals usually apply equally to all classifications, or to the majority classifications? Is contract ratification solely dependent upon membership vote, or is there some form of veto provision for craft employees?

8. At one time was your organization privately (or publicly) owned?
Yes _____ No _____ If answer is Yes, how has this change affected the bargaining process and bargaining outcome?

9. A. Do you presently have a management service company representing your interest? Yes _____ No _____ If answer is Yes, describe relationship and functions involved

(ask for a copy of the contract) and how and why was the
management service company selected? If answer is No, have you
ever had a management service company representing your company
(dates and description of relationship, or employed an outside consultant to represent your interest in labor negotiations? Who?

B. How has the management service company or the outside
consultant affected the collective bargaining relationships
at your facility?

10. A. How long has the bargaining unit been recognized?

B. How long has the bargaining unit been formally organized?

C. How many years has collective bargaining between management and union officials taken place at your organization?
Formal collective bargaining _____ (years), informal
collective bargaining _____ (years)

D. Approximately how many formal agreements (and dates of
these agreements if possible) have been negotiated since
inception? _____

11. Regarding your most recent negotiations:

A. What officials comprise the management's bargaining team?
How were these individuals selected?
What are their respective roles?

B. What officials comprise the union's bargaining team?
How were these individuals selected?
What are their respective roles?

C. How does this arrangement aid as well as hinder the collective
bargaining process? (Should various officials be added to or
deleted from the bargaining team? Why? Are the teams too
large or unrepresentative?)

Questions 12, 15, and 16 relate to the negotiation of the labor agreement presently in effect. After each question, ask respondent if this
was somewhat typical for other negotiations, obtaining explanations
for differences when appropriate.

12. A. When did collective bargaining commence? (date) _____
and end? (date) _____

B.   Does the length of negotiations favor management? The
union? Both? Or neither? Why?

C.   What is your fiscal year? _____

D.   What is the date that budget information must be submitted
for final approval? _____

E.   How does the budget-making process affect bargaining?
(e.g., have negotiations ever extended into another fiscal
year?)
Is retroactivity on wages permissible?
Are contract starting, expiration, and/or settlement dates
tied to the fiscal year?
Does the budget submission date put more pressure on manage-
ment or the union to resolve differences? Why?
Can negotiation demands cause a change in the budget?
Can settlement extend into another fiscal year?
Describe the final authority who approves the budget.
How does this composition affect bargaining? (e.g., is there
a labor or management bias present?)

13. A.   How often in the past five years has 13(c) of the Urban Mass
Transportation Act as amended in 1974 been implemented
at your agency? (obtain a copy of the 13(c) provisions)

B.   What are the advantages and disadvantages to management
under 13(c)?

C.   What are the advantages and disadvantages to labor under
13(c)?

D.   How do you assess the role of the Department of Labor in
administering 13(c)?

14. A.   How are union proposals drafted? (by bargaining committee,
total union membership, or international union)

B.   How well is the union strategy developed prior to negotiations?

C.   How well is management's strategy developed prior to negotiations?

D.   Have union and management developed any ground rules
regarding how negotiations are to be conducted (e.g.,

blackout of the press, inclusion of the general public, length
of negotiations, etc.)? If so, what are they?

15. A. Describe the three major issues in the last negotiation. (obtain
    amounts and relevant data)

    B. How were these issues issues resolved? (obtain the amount
       and percent of settlement)

    C. Did you grant an across-the-board wage increase? Yes _____
       No _____ If Yes, was the wage increase in percentage
       or in cents per hour? If No, what was respective wage
       distribution in percent or cents per hour?

16. A. To what extent was comparability used (e.g., wages and
    specific noneconomic issues)?

    B. How was "comparability" defined by management and the
       union in negotiations?

—	Management		Union	
—geographically	Yes	No	Yes	No
—cost of living	Yes	No	Yes	No
—in terms of other bar-gaining unit at same facility	Yes	No	Yes	No
—size of company	Yes	No	Yes	No
—revenues	Yes	No	Yes	No
—best negotiated settle-ment by specific issue by other parties	Yes	No	Yes	No
—other (please indicate)	Yes	No	Yes	No

    C. Have management and union reached agreement on how
       comparability is to be defined? If so, what is the definition
       and the relative priorities attached?

17. There are various procedures which have been used to resolve
    negotiation impasses, such as:

    —mediation
    —compulsory and binding arbitration
    —voluntary and binding arbitration
    —advisory arbitration
    —job action (strikes, slowdowns, collective absenteeism,
      etc.)

A. Are there any state or local statutes which affect (either mandate or prohibit) the use of any of the above procedures? Yes_____ No_____
If answer is Yes, indicate the specific procedures affected and obtain a copy of appropriate legislation.

B. Have you ever used (repeat for each item above)? When were you involved with each procedure? Describe the procedure along with the advantages and disadvantages it offers.

C. Have any governmental officials ever participated in impasse resolution procedures? Yes_____ No_____ If answer is Yes, what officials were involved, when did they become involved, and what was the effectiveness of their participation?

D. Have you ever used another impasse resolution procedure which has not been mentioned above? Yes _____
No_____ If answer is Yes, describe the procedure as well as its advantages and disadvantages.

18. A. Would involvement of local governmental officials assist or deter the collective bargaining process?

B. Would involvement of state governmental officials assist or deter the collective bargaining process?

C. Would involvement of federal governmental officials assist or deter the collective bargaining process?

19. In what ways do you think collective bargaining could be made more effective at your facility?

20. Present respondent with a card reflecting a 5-point scale: 1 = never; 2 = seldom; 3 = sometimes; 4 = frequently; 5 = always

A. Describe the degree that management and union use the following tactics in a typical contract negotiation (obtain scale response to each item for management and the union).

	Management	Union
—lobbying with councilmen and/or other government officials	_____	_____
—enlisting the support of the press	_____	_____

—enlisting public opinion   _____   _____

—lobbying with legislators
and/or other state governmental officials   _____   _____

B. How effective has _____ (repeat for each cited tactic) been for management?

C. How effective has _____ (repeat for each cited tactic) been for union?

21. Present respondent with card indicating the following attitudes:

A. General acceptance of the collective bargaining process
B. Conflicting attitudes over the desirability of collective bar-
gaining with limited expectations
C. Predominantly unfavorable attitudes toward collective bar-
gaining
D. No real concern either way regarding collective bargaining

Indicate for the following groups of individuals their overall
attitude toward the collective bargaining process at your facility:

—U.S. Department of Labor_____
—Operating management officials at your facility _____
—State governmental agencies_____
—Federal Department of Transportation_____
—Local government officials_____
—Union rank-and-file members_____
—The local community_____

22. (IN STATES OR LOCALITIES WITH PUBLIC EMPLOYEE
BARGAINING LAWS) Are there any changes you would like to
see in your state's or locality's existing public employee bargaining law? Yes_____ No_____If answer if Yes, how
would these changes affect the collective bargaining process?

23. (IN STATES OR LOCALITIES WITH NO EXISTING PUBLIC
EMPLOYEE BARGAINING) Would you favor legislation affecting
collective bargaining? Yes_____ No_____ If
answer is Yes, what major provisions would you include and
how would this affect the collective bargaining process?
If answer is No, what might be some of your reasons for your
answer?

24. A. What is your opinion regarding extending the Fair Labor
        Standards Act to mass transit employees?

    B. What is your opinion regarding proposed federal public
        employee bargaining laws which would include mass transit
        employees?

25. A. Cite and describe two instances where union-management
        cooperation is relatively high in your firm, indicating the
        reasons for this cooperation. (e.g., bidding schedules,
        provision for call-backs, split schedules, etc.)

    B. Cite and describe two instances where union-management
        cooperation is relatively low in your firm, indicating the
        reasons for this lack of cooperation. How was the problem
        addressed (informally or formally)? How was the problem
        resolved?

    C. Present respondent with a card reflecting a 7-point scale:

1	3	5	7
No attempt to cooperate and resolve differences	Little attempt to cooperate and resolve differences	Some attempt to cooperate and resolve differences	Great deal of effort to cooperate and resolve differences

How would you characterize union-management cooperation on
the following items?

	Management	Union
—implementation of technological change	_____	_____
—negotiation of the labor agreement	_____	_____
—administration of the labor agreement	_____	_____
—miscellaneous labor-management problems (e.g., how to handle employee with regard to personal problems, United Fund contributions, etc.)	_____	_____

    D. What steps could be taken to improve overall management-
        union cooperation in the administration of the contract at
        your facility?

26. A.   Describe two or three of the most recent technological changes
         for your operation.

         Change 1_____

         Change 2_____

         Change 3_____

   B.   Present respondent with card indicating following responses:

         1. controlling influence
         2. great deal of influence
         3. some influence
         4. little influence
         5. was not a factor

	Suggesting the change	Planning the change	Implementing the change
For innovation 1 what was the degree of influence exerted by the union in—	_____	_____	_____
For innovation 2 what was the degree of influence exerted by the union in—	_____	_____	_____
For innovation 3 what was the degree of influence exerted by the union in—	_____	_____	_____

   C.   How would you describe the overall influence of unions in
         technological change for your operations?

27. A.   What do you regard as management's unilateral right(s) in
         the labor-management relationship as well as the operation
         of the facility?

   B.   What do you regard as the union's unilateral right(s) in the
         labor-management relationship as well as the operation of
         the facility?

28. Present respondent with card indicating the alternative responses
    to this question:

   A.   Unilateral management right

  B.   Present labor agreement provisions pertaining to the issue
  C.   Union has right to petition or grieve to management officials
  D.   Management has obligation to meet and confer with union over issue but does not need the union's agreement
  E.   Management must receive union approval on the issue
  F.   Union has the right to negotiate the issue

What are management and union involvements on the following issues?

  a.   selection of employees _____
  b.   layoffs oı employees _____
  c.   implementation of affirmative action programs _____
  d.   length of runs _____
  e.   application for capital grants _____
  f.   revenue charges (fares and advertising) _____
  g.   scheduling changes (routes) _____
  h.   scheduling changes (times) _____
  i.   technological changes (new bus design, etc.) _____
  j.   time standards (run times) of routes _____
  k.   training and apprenticeship _____
  l.   bidding of runs _____
  m.   spread time (maximum time in which 8 hours of work can be scheduled at base hourly rate) _____

29. A.   "Public interest" is commonly cited as an important factor in labor-management relationships, but is seldom defined. How do you define the public interest? (special attention to items which are somewhat measurable)

    B.   (If management respondent) How do you think the union defines the public interest?

    C.   (If union respondent) How do you think management defines the public interest?

30. Present respondent the list indicating the following measures of the public interest:

    _____1.   improved safety of the vehicle
    _____2.   reduced fares for disadvantaged groups (please indicate the eligible groups)

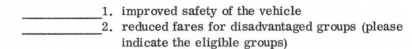

             _____physically handicapped
             _____elderly

_____welfare recipients
_____students
_____others (please specify)_____

_____3. guaranteeing uninterrupted service by binding
arbitration for every unresolved negotiation
item and grievance

_____4. training programs for upgrading and promoting
(please indicate eligible groups)

   _____minority employees
   _____hourly operating employees
   _____hourly craft employees
   _____nonmanagerial salaried employees
   _____managerial employees

_____5. improved efficiency of operations (for example,
service inventory maintenance systems, run
cutting and scheduling system)

_____6. guarantees protecting employees' jobs in case
of technological change or layoffs

_____7. improved environmental impact of buses (for
example, less noise and air pollution)

_____8. insuring that your transit employees' wages are
equal to, or better than, other agencies having
similar working conditions and cost of living

_____9. increased services

   _____new and better buses
   _____special vehicles for the transit
   disadvantaged
   _____increased number of miles covered
   by bus service

A. Given your knowledge of these factors, and your awareness
that each dollar spent on each factor does not yield equal
benefit, suppose that you have an additional amount of funds
to spend in a typical year. Assume that these funds equal
100 units. How would you distribute these units across the
following items [above] ?

B.   Rank these items 1 to 9 in terms of how you feel they contribute to the public interest (1 being most important, 9 being least important). (Ask for explanations of any major discrepancies between A and B.)

31. Do you think that strikes of mass transit employees affect the public interest? If yes, how?

32. (Return to questions 7A and B)

A.   What is the racial composition of employees by classification?

B.   How does this distribution affect the collective bargaining process?

C.   What proportion of union membership are minority individuals?

D.   What portion of union leadership are minority individuals?

33. A.   Are there work rules or memorandums of understanding outside of the labor contract? Yes_____ No_____

B.   If Yes, what issues are covered by above? What was the reason for their origin (e.g., issue occurred after formal agreement was signed, or before collective bargaining occurred; unresolved at time of contract expiration date).

AGREEMENT PURSUANT TO SECTION 13 (c) OF
THE URBAN MASS TRANSPORTATION ACT OF 1964,
AS AMENDED

WHEREAS, the Congress recognized in the National Mass
Transportation Assistance Act of 1974 that the urban mass transportation industry required operating assistance to maintain service to the
public, stimulate ridership and assist communities in meeting their
overall development aims, and

WHEREAS, Sections 3 (e) (4), 5 (n) (1) and 13 (c) of the Act
require, as a condition of any such assistance, that suitable fair and
equitable arrangements be made to protect urban mass transportation
industry employees affected by such assistance; and

WHEREAS, the fundamental purpose and scope of this agreement
is to establish such fair and equitable employee protective arrangements on a national and uniform basis for application throughout the
urban mass transportation industry to those employees and employees
represented by the labor organizations signatory hereto; and

WHEREAS, the undersigned American Public Transit Association and the national labor organizations signatory hereto have agreed
upon the following arrangements as fair and equitable for application
to any urban mass transportation employer ("Recipient") who is a
signatory hereto and who has been designated to receive federal
operating assistance under the Urban Mass Transportation Act of 1964,
as amended ("Act");

NOW, THEREFORE, it is agreed that the following terms and
conditions shall apply and shall be specified in any contract governing
such federal assistance to the Recipient:

(1) The term "Project" as used in this agreement, shall not be
limited to the particular facility, service, or operation assisted by
federal funds, but shall include any changes, whether organizational,
operational, technological, or otherwise, which are a result of the
assistance provided. The phrase "as a result of the Project" shall,
when used in this agreement, include events occurring in anticipation
of, during, and subsequent to the Project and any program of efficiencies or economies related thereto; provided, however, that volume

---

This agreement was provided by the American Public Transit
Association.

rises and falls of business, or changes in volume and character of employment brought about by causes other than the Project (including any economies or efficiencies unrelated to the Project) are not within the purview of this agreement.

(2) The Project, as defined in paragraph (1), shall be performed and carried out in full compliance with the protective conditions described herein.

(3) All rights, privileges, and benefits (including pension rights and benefits) of employees covered by this agreement (including employees having already retired) under existing collective bargaining agreements or otherwise, or under any revision or renewal thereof, shall be preserved and continued: provided, however, that such rights, privileges and benefits which are not foreclosed from further bargaining under applicable law or contract may be modified by collective bargaining and agreement by the Recipient and the union involved to substitute other rights, privileges and benefits. Unless otherwise provided, nothing in this agreement shall be deemed to restrict any rights the Recipient may otherwise have to direct the working forces and manage its business as it deems best, in accordance with the applicable collective bargaining agreement.

(4) The collective bargaining rights of employees covered by this agreement, including the right to arbitrate labor disputes and to maintain union security and checkoff arrangements, as provided by applicable laws, policies and/or existing collective bargaining agreements, shall be preserved and continued.* Provided, however, that this provision shall not be interpreted so as to require the Recipient to retain any such rights which exist by virtue of a collective bargaining agreement after such agreement is no longer in effect.

The Recipient agrees that it will bargain collectively with the union or otherwise arrange for the continuation of collective bargaining, and that it will enter into agreement with the union or arrange for such agreements to be entered into, relative to all subjects which are or may be proper subjects of collective bargaining. If, at any time, applicable law or contracts permit or grant to employees covered by this agreement the right to utilize any economic measures, nothing in this agreement shall be deemed to foreclose the exercise of such right.

---

* As an addendum to this agreement, there shall be attached where applicable the arbitration or other dispute settlement procedures or arrangements provided for in the existing collective bargaining agreements or any other existing agreements between the Recipient and the Union, subject to any changes in such agreements as may be agreed upon or determined by interest arbitration proceedings.

(5) (a) In the event the Recipient contemplates any change in the organization or operation of its system which may result in the dismissal or displacement of employees, or rearrangement of the working forces covered by this agreement, as a result of the Project, the Recipient shall do so only in accordance with the provisions of subparagraph (b) hereof. Provided, however, that changes which are not a result of the Project, but which grow out of the normal exercise of seniority rights occasioned by seasonal or other normal schedule changes and regular picking procedures under the applicable collective bargaining agreement, shall not be considered within the purview of this paragraph.

(b) The Recipient shall give to the unions representing the employees affected thereby, at least sixty (60) days; written notice of each proposed change, which may result in the dismissal or displacement of such employees or rearrangement of the working forces as a result of the Project, by sending certified mail notice to the union representatives of such employees. Such notice shall contain a full and adequate statement of the proposed changes, including an estimate of the number of employees affected by the intended changes, and the number and classifications of any jobs in the Recipient's employment available to be filled by such employees.

At the request of either the Recipient or the representatives of the affected employees, negotiations for the purpose of reaching agreement with respect to application of the terms and conditions of this agreement shall commence immediately. These negotiations shall include determining the selection of forces from among the employees of other urban mass transportation employers who may be affected as a result of the Project, to establish which such employees shall be offered employment with the Recipient for which they are qualified or can be trained; not, however, in contravention of collective bargaining agreements relating thereto. If no agreement is reached within twenty (20) days from the commencement of negotiations, any party to the dispute may submit it to arbitration in accordance with the procedures contained in paragraph (15) hereof. In any such arbitration, final decision must be reached within sixty (60) days after selection or appointment of the neutral arbitrator. In any such arbitration, the terms of this agreement are to be interpreted and applied in favor of providing employee protections and benefits no less than those established pursuant to SS 5 (2) (f) of the Interstate Commerce Act.

(6) (a) Whenever an employee, retained in service, recalled to service, or employed by the Recipient pursuant to paragraphs (5), (7) (e), or (18) hereof is placed in a worse position with respect to compensation as a result of the Project, he shall be considered a "displaced employee," and shall be paid a monthly "displacement

allowance" to be determined in accordance with this paragraph. Said displacement allowance shall be paid each displaced employee during the protective period so long as the employee is unable, in the exercise of his seniority rights, to obtain a position producing compensation equal to or exceeding the compensation he received in the position from which he was displaced, adjusted to reflect subsequent general wage adjustments, including cost of living adjustments where provided for.

(b) The displacement allowance shall be a monthly allowance determined by computing the total compensation received by the employee, including vacation allowances and monthly compensation guarantees, and his total time paid for during the last twelve (12) months in which he performed compensated service more than fifty per centum of each such months, based upon his normal work schedule, immediately preceding the date of his displacement as a result of the Project, and by dividing separately the total compensation and the total time paid for by twelve, thereby producing the average monthly compensation and the average monthly time paid for. Such allowance shall be adjusted to reflect subsequent general wage adjustments, including cost of living adjustments where provided for. If the displaced employee's compensation in his current position is less in any month during his protective period than the aforesaid average compensation (adjusted to reflect subsequent general wage adjustments, including cost of living adjustments where provided for), he shall be paid the difference, less compensation for any time lost on account of voluntary absences to the extent that he is not available for service equivalent to his average monthly time, but he shall be compensated in addition thereto at the rate of the current position for any time worked in excess of the average monthly time paid for. If a displaced employee fails to exercise his seniority rights to secure another position to which he is entitled under the then existing collective bargaining agreement, and which carries a wage rate and compensation exceeding that of the position which he elects to retain, he shall thereafter be treated, for the purposes of this paragraph, as occupying the position he elects to decline.

(c) The displacement allowance shall cease prior to the expiration of the protective period in the event of the displaced employee's resignation, death, retirement, or dismissal for cause in accordance with any labor agreement applicable to his employment.

(7)(a) Whenever any employee is laid off or otherwise deprived of employment as a result of the Project, in accordance with any collective bargaining agreement applicable to his employment, he shall be considered a "dismissed employee" and shall be paid a monthly dismissal allowance to be determined in accordance with this paragraph. Said dismissal allowance shall first be paid each dismissed employee on the thirtieth (30th) day following the day on which he is "dismissed" and shall continue during the protective period, as follows:

Employee's length of service prior to adverse effect	Period of protection
1 day to 6 years	equivalent period
6 years or more	6 years

The monthly dismissal allowance shall be equivalent to one-twelfth (1/12th) of the total compensation received by him in the last twelve (12) months of his employment in which he performed compensation service more than fifty per centum of each such months based on his normal work schedule to the date on which he was first deprived of employment as a result of the Project. Such allowance shall be adjusted to reflect subsequent general wage adjustments, including cost of living adjustments where provided for.

(b) An employee shall be regarded as deprived of employment and entitled to a dismissal allowance when the position he holds is abolished as a result of the Project, or when the position he holds is not abolished but he loses that position as a result of the exercise of seniority rights by an employee whose position is abolished as a result of the Project or as a result of the exercise of seniority rights by other employees brought about as a result of the Project, and he is unable to obtain another position, either by the exercise of his seniority rights, or through the Recipient, in accordance with subparagraph (e). In the absence of proper notice followed by an agreement or decision pursuant to paragraph (5) hereof, no employee who has been deprived of employment as a result of the Project shall be required to exercise his seniority rights to secure another position in order to qualify for a dismissal allowance hereunder.

(c) Each employee receiving a dismissal allowance shall keep the Recipient informed as to his current address and the current name and address of any other person by whom he may be regularly employed, or if he is self-employed.

(d) The dismissal allowance shall be paid to the regularly assigned incumbent of the position abolished. If the position of an employee is abolished when he is absent from service, he will be entitled to the dismissal allowance when he is available for service. The employee temporarily filling said position at the time it was abolished will be given a dismissal allowance on the basis of that position, until the regular employee is available for service, and thereafter shall revert to his previous status and will be given the protections of the agreement in said position, if any are due him.

(e) An employee receiving a dismissal allowance shall be subject to call to return to service by his former employer after being notified in accordance with the terms of the then-existing collective bargaining agreement. Prior to such call to return to work by his employer, he may be required by the Recipient to accept reasonably comparable employment for which he is physically and mentally qualified, or for which he can become qualified after a reasonable training or retraining period, provided it does not require a change in residence or infringe upon the employment rights of other employees under then-existing collective bargaining agreements.

(f) When an employee who is receiving a dismissal allowance again commences employment in accordance with subparagraph (e) above, said allowance shall cease while he is so reemployed, and the period of time during which he is so reemployed shall be deducted from the total period for which he is entitled to receive a dismissal allowance. During the time of such reemployment, he shall be entitled to the protections of this agreement to the extent they are applicable.

(g) The dismissal allowance of any employee who is otherwise employed shall be reduced to the extent that his combined monthly earnings from such other employment or self-employment, any benefits received from any unemployment insurance law, and his dismissal allowance exceed the amount upon which his dismissal allowance is based. Such employee, or his union representative, and the Recipient shall agree upon a procedure by which the Recipient shall be kept currently informed of the earnings of such employee in employment other than with his former employer, including self-employment, and the benefits received.

(h) The dismissal allowance shall cease prior to the expiration of the protective period in the event of the failure of the employee without good cause to return to service in accordance with the applicable labor agreement, or to accept employment as provided under subparagraph (e) above, or in the event of his resignation, death, retirement, or dismissal for cause in accordance with any labor agreement applicable to his employment.

(i) A dismissed employee receiving a dismissal allowance shall actively seek and not refuse other reasonably comparable employment offered him for which he is physically and mentally qualified and does not require a change in his place of residence. Failure of the dismissed employee to comply with this obligation shall be grounds for discontinuance of his allowance; provided that said dismissal allowance shall not be discontinued until final determination is made either by agreement between the Recipient and the employee or his representative, or by final arbitration decision rendered in accordance with paragraph (15) of this agreement that such employee did not comply with this obligation.

(8) In determining length of service of a displaced or dismissed employee for purposes of this agreement, such employee shall be given

full service credits in accordance with the records and labor agreements applicable to him and he shall be given additional service
credits for each month in which he receives a dismissal or displacement allowance as if he were continuing to perform services in his
former position.

(9) No employee shall be entitled to either a displacement or
dismissal allowance under paragraphs (6) or (7) hereof because of
the abolishment of a position to which, at some future time, he could
have bid, been transferred, or promoted.

(10) No employee receiving a dismissal or displacement allowance shall be deprived, during his protected period, of any rights,
privileges, or benefits attaching to his employment, including, without limitation, group life insurance, hospitalization and medical care,
free transportation for himself and his family, sick leave, continued
status and participation under any disability or retirement program,
and such other employee benefits as Railroad Retirement, Social
Security, Workmen's Compensation, and unemployment compensation,
as well as any other benefits to which he may be entitled under the
same conditions and so long as such benefits continue to be accorded
to other employees of the bargaining unit, in active service or fur-
loughed as the case may be.

(11)(a) Any employee covered by this agreement who is retained
in the service of his employer, or who is later restored to service
after being entitled to receive a dismissal allowance, and who is
required to change the point of his employment in order to retain or
secure active employment with the Recipient in accordance with this
agreement, and who is required to move his place of residence, shall
be reimbursed for all expenses of moving his household and other
personal effects, for the travelling expenses for himself and members
of his immediate family, including living expenses for himself and
his immediate family, and for his own actual wage loss during the
time necessary for such transfer and for a reasonable time thereafter,
not to exceed five (5) working days. The exact extent of the responsibility of the Recipient under this paragraph, and the ways and means
of transportation, shall be agreed upon in advance between the Recipient and the affected employee or his representatives.

(b) If any such employee is laid off within three (3) years after
changing his point of employment in accordance with paragraph (a)
hereof, and elects to move his place of residence back to his original
point of employment, the Recipient shall assume the expenses, losses
and costs of moving to the same extent provided in subparagraph (a)
of this paragraph (11) and paragraph (12)(a) hereof.

(c) No claim for reimbursement shall be paid under the provisions of this paragraph unless such claim is presented to the Recipient
within ninety (90) days after the date on which the expenses were
incurred.

(d) Except as otherwise provided in subparagraph (b), changes in place of residence, subsequent to the initial changes as a result of the Project, which are not a result of the Project but grow out of the normal exercise of seniority rights, shall not be considered within the purview of this paragraph.

(12)(a) The following conditions shall apply to the extent they are applicable in each instance to any employee who is retained in the service of the employer (or who is later restored to service after being entitled to receive a dismissal allowance), who is required to change the point of his employment as a result of the Project, and is thereby required to move his place of residence.

If the employee owns his own home in the locality from which he is required to move, he shall, at his option, be reimbursed by the Recipient for any loss suffered in the sale of his home for less than its fair market value, plus conventional fees and closing costs, such loss to be paid within thirty (30) days of settlement or closing on the sale of the home. In each case, the fair market value of the home in question shall be determined as of a date sufficiently prior to the date of the Project, so as to be unaffected thereby. The Recipient shall, in each instance, be afforded an opportunity to purchase the home at such fair market value before it is sold by the employee to any other person and to reimburse the seller for his conventional fees and closing costs.

If the employee is under a contract to purchase his home, the Recipient shall protect him against loss under such contract, and in addition, shall relieve him from any further obligation thereunder.

If the employee holds an unexpired lease of a dwelling occupied by him as his home, the Recipient shall protect him from all loss and cost in securing the cancellation of said lease.

(b) No claim for loss shall be paid under the provisions of this paragraph unless such claim is presented to the Recipient within one year after the effective date of the change in residence.

(c) Should a controversy arise in respect to the value of the home, the loss sustained in its sale, the loss under a contract for purchase, loss and cost in securing termination of a lease, or any other question in connection with these matters, it shall be decided through a joint conference between the employee, or his union, and the Recipient. In the event they are unable to agree, the dispute or controversy may be referred by the Recipient or the union to a board of competent real estate appraisers selected in the following manner: one (1) to be selected by the representatives of the employee, and one (1) by the Recipient, and these two, if unable to agree within thirty (30) days upon the valuation, shall endeavor by agreement within ten (10) days thereafter to select a third appraiser or to agree to a method by which a third appraiser shall be selected, and failing such agreement, either party may request the State or local Board of Real Estate Commissioners to designate within ten (10) days a third appraiser, whose designation will be binding upon the parties and whose jurisdiction shall be limited to determination of the issues raised in this paragraph only. A decision of a majority of the appraisers shall be required and said decision shall be final, binding, and conclusive. The compensation and expenses of the neutral appraiser, including expenses of the appraisal board, shall be borne equally by the parties to the proceedings. All other expenses shall be paid by the party incurring them, including the compensation of the appraiser selected by such party.

(d) Except as otherwise provided in paragraph (11)(b) hereof, changes in place of residence, subsequent to the initial changes as a result of the Project, which are not a result of the Project but grow out of the normal exercise of seniority rights, shall not be considered within the purview of this paragraph.

(e) "Change in residence" means transfer to a work location which is either (A) outside a radius of twenty (20) miles of the employee's former work location and farther from his residence than was his former work location, or (B) is more than thirty (30) normal highway route miles from his residence and also farther from his residence than was his former work location.

(13) A dismissed employee entitled to protection under this agreement may, at his option within twenty-one (21) days of his dismissal, resign and (in lieu of all other benefits and protections provided in this agreement) accept a lump sum payment computed in accordance with section (9) of the Washington Job Protection Agreement of May 1936:

Length of Service	Separation Allowance
1 year and less than 2 years	3 months' pay
2 years " " " 3 "	6 " "
3 " " " " 5 "	9 " "
5 " " " " 10 "	12 " "
10 " " " " 15 "	12 " "
15 " " over	12 " "

In the case of an employee with less than one year's service, five days' pay, computed by multiplying by 5 the normal daily earnings (including regularly scheduled overtime, but excluding other over-time payments) received by the employee in the position last occupied, for each month in which he performed service, will be paid as the lump sum.

(a) Length of service shall be computed as provided in Section 7(b) of the Washington Job Protection Agreement, as follows:

For the purposes of this agreement, the length of service of the employee shall be determined from the date he last acquired an employment status with the employing carrier and he shall be given credit for one month's service for each month in which he performed any service (in any capacity whatsoever) and twelve (12) such months shall be credited as one year's service. The employment status of an employee shall not be interrupted by furlough in instances where the employee has a right to and does return to service when called. In determining length of service of an employee acting as an officer or other official representative of an employee organization, he will be given credit for performing service while so engaged on leave of absence from the service of a carrier.

(b) One month's pay shall be computed by multiplying by 30 the normal daily earnings (including regularly scheduled overtime, but excluding other overtime payments) received by the employee in the position last occupied prior to time of his dismissal as a result of the Project.

(14) Whenever used herein, unless the context requires otherwise, the term "protective period" means that period of time during which a displaced or dismissed employee is to be provided protection hereunder and extends from the date on which an employee is displaced or dismissed to the expiration of six (6) years therefrom, provided, however, that the protective period for any particular employee during which he is entitled to receive the benefits of these provisions shall not continue for a longer period following the date he was displaced or dismissed than the employee's length of service, as shown by the records and labor agreements applicable to his employment prior to the date of his displacement or his dismissal.

(15)(a) In the event there arises any labor dispute with respect to the protection afforded by this agreement, or with respect to the interpretation, application or enforcement of the provisions of this agreement, not otherwise governed by Section (12) (c) hereof, the Labor-Management Relations Act, as amended, Railway Labor Act, as amended, or by impasse resolution provisions in a collective bargaining or protective agreement involving the Recipient and the union, which cannot be settled by the parties thereto within thirty (30) days after the dispute or controversy arises, it may be submitted at the written request of the Recipient or the union to a board of arbitration to be selected as hereinafter provided. One arbitrator is to be chosen by each interested party, and the arbitrators thus selected shall endeavor to select a neutral arbitrator who shall serve as chairman. Each party shall appoint its arbitrator within five (5) days after notice of submission to arbitration has been given. Should the arbitrators selected by the parties by unable to agree upon the selection of the neutral arbitrator within ten (10) days after notice

of submission to arbitration has been given, then the arbitrator selected
by any party may request the American Arbitration Association to
furnish, from among members of the National Academy of Arbitrators
who are then available to serve, five (5) arbitrators from which the
neutral arbitrator shall be selected. The arbitrators appointed by
the parties shall, within five (5) days after the receipt of such list,
determine by lot the order of elimination and thereafter each shall,
in that order, alternately eliminate one name until only one name
remains. The remaining person on the list shall be the neutral
arbitrator. If any party fails to select its arbitrator within the pre-
scribed time limit, the highest officer of the Union or of the Recipient
or their nominees, as the case may be, shall be deemed to be the
selected arbitrator, and the board of arbitration shall then function
and its decision shall have the same force and effect as though all
parties had selected their arbitrators. Unless otherwise provided,
in the case of arbitration proceedings, under paragraph (5) of this
agreement, the board of arbitration shall meet within fifteen (15) days
after selection or appointment of the neutral arbitrator and shall render its decision within forty-five (45) days after the hearing of the
dispute has been concluded and the record closed. The decision by
majority vote of the arbitration board shall be final and binding as
the decision of the arbitration board, except as provided in subparagraph (b) below. All the conditions of the agreement shall continue
to be effective during the arbitration proceedings.

(b) In the case of any labor dispute otherwise covered by subparagraph (a) but involving multiple parties, or employees of urban
mass transportation employers other than those of the Recipient,
which cannot be settled by collective bargaining, such labor dispute
may be submitted, at the written request of any of the parties to this
agreement involved in the dispute, to a single arbitrator who is mutually acceptable to the parties. Failing mutual agreement within (10)
days as to the selection of an arbitrator, any of the parties involved
may request the American Arbitration Association to furnish an
impartial arbitrator from among members of the National Academy
of Arbitrators who is then available to serve. Unless otherwise provided, in the case of arbitration proceedings under paragraph (5) of
this agreement, the arbitrator thus appointed shall convene the
hearing within fifteen (15) days after his selection or appointment
and shall render his decision within forty-five (45) days after the
hearing of the dispute or controversy has been concluded and the
record closed. The decision of the neutral arbitrator shall be final,
binding, and conclusive upon all parties to the dispute. All the conditions of the agreement shall continue to be effective during the arbitration proceeding. Authority of the arbitrator shall be limited to the
determination of the dispute arising out of the interpretation,

application, or operation of the provisions of this agreement. The arbitrator shall not have any authority whatsoever to alter, amend, or modify any of the provisions of any collective bargaining agreement.

(c) The compensation and expenses of the neutral arbitrator, and any other jointly incurred expenses, shall be borne equally by the parties to the proceeding and all other expenses shall be paid by the party incurring them.

(d) In the event of any dispute as to whether or not a particular employee was affected by the Project, it shall be his obligation to identify the Project and specify the pertinent facts of the Project relied upon. It shall then be the Recipient's burden to prove that factors other than the Project affected the employee. The claiming employee shall prevail if it is established that the Project had an effect upon the employee even if other factors may also have affected the employee (Hodgson's Affidavit in Civil Action No. 825-71).

(e) Nothing in this agreement shall be construed to enlarge or limit the right of any party to utilize, upon the expiration of any collective bargaining agreement or otherwise, any economic measures which are not inconsistent or in conflict with applicable laws or this agreement.

(16) Nothing in this agreement shall be construed as depriving any employee of any rights or benefits which such employee may have under any existing job security or other protective conditions or arrangements by collective bargaining agreement or law where applicable, including P. L. 93-236, enacted January 2, 1974; provided that there shall be no duplication of benefits to any employees, and, provided further, that any benefit under the agreement shall be construed to include the conditions, responsibilities, and obligations accompanying such benefit.

(17) The Recipient shall be financially responsible for the application of these conditions and will make the necessary arrangements so that any employee affected as a result of the Project may file a claim through his union representative with the Recipient within sixty (60) days of the date he is terminated or laid off as a result of the Project, or within eighteen (18) months of the date his position with respect to his employment is otherwise worsened as a result of the Project; provided, in the latter case, if the events giving rise to the claim have occurred over an extended period, the 18-month limitation shall be measured from the last such event; provided, further, that no benefits shall be payable for any period prior to six (6) months from the date of the filing of the claim. Unless such claims are filed with the Recipient within said time limitations, the Recipient shall thereafter be relieved of all liabilities and obligations related to said claims. The Recipient will fully honor the claim, making appropriate

payments, or will give notice to the claimant and his representative
of the basis for denying or modifying such claim, giving reasons
therefor. In the event the Recipient fails to honor such claim, the
Union may invoke the following procedures for further joint investigation of the claim by giving notice in writing of its desire to pursue
such procedures. Within ten (10) days from the receipt of such notice,
the parties shall exchange such factual material as may be requested
of them relevant to the disposition of the claim and shall jointly take
such steps as may be necessary or desirable to obtain from any third
party such additional factual material as may be relevant. In the event
the claim is so rejected by the Recipient, the claim may be processed
to arbitration as hereinabove provided by paragraph (15). Prior to
the arbitration hearing, the parties shall exchange a list of intended
witnesses. In conjunction with such proceedings, the impartial arbitrator shall have the power to subpoena witnesses upon the request of
any party and to compel the production of documents and other information denied in the pre-arbitration period which is relevant to the
disposition of the claim.

    Nothing included herein as an obligation of the Recipient
shall be construed to relieve any other urban mass transportation employer of the employees covered hereby of any obligations which it has under existing collective bargaining agreements,
including but not limited to obligations arising from the benefits referred to in paragraph (10) hereof, nor make any such employer a third-party beneficiary of the Recipient's obligations
contained herein, nor deprive the Recipient of any right of
subrogation.

    (18) During the employee's protective period, a dismissed
employee shall, if he so requests, in writing, be granted priority of
employment to fill any vacant position within the jurisdiction and
control of the Recipient, reasonably comparable to that which he held
when dismissed, for which he is, or by training or retraining can
become, qualified; not, however, in contravention of collective bargaining agreements relating thereto. In the event such employee
requests such training or re-training to fill such vacant position, the
Recipient shall provide for such training or re-training at no cost to
the employee. The employee shall be paid the salary or hourly rate
provided for in the applicable collective bargaining agreement for
such position, plus any displacement allowance to which he may be
otherwise entitled. If such dismissed employee who has made such
request fails, without good cause, within ten (10) days to accept an
offer of a position comparable to that which he held when dismissed
for which he is qualified, or for which he has satisfactorily completed
such training, he shall, effective at the expiration of such ten-day
period, forfeit all rights and benefits under this agreement.

As between employees who request employment pursuant to this paragraph, the following order where applicable shall prevail in hiring such employees:

(a) Employees in the craft or class of the vacancy shall be given priority over employees without seniority in such craft or class;

(b) As between employees having seniority in the craft or class of the vacancy, the senior employees, based upon their service in that craft or class, as shown on the appropriate seniority roster, shall prevail over junior employees;

(c) As between employees not having seniority in the craft or class of the vacancy, the senior employees, based upon their service in the crafts or classes in which they do have seniority as shown on the appropriate seniority rosters, shall prevail over junior employees.

(19) This agreement shall be binding upon the successors and assigns of the parties hereto, and no provisions, terms, or obligations herein contained shall be affected, modified, altered or changed in any respect whatsoever by reason of the arrangements made by or for the Recipient to manage and operate the system.

Any such person, enterprise, body, or agency, whether publicly- or privately-owned, which shall undertake the management or operation of the system, shall agree to be bound by the terms of this agreement and accept the responsibility for full performance of these conditions.

(20) The employees covered by this agreement shall continue to receive any applicable coverage under Social Security, Railroad Retirement, Workmen's Compensation, unemployment compensation, and the like. In no event shall these benefits be worsened as a result of the Project.

(21) In the event any provision of this agreement is held to be invalid, or otherwise unenforceable under the federal, State, or local law, in the context of a particular Project, the remaining provisions of this agreement shall not be affected and the invalid or unenforceable provision shall be renegotiated by the Recipient and the interested union representatives of the employees involved for purpose of adequate replacement under S 13(c) of the Act. If such negotiation shall not result in mutually satisfactory agreement, any party may invoke the jurisdiction of the Secretary of Labor to determine substitute fair and equitable employee protective arrangements for application only to the particular Project, which shall be incorporated in this agreement only as applied to that Project, and any other appropriate action, remedy, or relief.

(22) This agreement establishes fair and equitable employee protective arrangements for application only to federal operating assistance Projects under SS3(h) and 5 of the Act and shall not be applied to other types of assistance under S5 or under other provisions of the Act, in the absence of further understandings and agreements to that effect.

(23) The designated Recipient, as hereinabove defined, signatory hereto, shall be the sole provider of mass transportation services to the Project and such services shall be provided exclusively by employees of the Recipient covered by this agreement, in accordance with this agreement and any applicable collective bargaining agreement. The parties recognize, however, that certain of the recipients signatory hereto, providing urban mass transportation services, have heretofore provided such services through contracts by purchase, leasing, or other arrangements and hereby agree that such practices may continue. When ever any other employer provides such services through contracts by purchase, leasing, or other arrangements with the Recipient, or on its behalf, the provisions of this agreement shall apply.

(24) An employee covered by this agreement, who is not dismissed, displaced, or otherwise worsened in his position with regard to his employment as a result of the Project, but who is dismissed, displaced, or otherwise worsened solely because of the total or partial termination of the Project, discontinuance of Project services, or exhaustion of Project funding, shall not be deemed eligible for a dismissal or displacement allowance within the meaning of paragraphs (6) and (7) of this agreement.

(25) If any employer of the employees covered by this agreement shall have rearranged or adjusted its forces in anticipation of the Project, with the effect of depriving an employee of benefits to which he should be entitled under this agreement, the provisions of this agreement shall apply to such employee as of the date when he was so affected.

(26) Any eligible employer not initially a party to this agreement may become a party by serving written notice of its desire to do so upon the Secretary of Labor, the American Public Transit Association, or in the event of any objection to the addition of such employer as a signatory, its designee, and the unions signatory hereto, or their designee. Then the dispute as to whether such employer shall become a signatory shall be determined by the Secretary of Labor.

(27) In the context of a particular Project, any other union which is the collective bargaining representative of urban mass transportation employees in the service area of the Recipient, and who may be affected by the assistance to the Recipient within the meaning of 49 U.S.C.A. 1609(c), may become a party to this agreement as applied to the Project, by serving written notice of its desire to do so upon the other union representatives of the employees affected by the Project, the Recipient, and the Secretary of Labor. In the event of any disagreement that labor organization should become a party to this agreement, as applied to the Project, then the dispute as to whether such labor organization shall participate shall be determined by the Secretary of Labor.

(28) This agreement shall be effective and be in full force and effect for the period from November 26, 1974 to and including September 30, 1977. It shall continue in effect thereafter from year to year unless terminated by the A.P.T.A. or by the national labor organizations signatory hereto upon one hundred twenty (120) days' written notice prior to the annual renewal date. Any signatory employer or labor organization may individually withdraw from the agreement effective October 1, 1977, or upon any annual renewal date thereafter, by serving written notice of its intention so to withdraw one hundred twenty (120) days prior to the annual renewal date; provided, however, that any rights of the parties hereto or of individuals established and fixed during the term of this agreement shall continue in full force and effect, notwithstanding the termination of the agreement or the exercise by any signatory of the right to withdraw therefrom. This agreement shall be subject to revision by mutual agreement of the parties hereto at any time, but only after the serving of a sixty (60) days' notice by either party upon the other.

(29) In the event any project to which this agreement applies is approved for assistance under the Act, the foregoing terms and conditions shall be made part of the contract of assistance between the federal government and the Recipient or other applicant for federal funds; provided, however, that this agreement shall not merge into the contract of assistance but shall be independently binding and enforceable by and upon the parties thereto, in accordance with its terms, nor shall any other employee protective agreement nor any collective bargaining agreement merge into this agreement, but each shall be independently binding and enforceable by and upon the parties thereto, in accordance with its terms.

BOOKS

Abond, Antone, and Grace Abond. The Right to Strike in Public
Employment. Ithaca: Cornell University Press, 1974.

Adler, Hans A. Economic Appraisal of Transport Projects. Bloomington: Indiana University Press, 1971.

Advisory Commission on Intergovernmental Relations. Labor-Management Policies for State and Local Government. Washington,
D.C.: U.S. Government Printing Office, 1969.

American Municipal Association. The Collapse of Commuter Service:
A Survey of Mass Transportation in Five Major Cities. Washington, D.C.: American Municipal Association, 1960.

Automotive Safety Foundation. Urban Transit Development in Twenty
Major Cities. Washington, D.C.: Automotive Safety Foundation,
1968.

Backman, Jules, and M. R. Gainesborough. Behavior of Wages.
New York: National Industrial Conference Board, 1948.

Banks, R. L., and Associates. Study and Evaluation of Urban Mass
Transportation Regulation and Regulatory Bodies. Springfield,
Va.: National Technical Information Service, 1972.

Beal, Edwin F., and Edward D. Wickersham. The Practice of
Collective Bargaining. 2d ed. Homewood, Ill.: Richard D.
Irwin, 1967.

Berry, Donald S., et al. The Technology of Urban Transit. Evanston:
Northwestern University Press, 1963.

Bleakney, Thomas P. Retirement Systems for Public Employees.
Homewood, Ill. Richard D. Irwin, 1972.

Bloom, Gordon F., and Herbert R. Northrup. Economics of Labor
Relations. Homewood, Ill.: Richard D. Irwin, Inc., 1969.

Bok, Derek C., and John T. Dunlop. Labor and the American Community. New York: Simon and Schuster, 1970.

Bowen, Don L., ed. Public Service Professional Associations and the Public Interest. Philadelphia: American Academy of Political and Social Science, 1973.

Boyd, Hayden J., Norman J. Asher, and Elliot S. Wetzler. Evaluation of Rail Rapid Transit and Express Bus Service in the Urban Commuter Market. Arlington, Va.: Institute for Defense Analyses, 1973.

Buel, Ronald A. Dead End: The Automobile in Mass Transportation. Englewood Cliffs, N.J.: Prentice-Hall, 1972.

Cantanese, Anthony J., ed. New Perspectives in Urban Transportation Research. Lexington, Mass.: Lexington Books, 1973.

Cantilli, Edmund J. Programming Environmental Improvements in Public Transportation. Lexington, Mass.: Lexington Books, 1973.

Carpenter, Jesse Thomas. Employers' Associations and Collective Bargaining in New York City. Ithaca: Cornell University Press, 1950.

Cartter, Allan M., and F. Ray Marshall. Labor Economics. Rev. ed. Homewood, Ill.: Richard D. Irwin, 1972.

Chamberlain, Neil W. Collective Bargaining. New York: McGraw-Hill, 1951.

_____. Labor. New York: McGraw-Hill, 1958.

_____. The Union Challenge to Management Control. New York: Harper, 1948.

Chandler, Margaret K. Management Rights and Union Interests. New York: McGraw-Hill, 1964.

Chernish, William N. Coalition Bargaining: A Study of Union Tactics and Public Policy. Philadelphia: University of Pennsylvania Press, 1969.

Coddington, Alan. Theories of the Bargaining Process. Chicago: Aldine, 1968.

Cohen, L. B. Work Staggering for Traffic Relief: An Analysis of Manhattan's Central Business District. New York: Praeger, 1968.

Cohen, Sanford. Labor in the United States. Columbus, Ohio: Charles E. Merrill, 1970.

Cooper, Norman L. Urban Transportation: An Answer. Bloomington: Indiana University Press, 1971.

Crouch, Winston W. Employer-Employee Relations in Council-Manager Cities. Washington, D.C.: International City Managers' Association, 1964.

Cullen, Donald. National Emergency Strikes. Ithaca: New York State School of Industrial and Labor Relations, Cornell University, 1968.

Curry, D. A., and R. G. McGillivray. Urban Transit Regulation and Planning in the San Francisco Bay Area. Palo Alto: Stanford Research Institute, 1971.

Dahl, Robert A., and Charles E. Lindblom. Politics, Economics and Welfare. New York: Harper & Row, 1953.

Danielson, Michael N. Federal-Metropolitan Politics and the Commuter Crisis. New York: Columbia University Press, 1965.

Davey, Harold W. Contemporary Collective Bargaining. 3d ed. Englewood Cliffs, N. J.: Prentice-Hall, 1972.

Davis, J. R. Elevated System and the Growth of Northern Chicago. Evanston: Northwestern University Press, 1965.

De Salvo, Joseph S., ed. Perspectives on Regional Transportation Planning. Lexington, Mass: Lexington Books, 1973.

Dickenson, S. Clark. Collective Wage Determination. New York: Ronald Press, 1941.

Domencich, Thomas A., and Gerald Kraft. Free Transit. Lexington, Mass. Lexington Books, 1970.

Domenico, Gagliardo. The Kansas Industrial Court, An Experiment in Compulsory Arbitration. Lawrence: University of Kansas Press, 1941.

Dunlop, John T. Collective Bargaining Principles and Cases. Chicago: Richard D. Irwin, 1949.

_____. Wage Determination Under Trade Unions. New York: Macmillan, 1944.

Dunlop, John T., and Neil W. Chamberlain. Frontiers of Collective Bargaining. New York: Harper & Row, 1967.

Estey, Marten. The Unions: Structure, Development and Management. 2d ed. New York: Harcourt, Brace and World, 1976.

Fitch, Lyle Craig. Urban Transportation and Public Policy. San Francisco: Chandler Publishing, 1964.

Fogel, Walter, and Archie Kleingartner. Contemporary Labor Issues. Belmont, Calif.: Wadsworth, 1968.

Foner, Philip. Organized Labor and the Black Worker, 1919-1973. New York: Praeger, 1974.

Friedman, Milton. Capitalism and Freedom. Chicago: University of Chicago Press, 1963.

Friedrich, Carl J., ed. The Public Interest. New York: Atherton Press, 1967.

Ginsberg, Eli, et al. Democratic Values and the Rights of Management. New York: Columbia University Press, 1963.

Gouldner, Alvin. Wildcat Strike. New York: Harper & Row, 1965.

Green, Constance M. The Secret City: A History of Race Relations in the Nation's Capital. Princeton: Princeton University Press, 1967.

Haefele, Edwin T., ed. Transport and National Goals. Washington, D.C.: Brookings Institution, 1969.

Haney, Dan G., et al. Traveler and Community Benefits from Proposed Los Angeles Rapid Transit System. Menlo Park: Stanford Research Institute, 1970.

Hanslowe, Kurt L. The Emerging Law of Labor Relations in Public Employment. Ithaca: New York State School of Industrial and Labor Relations, Cornell University, 1967.

Heistand, Dale L. Economic Growth and Employment Opportunities for Minorities. New York: Columbia University Press, 1964.

Held, Virginia. The Public Interest and Individual Interests. New York: Basic Books, 1970.

Henderson, Clark, et al. Final Report I—Future Urban Transportation Systems: Descriptions, Evaluations and Programs. Menlo Park: Stanford Reserach Institute, 1968.

Heyne, Paul T. Private Keepers of the Public Interest. New York: McGraw-Hill, 1968.

Hicks, J. R. The Theory of Wages. New York: Peter Smith, 1948.

Hilton, George W. Federal Transit Subsidies. Washington, D. C.: American Enterprise Institute for Public Policy Research, 1974.

Hilton, George W., and John F. Due. The Electric Interurban Railways in America. Palo Alto: Stanford University Press, 1960.

Homburger, Wolfgang S., ed. Urban Mass Transit Planning. Berkeley: University of California Press, 1967.

Horowitz, Morris Aaron. Manpower Utilization in the Railroad Industry: An Analysis of Working Rules and Practices. Boston: Northeastern University Press, 1960.

Horton, Raymond D. Municipal Labor Relations in New York City. New York: Praeger, 1973.

Huberman, Leo. The Great Bus Strike, New York: Modern Age Books, 1941.

Institute of Transportation and Traffic Engineering. New and Novel Transportation Systems—Planning Principles, Operating Characteristics and Costs. Berkeley: University of California, 1970.

International Labor Organization. Collective Bargaining and the Challenge of New Technology. Geneva: International Labor Organization, 1972.

Kennedy, Norman, and Wolfgang S. Homburger. The Organization of Metropolitan Transit Agencies. Berkeley: Institute of Transportation and Traffic Engineering, University of California, 1961.

Kennedy, Thomas. The Significance of Wage Uniformity. Philadelphia: University of Pennsylvania Press, 1948.

Kheel, Theodore W. Transit and Arbitration. Englewood Cliffs, N.J.: Prentice-Hall, 1960.

Kimley-Horn and Associates. Financial Resources Available for Transportation—Jacksonville Urban Area. Jacksonville: Jacksonville Area Planning Board, 1971.

Kirby, Ronald R., et al. Para-Transit: Neglected Options for Urban Mobility. Washington, D.C.: Urban Institute.

Kochan, Thomas A. City Employee Bargaining with a Divided Management. Madison: Industrial Relations Research Institute, University of Wisconsin, 1971.

Kruger, Daniel H. Collective Bargaining in the Public Service. New York: Random House, 1969.

Kuhn, Alfred. Arbitration in Transit: An Evaluation of Wage Criteria. Philadelphia: University of Pennsylvania Press, 1952.

_____. Labor Institutions and Economics. New York: Rinehart, 1956.

Kuhn, James W. Bargaining in Grievance Settlement. New York: Columbia University Press, 1961.

Kuhn, Tillo. Public Enterprise: Economics and Transport Problems. Berkeley: University of California Press, 1962.

Landsberg, Hans H., Leonard L. Fischman, and Joseph L. Fisher. Resources in America's Future, Patterns of Requirements and Availabilities, 1960-2000. Baltimore: Johns Hopkins Press, for Resources for the Future, Inc., 1963.

Lang, A. Scheffer, and Richard M. Soberman. Urban Rail Transit: Its Economics and Technology. Cambridge: M.I.T. Press, 1964.

Lasson, K. The Workers. New York: Grossman, 1971.

Levin, Myron J. Survey of Equal Employment Opportunities in New
Jersey Investor-Owned Public Utilities. Trenton: Division of
Civil Rights, Department of Law and Public Safety, 1966.

Levinson, Harold M. Determining Forces in Collective Bargaining.
New York: John Wiley, 1966.

Levinson, Harold M., et al. Collective Bargaining and Technological
Change in American Transportation. Evanston: Northwestern
University Press, 1971.

Lewis, H. Gregg. Unionism and Relative Wages in the U.S. Chicago:
University of Chicago Press, 1963.

Lieb, Robert C. Labor in the Transit Industry. Washington, D.C.:
Office of Transportation Systems Analysis and Information,
U.S. Department of Transportation, 1976.

_____. Labor in the Transportation Industries. New York:
Praeger, 1974.

Lindblom, Charles E. Unions and Capitalism. New Haven: Yale
University Press, 1949.

Lowenberg, J. Joseph, and Michael H. Moskow, eds. Collective
Bargaining in Government: Readings and Cases. Englewood
Cliffs, N.J.: Prentice-Hall, 1972.

McGinley, James J. Labor Relations in the New York Rapid Transit
Systems, 1904-1944. New York: Kings Crown Press, Columbia
University, 1949.

McKelvey, Jean T. Management Rights and the Arbitration Process.
Washington, D.C.: Bureau of National Affairs, 1956.

Marshall, Ray. The Negro Worker. New York: Random House, 1967.

_____. The Negro and Organized Labor. New York: John
Wiley, 1965.

Margolis, Julius., ed. The Analysis of Public Output. New York:
Columbia University Press, 1970.

Mason, Edward S. The Street Railway in Massachusetts. Cambridge:
    Harvard University Press, 1932.

Metropolitan Rapid Transit Commission. Metropolitan Rapid Transit
    Financing. New York: Metropolitan Rapid Transit Commission,
    1957.

Meyer, John R., J. F. Kain, and M. Wohl. The Urban Transportation
    Problem. Cambridge: Harvard University Press, 1965.

Meyer, John R., and M. R. Straszheim. Technique of Transport
    Planning. Vol. 1, "Pricing and Project Evaluation." Washing-
    ton, D.C.: Brookings Institution, 1971.

Miller, David R., ed. Urban Transportation Policy: New Perspectives.
    Lexington, Mass.: Lexington Books, 1973.

Miller, John. Fares Please. New York: Dover, 1960.

Morton, Herbert Charles. Public Contracts and Private Wages:
    Experience Under the Walsh-Healey Act. Washington, D.C.:
    Brookings Institution, 1965.

Moskow, Michael H., J. Joseph Lowenberg, and Edward Koziara,
    eds., Collective Bargaining in Public Employment. New York:
    Random House, 1970.

Morris, Charles J., ed. The Developing Labor Law. Washington,
    D.C.: Bureau of National Affairs, 1971.

Murin, William J. Mass Transit Policy Planning: An Incremental
    Approach. Lexington, Mass.: Heath-Lexington Books, 1971.

Nader, Ralph, et al., eds. Conference on Professional Responsibility,
    Washington 1971. New York: Grossman, 1972.

National Commission on Productivity and Work Quality. Employee
    Incentives to Improve State and Local Government Productivity.
    Washington, D.C.: U.S. Government Printing Office, 1975.

National Commission on Technology. The Outlook for Technological
    Change and Employment. Washington, D.C.: National Commis-
    sion on Technology, 1966.

Nigro, Felix A. Management-Employee Relations in the Public Service.
    Chicago: Public Personnel Association, 1969.

Northrup, Herbert R. Compulsory Arbitration and Government Intervention in Labor Disputes. Washington, D.C.: Labor Policy Association, 1966.

_____. Organized Labor and the Negro. New York: Harper and Brothers, 1944.

_____. Strike Controls in Essential Industries. Studies in Business Economics, no. 30. New York: National Industrial Conference Board, 1951.

Northrup, Herbert R. et al. Negro Employment in Basic Industry. Studies of Negro Employment. Vols. 1 and 5. Philadelphia: Industrial Research Unit, Wharton School of Finance and Commerce, University of Pennsylvania, 1970.

Northrup, Herbert R., and Gordon F. Bloom, Government and Labor. Homewood, Ill.: Richard D. Irwin, 1963.

Norton, Hugh S. National Transportation Policy: Formation and Implementation. Berkeley: McCutcheon, 1967.

O'Connell, W. H. Ride Free, Drive Free: The Transit Trust Fund and the Robin Hood Principle. New York: John Day, 1973.

Oi, Walter Y., and Paul W. Shuldiner. An Analysis of Urban Travel Demands. Evanston: Transportation Center, Northwestern University, 1962.

Owen, Wilfred. The Accessible City. Washington, D.C.: Brookings Institution, 1972.

_____. The Metropolitan Transportation Problem. Garden City, N.Y.: Doubleday, 1966.

Paranka, Stephen. Urban Transportation Dilemma. Atlanta: Georgia State College of Business Administration, 1961.

Pegrum, D. F. Transportation Economics and Public Policy. 3d ed. Homewood, Ill. : Richard D. Irwin, 1973.

Pen, J. The Wage Rate under Collective Bargaining. Cambridge: Harvard University Press, 1959.

Perlman, Richard. Wage Determination. Boston: D.C. Heath, 1965.

Peters, Charles, and Branch Taylor. Blowing the Whistle: Dissent in the Public Interest. New York: Praeger, 1972.

Rees, Albert. The Economics of Trade Unions. Chicago: University of Chicago Press, 1962.

Reische, Diana L., ed. Problems of Mass Transportation. New York: H. W. Wilson, 1970.

Reynolds, Lloyd G. Labor Economics and Labor Relations. New York: Prentice-Hall, 1949.

Richards, Brian. New Movement in Cities. London: Studio Vista, New York: Reinhold, 1966.

Risher, H. W. The Crises in Railroad Collective Bargaining: A Study of the Institutional Impediments to Change in the Industrial Relation System. Springfield, Virginia: National Technical Information Service, U. S. Department of Commerce, 1972.

Roberts, Harold S. Labor-Management Relations in the Public Service. Honolulu: Industrial Relations Center, University of Hawaii, 1968.

Ross, Arthur M. Trade Union Wage Policy. Berkeley: University of California Press, 1948.

Ross, Philip. The Government as A Source of Union Power: The Role of Public Policy in Collective Bargaining. Providence: Brown University Press, 1965.

Rubin, Richard S. A Summary of State Collective Bargaining Law in Public Employment. Public Employee Relations Report, no. 3. Ithaca: Cornell University Press, 1968.

Saso, Carmen D. Coping with Public Employee Strikes. Chicago: Public Personnel Association, 1970.

Schmidt, Emerson P. Industrial Relations in Urban Transportation. Minneapolis: University of Minnesota Press, 1937.

_____. Union Power and the Public Interest. Los Angeles: Nash, 1973.

Schneider, Lewis M. Marketing Urban Mass Transit. Boston: Division of Research, Graduate School of Business Administration, Harvard University, 1965.

Schroeder, Werner W. Metropolitan Transit Research Study. Chicago: Chicago Transit Authority, 1954.

Seidman, Joel, et al. The Worker Views His Union. Chicago: University of Chicago Press, 1958.

Seminar Research Bureau. Studies of Urban Transportation: Travel in the Boston Region 1959-1980. Chestnut Hill: Boston College, 1960-61.

Sharp, Clifford. Problems of Urban Passenger Transport. Leicester, Mass.: Leicester University Press, 1967.

Sheldon, Nancy W. The Economic and Social Impact of Investments in Public Transit. Lexington, Mass.: Lexington Books, 1973.

Slichter, Sumner. Basic Criteria Used in Wage Negotiations. Chicago: Association of Commerce and Industry, 1947.

_____. The Impact of Collective Bargaining on Management. Washington, D.C.: Brookings Institution, 1960.

_____. Union Policies and Industrial Management. Washington, D.C.: Brookings Institution, 1941.

Slichter, Sumner, James J. Healy, and E. Robert Livernash. The Impact of Collective Bargaining on Management. Washington, D.C.: Brookings Institution, 1960.

Smerk, George M. Readings in Urban Transportation. Bloomington: Indiana University Press, 1968.

_____. Urban Transportation: The Federal Role. Bloomington: Indiana University Press, 1965.

Smith, Bruce L. R., and D. C. Hague, eds. The Dilemma of Accountability in Modern Government: Independence Versus Control. London: Macmillan, 1971.

Smith, Leonard J. Collective Bargaining. New York: Prentice-Hall, 1946.

Smith, Russell, Harry Edwards, and R. Theodore Clark, Jr.
Labor Relations Law in the Public Sector—Cases and Materials.
Indianapolis: Bobbs-Merrill, 1974.

Smith, Wilbur, and Associates. Future Highways and Urban Growth.
New Haven: Wilbur Smith and Associates, 1961.

Stanford Research Institute. Future Urban Transportation Systems:
Descriptions, Evaluations, and Programs. Menlo Park:
Stanford Research Institute, 1968.

Stanley, David T. Managing Local Government Under Union Pressure.
Washington, D.C.: Brookings Institution, 1972.

Stolberg, Benjamin. The Story of the CIO. New York: Viking Press,
1938.

Stone, Tabor R. Beyond the Automobile: Reshaping the Transportation
Environment. Englewood Cliffs, N.J.: Prentice-Hall, 1971.

Tax Foundation. Urban Mass Transportation in Perspective. New
York: Tax Foundation, 1968.

Taylor, George W. Government Regulation of Industrial Relations.
New York: Prentice-Hall, 1948.

Troy, Leo. Trade Union Membership, 1897-1962. National Bureau
of Economic Research, Occasional Paper 92. New York: Columbia
University Press, 1965.

Turcott, J.K. The Path to Transit Peace. Englewood Cliffs, N.J.:
Prentice-Hall, 1960.

Vosloo, William B. Collective Bargaining in the Public Sector.
Chicago: Public Personnel Association, 1966.

Warner, Stanley L. Stochastic Choice of Mode in Urban Travel: A
Study in Binary Choice. Chicago: Northwestern University
Press, 1962.

Wellington, Harry H. The Unions and the Cities. Washington, D.C.:
Brookings Institution, 1972.

Whittemore, L. H. The Man Who Ran the Subways. New York: Holt,
Rinehart and Winston, 1968.

Whyte, William F. The Grievance Process. Lansing: Industrial
Relations Research Center, 1956.

Winnie, Richard E. Measuring the Effectiveness of Local Government
Services: Transportation. Washington, D.C.: Urban Institute,
1972.

Wirtz, W. Willard. Labor and the Public Interest. New York:
Harper & Row, 1964.

Wolkinson, Benjamin W. Blacks, Unions, and the EEOC. Lexington,
Mass.: Lexington Books, 1973.

Woodworth, Robert T., and Richard B. Peterson, eds. Collective
Negotiation for Public and Professional Employees. Glenview,
Illinois: Scott, Foresman, 1969.

Zagoria, Sam, ed. Public Workers and Public Unions. Englewood
Cliffs, N.J.: Prentice-Hall, 1972.

Zettel, Richard M., and Richard R. Carll. Summary Review of
Major Metropolitan Area Transportation Studies in the United
States. Berkeley: Institute of Transportation and Traffic
Engineering, University of California, 1962.

Zwerling, Stephen. Mass Transit and the Politics of Technology: A
Study of BART and the San Francisco Bay Area. New York:
Praeger, 1974.

ARTICLES

Ackley, Gardner. "Automation: Threat and Promise." New York
Times Magazine, March 22, 1964, pp. 16, 52, 54, 57.

Allen, W. B., and R. R. Mudge. "Technique to Assess the Micro-
Impact of a Transportation Investment." Appraisal Journal
43 (April 1975): 274-92.

Alpert, Jonathan. "Labor Relations in Public Employment—Can
Government Govern Itself?" Maryland Law Review 29 (1969):
40-58.

Altshuler, Alan. "The Federal Government and Paratransit." In
    Paratransit, Special Report 164, ed. Sandra Rosenbloom, pp.
    89-104. Washington, D.C.: Transportation Research Board,
    1976.

Annable, James E., Jr. "A Theory of Wage Determination in Public
    Employment." The Quarterly Review of Economics and Business
    14 (Winter 1974): 43-58.

Anderson, Arvid. "The Structure of Public Sector Bargaining." In
    Public Workers and Public Unions, ed. Sam Zagoria, pp. 37-
    52. Englewood Cliffs, N.J.: Prentice-Hall, 1972.

_____. "Strikes and Impasse Resolution in Public Employment."
    Michigan Law Review 67 (1969): 943-70.

Ashenfeter, Orley. "Racial Discrimination and Trade Unionism."
    Journal of Political Economy (May-June 1972): 491-504.

Atwood, Jay F. "Collective Bargaining's Challenge: Five Imperatives
    for Public Managers." Public Personnel Management (January-
    February 1976): 24-31.

Barbash, Jack. "Rationalization in the American Union." In Essays
    in Industrial Relations Theory, ed. Gerald G. Somers, pp. 147-
    62. Ames: Iowa State University Press, 1969.

_____. "The Impact of Technology on Labor-Management
    Relations." In Contemporary Labor Issues, ed. Walter Fogel
    and Archie Kleingartner, pp. 338-43. Belmont, Calif.:
    Wadsworth, 1968.

Barnum, Darold T. "From Private to Public: Labor Relations in
    Urban Transit." Industrial and Labor Relations Review 25
    (October 1971): 95-115.

_____. "National Public Labor Relations Legislation: The
    Case of Urban Mass Transit." Labor Law Journal 27 (March
    1976): 168-76.

Bennett, George. "The Public Interest and Public Unions." Public
    Personnel Management 3 (November-December 1974): 545-50.

Berg, John T., Stanley Miller, and Edward Fleishman. "Labor Costs and Productivity for the Lindenwold Rapid Rail Line and the Shirley Highway Rapid Bus Demonstration Project: Some Preliminary Findings." Transportation Journal 14 (Fall 1974): 46-50.

Bernstein, Merton C. "Alternatives to the Strike in Public Labor Relations." Harvard Law Review 85 (1971): 459-75.

Bers, Melvin. "The Right to Strike in the Public Sector." Labor Law Journal 21 (1970): 482-84.

Biles, George E. "Allegiances of Unionized Public Employees Toward Employer and Union." Public Personnel Management 3 (March-April 1974): 165-69.

Bilik, A. "Close the Gap: NLRB and Public Employees." Ohio State Law Journal 31 (Summer 1970): 456-89.

Blasingame, Ernest N. "Public Employees: No Right to Strike." Tennessee Law Review 38 (1971): 403-39.

Bloch, Marc J. "Public Employees' Right to Strike." Cleveland-Marshall Law Review 18 (1969): 392-406.

Bloedorn, John. "The Strike and the Public Sector." Labor Law Journal 20 (1969): 151-60.

Burton, John F., Jr. "Can Public Employees be Given the Right to Strike?" Labor Law Journal 21 (1970): 472-78.

_____. "Local Government Bargaining and Management Structure." Industrial Relations 2 (May 1972), 123-39.

Burton, John F., Jr. and Charles Krider. "The Role and Consequences of Strikes by Public Employees." The Yale Law Journal 74 (January 1970): 428-32.

Carr, Robert B. "MBTA Must Negotiate 26 Separate Contracts." Boston Sunday Globe, February 7, 1971, pp. 29, 47.

Chamberlain, Neil W. "Comparability Pay and Compulsory Arbitration in Municipal Bargaining." In Collective Bargaining in Government: Readings and Cases, ed. J. Joseph Lowenberg and Michael Moskow, pp. 342-46. Englewood Cliffs, N.J.: Prentice-Hall, 1972.

_____. "Public vs. Private Sector Bargaining." In Collective Bargaining in Government: Readings and Cases, ed. J. Joseph Lowenberg and Michael Moskow. Englewood Cliffs, N.J.: Prentice-Hall, 1972.

_____. "The Union Challenge to Management Control." Industrial and Labor Relations Review 17 (January 1963): 184-92.

Chatterjee, A., and K. C. Sinha. "Distribution of Benefits of Public Transit Projects." Transportation Engineering Journal 101 (August 1975), 505-19.

Clary, Jack R. "Pitfalls of Collective Bargaining in Public Employment." Labor Law Journal 18 (July 1967): 401-11.

Conway, Thomas, "Franchises and Public Regulation." In Principles of Urban Transportation, ed. Frank H. Mossman. Cleveland: Western Reserve University, 1951.

Cook, A. H. "Union Structure in Municipal Collective Bargaining." Monthly Labor Review 89 (June 1966): 606-08.

Copozza, D. R. "Measuring the Benefits of Urban Improvements." Annals of Regional Science 9 (July 1975): 46-60.

Crouch, Winston W. "The American City and its Organized Employees." In Collective Bargaining in Government: Readings and Cases, ed. J. Joseph Lowenberg and Michael H. Moskow, pp. 72-80. Englewood Cliffs, N. J.: Prentice-Hall, 1972.

Davey, Harold B. "Hazards in Labor Arbitration." Industrial and Labor Relations Review, April 1948, pp. 386-405.

Davis, J. A. "Employment of Negroes in Local Transit Industry." Opportunity 22 (April-June 1944): 63-65.

Davis, Pearce, and Gopal C. Pati. "Elapsed Grievance Time, 1942-1972." Arbitration Journal, March 1974, p. 21.

Denise, M. L., and R. H. Sarry. "Collective Bargaining and the National Interest." Personnel 39 (November 1962): 15-32.

Derber, Milton, W. Ellison Chalmers, and Ross Stagner. "Collective Bargaining and Management Functions: An Empirical Study." Journal of Business 31 (April 1958): 107-20.

Derber, Milton, et al. "Bargaining and Budget Making in Illinois
    Public Institutions." Industrial and Labor Review 27 (October
    1973): 49-62.

"Does This Man Have the U.S. by the Throat?" Skeptic, May-June,
    1976, pp. 54-55.

Douglas, G. W. "Price Regulation and Optimal Service Standards."
    Journal of Transport Economics and Policy 6 (1972): 116-27.

Due, John F. "Urban Mass Transit Policy: A Review Article." The
    Quarterly Review of Economics and Business 16 (Spring 1976):
    93-105.

Dunlop, John T. "The Economics of Wage Dispute Settlement." Law
    and Contemporary Problems, Spring 1947, pp. 281-96.

_____. "The Function of A Strike." In Frontiers of Collective
    Bargaining, ed. John T. Dunlop and Neil Chamberlain, pp.
    103-121. New York: Harper & Row, 1967.

Erstling, J. "Federal Regulation of Non-Federal Public Employment."
    Labor Law Journal 24 (November 1973): 739-54.

Fallon, William J. "For Some Order in Public Employee Bargaining."
    Labor Law Journal 21 (1970): 434-37.

Feigenbaum, Charles. "Civil Service and Collective Bargaining:
    Conflict or Compatibility." Public Personnel Management 3
    (May-June 1974): 165-69.

Fogel, Walter, and David Lewin. "Wage Determination in the Public
    Sector." Industrial and Labor Relations Review 27 (April 1974):
    410-31.

Fosser, P. T., Jr. "Right to Union Representation Under Executive
    Order 11491." Labor Law Journal 25 (September 1974): 531-39.

Frankel, Saul. "Employer-Employee Relations in the Public Service."
    Public Personnel Review 25 (1964): 220-25.

Freeman, Lee A. "Fringe Issues and Their Cost." Mass Transporta-
    tion, November 1947, pp. 570-74.

Friedman, Milton. "Some Comments on the Significance of Labor Unions for Economic Policy." The Impact of the Union., ed. David McCord Wright. New York: Harcourt, Brace, 1951.

Friend, Edward H. "First National Municipal Employee Benefit Survey Shows Cities Pay More Than Industry." LMRS Newsletter, October 1972, pp. 1-3.

Freund, J. L. "Market and Union Influences on Municipal Employee Wages." Industrial and Labor Relations Review 27 (May-June 1974): 391-404.

Frey, Alexander H. "The Logic of Collective Bargaining and Arbitration." Law and Contemporary Problems, Spring 1947, pp. 264-80.

Frye, Jack. "Attrition in Job Elimination." Labor Law Journal 14 (September 1963): 809-17.

Fusilier, H. L., and Lawrence Steinmetz. "Public Employee Strikes: An Operational Solution." Quarterly Review of Economics and Business 7 (1967): 29-36.

Gilbert, Henderson. "Bankruptcy—Socialization—Profit—Which?" Passenger Transport, Convention Issue (1949): 9.

Gilroy, Thomas, and Anthony Sinicropi. "Impasse Resolution in Public Employment: A Current Assessment." Industrial and Labor Relations Review 25 (1972): 496-511.

Goble, George. "The Non-Stoppage Strike," Labor Law Journal 2 (1951): 105-14.

Goldberg, Joseph P. "Changing Policies in Public Employee Labor Relations." Monthly Labor Review 93 (July 1970): 5-14.

_____. "Labor Management Relations Laws in Public Service." Monthly Labor Review 91 (June 1968): 984-86.

Golob, T. F., and R. L. Gustafson. "Economic Analysis of a Demand-Responsive Public Transportation System." In Highway Research Record 367. Washington, D.C.: Highway Research Board, 1971.

Gotbaum, Victor. "Collective Bargaining and the Union Leader."
In Public Workers and Public Unions, ed. Sam Zagoria, pp.
77-88. Englewood Cliffs, N.J.: Prentice-Hall, 1972.

Gould, W. B. "Labor Relations and Race Relations." In Public
Workers and Public Unions, ed. Sam Zagoria. Englewood
Cliffs, N.J.: Prentice-Hall, 1972.

Gray, D. W. "It's the Law—No Utilities Strikes in Virginia." Bus
Transportation, December 1949, p. 63.

Gregory, Charles O. "Injunctions, Seizure and Compulsory Arbitration." Temple Law Quarterly 26 (1953): 397-405.

Grodin, Joseph R. "Arbitration of Public Sector Labor Disputes:
the Nevada Experiment." Industrial and Labor Relations Review
28 (October 1974): 89-102.

_____. "Either-Or Arbitration for Public Employee Disputes."
Industrial Relations 11 (May 1972): 260-266.

Haemmel, William. "Government Employees and the Right to Strike—
The Final Necessary Step." Tennessee Law Review 39 (1971):
75-88.

Hall, James T. "Work Stoppages in Government." Monthly Labor
Review 91 (1969): 53-54.

Halligan, Patrick D. "Enjoining Public Employees' Strikes: Dealing
with Recalcitrant Defendants." DePaul Law Review 19 (1969):
298-317.

Hamermesh, Daniel S. "The Effect of Government Ownership on
Wages." In Labor in the Public and Nonprofit Sectors, ed. Daniel
S. Hamermesh. Princeton: Princeton University Press, 1975.

Hardman, J. B. S. "Union Objectives and Social Power." In
American Labor Dynamics, ed. J. B. S. Hardman. New York:
Harcourt, Brace, 1928.

Hartman, Paul. "Industrial Relations in the News Media." Industrial
Relations Journal 6 (Winter 1975-76): 4-18.

Kain, John. "The Unexplored Potential of Freeway Rapid Transit in
    Regional Transportation Planning: An Atlanta Case Study." In
    Unorthodox Approaches to Urban Transportation: The Emerging
    Challenge to Conventional Planning, ed. Andrew Hamer. Atlanta:
    Bureau of Business and Economic Research, Georgia State
    University, 1972.

Kain, John, and John R. Meyer. "Transportation and Poverty." The
    Public Interest (1970).

Kanwit. Edmond L. "The Urban Mass Transportation Administration:
    Its Problems and Promises." In Urban Transportation Policy:
    New Perspectives, ed. David R. Miller. Lexington, Mass.:
    Lexington Books, 1972.

Karr Robert. "Labor Law—Strikes by Public Employees—The
    Invalidity of the Prohibition." DePaul Law Review 19 (1969):
    377-93.

Kennedy, Van Dusen. "Grievance Negotiation." In Industrial Conflict,
    ed. Arthur Kornhauser, Robert Dubin, and Arthur Ross. New
    York: McGraw-Hill, 1954.

Kheel, Theodore. "Strikes in Public Employment." Michigan Law
    Review 67 (March 1969): 931-42.

Kochan, T. A. "A Theory of Multilateral Collective Bargaining in
    City Governments." Industrial and Labor Relations Review 27
    (July 1974): 525-42.

_____. "Correlates of State Public Employee Bargaining
    Laws." Industrial and Labor Relations Review 12 (October 1973);
    322-37.

Kochan, T. A., et al. "Determinants of Intraorganizational Conflict
    in Collective Bargaining in the Public Sector." Administrative
    Science Quarterly 20 (March 1975): 10-23.

Koczak, Stephen A. "Collective Bargaining and Comparability in the
    Federal Sector." In Industrial Relations Research Proceedings
    of the Twenty-Eighth Annual Winter Meeting, ed. James Stern
    and Barbara Dennis, pp. 197-204. Madison: Industrial Relations
    Research Association, 1976.

Kovner, Joseph, and Herbert Lahne. "Shop Society and the Union."
    Industrial and Labor Relations Review 7 (October 1953): 3-14.

Krislov, Joseph. "The Cleveland Transit Strike of 1949." Personnel
    Administration 13 (November 1950): 25-30.

_____. "Work Stoppages of Government Employees, 1942-
    1959." Quarterly Review of Economics and Business 1 (1961):
    87-92.

Kuhn, James W. "Encroachments on the Right to Manage." California
    Management Review 5 (Fall 1962): 23-27.

_____. "The Grievance Process." In Frontiers of Collective
    Bargaining, ed. John Dunlop and Neil W. Chamberlain. New
    York: Harper & Row, 1967.

Hayes, Frederick O'R. "Collective Bargaining and the Budget
    Director." In Public Workers and Public Unions, ed. Sam
    Zagoria, pp. 89-100. Englewood Cliffs, N.J.: Prentice-Hall,
    1972.

Heathington, K. W., et al. "An Example of Demand-Responsive
    Transportation Systems in the Private Sector." In Transporta-
    tion Research Record 522. Washington, D.C.: Transportation
    Research Board, 1974.

Herman, Joseph. "Strikes by Public Employees: The Search for
    Right Principles." Chicago Bar Record 53 (1971): 57-67.

Hildebrand, George H. "The Public Sector." In Frontiers of
    Collective Bargaining, ed. John T. Dunlop and Neil W. Chamber-
    lain. New York: Harper & Row, 1967.

Hilton, George W. "Rail Transit and the Pattern of Modern Cities:
    The California Case." Traffic Quarterly 21 (1967): 379-93.

Hoelling, Michael F. "Expediated Grievance Arbitration: The First
    Steps." In Industrial Relations Research Proceedings of the
    Twenty-Seventh Annual Winter Meeting, ed. James Stern and
    Barbara Dennis. Madison: Industrial Relations Research
    Association, 1975.

Holley, William H., Jr. "Unique Complexities of Public Sector Labor
    Relations." Personnel Journal 55 (February 1976): 72-75.

Houseman, K. A. "Compulsory Arbitration in the Public Sector: Constitutionality and Enforcement Issues." Public Personnel Management 2 (May-June 1973): 194-99.

Howlett, Robert G. "Right to Strike in the Public Sector." Chicago Bar Record 53 (1971): 108-16.

Imundo, Louis V. "Federal Government Sovereignty and Its Effect on Labor-Management Relations." Labor Law Journal 26 (March 1975): 146-51.

_____. "Some Comparisons Between Public Sector and Private Sector Bargaining." Labor Law Journal 24 (December 1973): 810-17.

Ives, R., et al. "Mass Transit and the Power Elite." Review of Radical Political Economics 4 (Summer 1972): 68-77.

Jedel, M. J., and W. T. Rutherford. "Public Labor Relations in the Southeast: Review, Synthesis and Prognosis." Labor Law Journal 28 (August 1974): 483-95.

Jensen, Edward. "Pittsburgh's Venture into Public Transit." Pittsburgh Business Review 37 (August 1967): 1-6.

Joseph, Myron L. "Approaches to Collective Bargaining in Industrial Relations Theory." In Essays in Industrial Relations Theory, ed. Gerald D. Somers. Ames: Iowa State University Press, 1969.

Lester, Richard A. "A Range Theory of Wage Differentials." Industrial and Labor Relations Review 5 (July 1952): 485.

_____. "Benefits as A Preferred Form of Compensation." Southern Economic Journal 33 (April 1967): 488-95.

Lehrer, Seymour H. "The Maryland Public Utilities Disputes Act." Labor Law Journal 7 (October 1956): 607-17.

Lev, Edward R. "Strikes by Government Employees: Problems and Solutions." American Bar Association Journal 57 (1971): 771-77.

Lewin, David. "Public Employment Relations: Confronting the Issues." Industrial Relations, October 1973, pp. 309-21.

Lisco, Thomas E. "Mass Transportation: Cinderella in Our Cities."
    The Public Interest 18 (1970): 52-74.

Livernash, E. R. "The Relation of Power to the Structure and Process
    of Collective Bargaining." The Journal of Law and Economics
    6 (October 1963): 10-40.

Long, Gary, and Peter Feuille. "Final Offer Arbitration: Sudden
    Death in Eugene." Industrial and Labor Relations Review 27
    (January 1974): 186-203.

Lovell, Hugh C. "The Pressure Lever in Mediation." Industrial
    and Labor Relations Review 6 (October 1952): 20-30.

Lowenberg, J. Joseph. "Compulsory Arbitration for Police and
    Firefighters in Pennsylvania in 1968." Industrial and Labor
    Relations Review 23 (April 1970): 337-70.

_____. "The Effect of Compulsory Arbitration on Collective
    Negotiations." Journal Of Collective Negotiations in the Public
    Sector, May 1972, pp. 177-90.

Lurie, Melvin. "Government Regulations and Union Power: A Case
    Study of the Boston Transit Industry." The Journal of Law
    and Economics 3 (October 1960): 118-35.

McKelvey, Jean T. "The Role of State Agencies in Public Employee
    Labor Relations." Industrial and Labor Relations Review 20
    (January 1967): 182-97.

McKersie, Robert B., and William M. Shropshire, Jr. "Avoiding
    Written Grievances: A Successful Program." Journal of
    Business 25 (April 1962): 135-52.

MacMahon, A. W. "The New York City Transit System: Public
    Ownership, Civil Service, and Collective Bargaining." Political
    Science Quarterly 56 (June 1941).

Maher, John E. "Union, Nonunion Wage Differentials." American
    Economic Review 46 (June 1956): 336-52.

Marceau, LeRoy, and Richard A. Musgrave. "Strikes in Essential
    Industries: A Way Out." Harvard Business Review 27 (1949):
    286-92.

Marshall, Howard D., and Natalie G. Marshall. "Non-Stoppage Strike Proposals—A Critique." Labor Law Journal 7 (1956): 299-304.

Marshall, Ray. "Union Racial Problems in the South." Industrial Relations 1 (May 1962): 117-28.

Mayer, H. M. "High-Speed Rail Passenger Transportation and Regional Development in the Midwest." Traffic Quarterly 21 (July 1967): 395-405.

Merewitz, Leonard. "Public Transportation: Wish Fulfillment and Reality in the San Francisco Bay Area." American Economic Review 62 (May 1972): 78-86.

Meyers, Frederic. "Organization and Collective Bargaining in the Local Mass Transportation Industry in the Southeast." Southern Economic Journal 15 (April 1949): 425-40.

Mobley, T. C. "Union Scales in Four Industries, July 1, 1961." Monthly Labor Review 85 (August 1962): 893-97.

_____. "Union Wage Scales of Local Transit Operating Employees 1959." Monthly Labor Review 83 (February 1960): 164-66.

Morris, Michael. "Public Employee Unions—The Political Imperative." Journal of Collective Negotiators in the Public Sectors 4 (1973): 369-80.

New, C. C. "Transport Fleet Planning for Multi-Period Operations." Operational Research Quarterly 26 (April 1975): 151-66.

Northrup, Herbert R. "Fact-Finding in Labor Disputes: The States' Experience." Industrial and Labor Relations Review 17 (October 1963).

_____. "The Railway Labor Act: A Critical Reappraisal." Industrial and Labor Relations Review 25 (October 1971).

Northrup, Herbert R., and Richard L. Rowan. "Arbitration and Collective Bargaining: An Analysis of State Experience." Labor Law Journal 14 (February 1963).

_____. "State Seizure in Public Interest Disputes." Journal of Business of the University of Chicago 26 (April 1963).

Notes. "Government Employees and Unionism." Harvard Law Review
    54 (1941): 1360-68.

_____. "Labor Relations in the Public Service." Harvard Law
    Review 75 (1961): 391-13.

_____. "New York Sends $2.5 Billion Bond to Voters." IRT
    Digest 5 (July-August 1971): 14-15.

_____. "The Due Process Rights of Public Employees." New
    York University Law Review 50 (May 1965): 310-65.

Palmer, Foster M. "The Literature of the Street Railway." Howard
    Library Bulletin 12 (Winter 1958): 117-38.

Parker, Hyman. "The Role of the Michigan Labor Mediation Board
    in Public Employee Labor Disputes." Labor Law Journal 10
    (September 1959): 633-42.

Peck, M. J., and J. R. Meyer. "The Determination of a Fair Return
    on Investment for Regulated Industries." In Transportation
    Economics. New York: National Bureau of Economic Research,
    1965.

Pollitt, Daniel H. "Union Security in America." The American
    Federationist 80 (October 1973): 16.

Prasow, Paul. "The Theory of Management Reserved Rights—Revi-
    sited." In Industrial Relations Research Association Proceedings
    of the Twenty-Sixth Annual Winter Meeting. Madison: Industrial
    Relations Research Association, 1974. 74-84.

"Public Employees vs. the Cities." Business Week, July 21, 1975.

Rainville, Walter, S., Jr. "Transit Faces the Future." Traffic
    Quarterly, April 1960.

Raskin, A. H. "Mayor and Governor: Knee-Deep in Trouble." In
    Collective Negotiation for Public and Professional Employees,
    ed. Robert T. Woodworth and Richard B. Peterson. Glenview,
    Ill.: Scott, Foresman, 1969.

_____. "Politics Up-Ends the Bargaining Table." In Public
    Workers and Public Unions, ed. Sam Zagoria. Englewood Cliffs,
    N.J.: Prentice-Hall, 1972.

Ray, Jack N. "The Compatibility of Public Employment Collective Bargaining with Public Interest." Labor Law Journal 18 (December 1967): 752-55.

Rees, Albert. "The Effects of Union on Resource Allocation." The Journal of Law and Economics 6 (October 1963): 69-78.

Rehmus, Charles M. "Constraints on Local Governments in Public Employee Bargaining." Michigan Law Review 67 (March 1969): 917-30.

_____. "Is A Final Offer Ever Final?" Monthly Labor Review 97 (September 1974): 43-45.

_____. "Legislated Interest Arbitration." In Proceedings of the Twenty-Seventh Annual Winter Meeting, ed. James Stern and Barbara Dennis. Madison: Industrial Relations Research Association, 1975.

Renshaw, E. F. "Alternate Sources of Financing for Mass Transit Subsidies: A Note." Land Economics 50 (May 1974): 171-76.

_____. "Note on Mass Transit Subsidies." National Tax Journal 26 (December 1973), 639-44.

Robins, Eva. "Some Comparisons of Mediation in the Public and Private Sector." In Collective Bargaining in Government: Readings and Cases, ed. J. Joseph Lowenberg and Michael Moskow. Englewood Cliffs, N. J.: Prentice-Hall, 1972.

Rock, E. "Research on Municipal Collective Bargaining." Monthly Labor Review 89 (June 1966): 615-16.

Ross, Arthur M. "Public Employee Unions and the Right to Strike." Monthly Labor Review 92 (March 1969): 14-18.

_____. "The Influence of Unionism Upon Earnings." Quarterly Journal of Economics 62 (February 1948): 263-86.

Ross, D. B. "The Arbitration of Public Employee Wage Disputes." Industrial And Labor Relations Review 23 (October 1969): 3-14.

Ryder, M. S. "Some Concepts Concerning Grievance Procedure." Labor Law Journal 7 (January 1956): 15-18.

Sastry, M. V. R. "Systems Approach to Cost-Benefit Analysis of
    Urban Transportation." Transportation Journal 12 (Spring
    1973): 39-45.

Schott, G. J., and L. L. Leisher. "Common Starting Point for
    Intercity Passenger Transportation Planning." Astronautics
    and Aeronautics 13 (July-August 1973): 38-55.

Schregel, J. "Labour Relations in the Public Section." International
    Labor Review 110 (November 1974): 381-404.

_____. "Workers' Participation in Management." Industrial
    and Labor Relations Review 9 (February 1970): 117-22.

Shils, Edward B. "Transportations's Labor Difficulties." Harvard
    Business Review (May-June 1964): 84-98.

_____. "Union Fragmentation: A Major Cause of Transportation
    Crises." Industrial and Labor Relations Review 25 (October
    1971): 32-52.

Shultz, George P. "Strategies for National Labor Policy." The
    Journal of Law and Economics 6 (October 1963): 1-9.

Siegel, Jay S., and Burton Kainen. "Political Forces in Public
    Sector Collective Bargaining." Catholic University Law Review
    21 (1972): 581-88.

Smardon, Raymond A. "Arbitration is No Bargain." Nation's Business
    62 (October 1974): 80-83.

Smerk, George M. "An Evaluation of Ten Years of Federal Policy
    in Urban Mass Transportation." Transportation Journal 11
    (Winter 1971): 45-57.

_____. "Development of Federal Mass Transportation Policy."
    Indiana Law Journal 47 (1972): 249-92.

_____. "Evaluation of Federal Effort in Mass Transportation."
    Traffic Quarterly, October 1972, pp. 501-16.

_____. "Federal Transit Policy: Speculation on the Future."
    Transit Journal 1 (August 1975): 5-20.

Statter, Robert. "Principles of Arbitration in Wage Rate Disputes." Industrial and Labor Relations Review 1 (April 1948): 385-94.

Staudohar, Paul D. "Individual and Collective Rights in Public Employment Appeals Procedures." Labor Law Journal, 26 (July 1975), 435-38.

_____. "Quasi-Strikes by Public Employees." Journal of Collective Negotiations in the Public Sector 3 (Fall 1974): 363-71.

_____. "Some Implications of Mediation for Resolution of Bargaining Impasses in Public Employment." Public Personnel Management 2 (July-August 1973): 299-304.

Steiber, Jack. "Collective Bargaining in the Public Sector." In Challenges to Collective Bargaining, ed. Lloyd Ulman. Englewood Cliffs, N.J.: Prentice-Hall, 1967.

Stephens, Waldo E. "Is Three-Man Arbitration Too Much Like A Packed Jury?" Mass Transportation, March 1947, p. 91.

Stepp, John R. "The Determinants of Southern Public Employee Recognition." Public Personnel Management 3 (January-February 1974): 59-69.

Smith, A. B., Jr. "Impact on Collective Bargaining of Equal Employment Opportunity Remedies." Industrial and Labor Relations Review 28 (April 1975): 376-94.

Smith, R. A. "State and Local Advisory Reports on Public Employment Labor Legislation: A Comparative Analysis." Michigan Law Review 67 (March 1969): 891-918.

Stern, James L. "Alternative Dispute Settlement Procedures." Wisconsin Law Review (1968): 1100-12.

_____. "Final Offer Arbitration—Initial Experience in Wisconsin." Monthly Labor Review 97 (September 1974): 39-43.

Stevens, Carl. "Mediation and the Role of the Neutral." In Frontiers of Collective Bargaining, ed. John T. Dunlop and Neil W. Chamberlain. New York: Harper & Row, 1967.

Sulzner, George T. "The Impact of Impasse Procedures in Public
    Sector Labor: An Overview." Journal of Collective Negotiations
    in the Public Sector 4 (1975): 3-22.

Sussna, Edward. "Collective Bargaining on the New York City Transit
    System, 1940-57." Industrial and Labor Relations Review 11
    (July 1958): 518-33.

Taylor, George W. "Can Wages Be Left to Collective Bargaining?"
    In Wages, Prices and the National Welfare, ed. University of
    California Institute of Industrial Relations. Berkeley: University
    of California Press, 1948.

_____. "Criteria in the Wage Bargain." In First Annual
    Conference on Labor. New York: New York University Press,
    1948.

_____. "Public Employment: Strikes or Procedures?"
    Industrial and Labor Relations Review 20 (1967): 617-36.

Tillery, Winston L. "Layoff and Recall Provisions in Major Agree-
    ments." Monthly Labor Review 94 (July 1971): 41-46.

Ullman, J. C., and J. P. Begin. "The Structure and Scope of Appeals
    Procedures for Public Employees." Industrial and Labor
    Relations Review 23 (April 1970): 323-40.

Veerapandian, M., and S. Ramani. "Simulation of a Metropolitan
    Bus System." Simulation: Technical Journal of Society for
    Computer Simulation 24 (June 1975): 133-36.

Vickrey, William. "Pricing as a Tool in Coordination of Local
    Transportation." In Transportation Economics. New York:
    Columbia University Press, 1965.

Wachs, Martin. "Fostering Technological Innovation in Urban
    Transportation." Traffic Quarterly, January 1971, pp. 39-53.

Warner, Kenneth O. "Financial Implications of Employee Bargaining
    in the Public Service." Municipal Finance 40 (August 1967):
    34-39.

Weber, Arnold R. "Public Policy and the Scope of Collective Bar-
    gaining." Labor Law Journal 13 (January 1962): 49-70.

_____. "Stability and Change in the Structure of Collective Bargaining." In Challenges to Collective Bargaining, ed. Lloyd Ulman. Englewood Cliffs, N.J.: Prentice-Hall, 1967.

Weissbrodt, Sylvia. "Changes in State Labor Laws in 1970." Monthly Labor Review 94 (January 1971): 15-16.

Wellington, Harry H., and R. K. Winter, Jr. "More on Strikes by Public Employees." Yale Law Journal 79 (January 1970): 441-43.

_____. "Structuring Collective Bargaining in Public Employment." Yale Law Journal 79 (April 1970).

_____. "The Limits of Collective Bargaining in Public Employment." Yale Law Journal 77 (June 1969): 1107-127.

White, Leonard. "Strikes in the Public Service." Public Personnel Review 10 (1949): 3-10.

White, Sheila C. "Work Stoppages of Government Employees." Monthly Labor Review 92 (December 1969): 29-34.

Wisehart, A. M. "Transportation Strike Control Legislation: A Congressional Challenge." Michigan Law Review 66 (June 1968): 1697-1722.

Witney, Fred. "Final Offer Arbitration: The Indianapolis Experience." Monthly Labor Review 96 (May 1973): 220-25.

Wolk, Stuart R. "Public Employee Strikes—A Survey of the Condon-Wadlin Acts." New York Law Forum 13 (1967): 69-79.

Young, Dallas M. "Fifty Years of Labor Arbitration in Cleveland Transit." Monthly Labor Review 83 (May 1960): 464-71.

Young, Stanley. "The Question of Managerial Prerogatives." Industrial and Labor Relations Review 17 (January 1963): 240-53.

Young, T. E., and B. L. Brewer. "Strikes by State and Local Government Employees." Industrial Relations 9 (May 1970): 356-61.

Zack, Arnold M. "Are Strikes of Public Employees Necessary?"
American Bar Association Journal 53 (1967): 808-10.

_____. "Impasses, Strikes, and Resolutions." In Public
Workers and Public Unions, ed. Sam Zagoria. Englewood
Cliffs, N.J.: Prentice-Hall, 1972.

_____. "Meeting the Rising Cost of Public Sector Settlements."
Monthly Labor Review 96 (May 1973): 38-40.

_____. "Why Public Employees Strike." Arbitration Journal
23 (1968): 69-84.

Zagoria, Sam. "Fringe Benefits—A 'Second' Paycheck." American
City, February 1973, pp. 48-50.

OFFICIAL SOURCES

Amalgamated Association v. Wisconsin Employment Relations Board.
340 U.S. 383 (1951).

Amalgamated Transit Union, Division 618 v. Rhode Island Public
Transit Authority. July 31, 1967.

City of Cleveland v. Division 268 of Amalgamated Association. 90
N.E. 2d 711.

City of Detroit v. Division 26 of Amalgamated Association. 332
Michigan 237, 51 N.W. 2d 228.

Commonwealth of Pennsylvania. An Act Protecting the Rights of
Employees of Existing Transportation Systems Which Are
Acquired by Cities of the Third Class or . . . P.L. 628,
(1967).

_____. Metropolitan Transportation Authorities Act of 1963.
P.L. 450 (1963).

Consent Order in Civil Action No. 70-2946, Section D. Henry Faggen
v. New Orleans Public Service Inc., et al. U.S. District Court,
Eastern District of Louisiana, entered March 8, 1974.

Dade County v. Motor Coach Employees. 157 So 2d 176.

Division 2187 Amalgamated Association v. State of Missouri. 374
    U.S. 74 (1963).

Fair Labor Standards Act. 52 Stat. 1060 (1970), SS 2(r) and 7(b)(7).

General Electric Company v. Callahan. 294 F. 2d 60 (1962).

Grand Rapids City Coach Lines v. Howlett. 137 F. Supp. 667 (1956).

Labor Management Relations Service. "A Spotlight on City Employee
    Benefits, First National Survey of Employee Benefits for Full-
    Time Personnel of U.S. Municipalities." Mimeographed.
    Washington: U.S. Civil Service Commission, 1972.

National Labor Relations Act, 29 U.S.C. SS 151-168.

National Labor Relations Board v. Baltimore Transit Company. 140
    F. 2d 51 (CA-4, 1944), cert. den., 64 S. Ct. 847 (1944).

New Orleans Union Passenger Terminal Case. 282 ICC 271 (1952).

New York City Transit Authority v. Loos. 2 Misc. 2d 733 (1956),
    154 N.Y.S. 2d 209, Affirmed 3 A.D. 2d 740, 161 N.Y.S. 2d
    564.

Oklahoma Ry. Company, Trustees Abandonment. 257 ICC 177 (1944).

Order of the Interstate Commerce Commission in Finance Docket No.
    15920. New Orleans Union Passenger Terminal Case, 282 ICC
    271 (January 16, 1952).

Tate v. Philadelphia Transportation Company. 190 A 2d 136 (1963),
    410 Pa. 490.

U.S., Bureau of the Budget, Office of Statistical Standards. Standard
    Industrial Classification Manual. Washington, D.C.: U.S.
    Government Printing Office, 1967.

U.S. Congress, House. Committee on Banking and Currency. Hear-
    ings, Metropolitan Mass Transportation. 86th Cong., 2d
    sess. Washington, D.C.: U.S. Government Printing Office,
    1960.

_____. Hearings, Urban Mass Transportation 1961. 87th
    Cong., 1st sess. Washington, D.C.: U.S. Government Printing
    Office, 1961.

_____ . Hearings, Urban Mass Transportation Act of 1962.
87th Cong. , 2nd sess. Washington, D.C.: U. S. Government Printing Office, 1962.

_____ . Urban Mass Transportation Act of 1962. Hearings
before Subcommittee No. 3 of the Committee on Banking and
Currency on H.R. 11158. pp. 519-20. 87th Cong. , 2d sess.
Washington, D.C.: U.S. Government Printing Office, 1962.

U.S. Congress, House. Committee of the Whole House on the State
of the Union. The Transportation System of Our Nation: Message
from the President of the United States. 87th Cong. , 2d sess.
H. Doc. 384, p. 9. Washington, D.C.: U.S. Government
Printing Office, 1962.

U.S. Congress, Office of Technology Assessment. Automated
Guideway Transit: An Assessment of PRT and Other New
Systems. Report prepared at the request of the Senate
Committee on Appropriations, Transportation Subcommittee.
Washington, D.C.: U.S. Government Printing Office, 1975.

U.S. Congress, Senate. Committee on Banking and Currency.
Hearings, Urban Mass Transportation 1961. 87th Cong. , 1st
sess. Washington, D.C.: U.S. Government Printing Office,
1961.

_____ . Hearings, Urban Mass Transportation, 1962. 87th
Cong. , 2d sess. Washington, D.C.: U.S. Government Printing
Office, 1962.

_____ . Report, Urban Mass Transportation Act Of 1963. 88th
Cong. , 1st sess. Washington, D.C.: U.S. Government Printing
Office, 1963.

_____ . Section-by-section summary of the Provisions of S.6,
the Urban Mass Transportation Act of 1963, as Passed by the
Senate on April 4, 1963. 88th Cong. , 1st sess. Washington,
D.C.: U.S. Government Printing Office, 1963.

_____ . Hearings on Urban Mass Transportation before the
Subcommittee of the Committee on Banking and Currency. 87th
Cong. , 1st sess. Washington, D.C.: U.S. Government Printing
Office, 1961.

_____ . Mass Transportation, 1969. Hearings before the
Subcommittee on Housing and Urban Affairs of the Committee

on Banking and Currency on S.676, S. 1032, S.2656, S.2821, S.3154. 91st Cong., 1st sess. Washington, D.C.: U.S. Government Printing Office, 1970.

_____. Emergency Urban Mass Transit Legislation. Hearings before the Subcommittee on Housing and Urban Affairs of the Committee on Banking and Currency. 92nd Cong., 2d sess. Washington, D.C.: U.S. Government Printing Office, 1972, 56.

U.S. Congress, Senate, Committee on Commerce Subcommittee on Surface Transportation. Hearings, Urban Mass Transportation, 1963. 88th Cong., 1st sess. Washington, D.C.: U.S. Government Printing Office, 1963.

U.S. Congress, Senate, Committee on Interstate and Foreign Commerce. Commuter Transportation. Study of passenger transportation in new Jersey-New York-Connecticut metropolitan region with particular reference to rapid-rail commutation. Prepared by Anthony Arpaia and the Regional Plan Association. 87th Cong., 1st sess. Washington, D.C.: U.S. Government Printing Office, 1961.

_____. National Transportation Policy; Preliminary Draft of a Report. Prepared by the Special Study Group on Transportation Policies in the United States. 87th Cong., 1st sess. Washington, D.C.: U.S. Government Printing Office, 1961.

U.S. Congress, Senate, Committee on Labor and Public Welfare, Subcommittee on Labor. Compilation of Selected Labor Laws Pertaining to Labor Relations. Washington, D.C.: U.S. Government Printing Office, 1974.

U.S. Department of Commerce, Bureau of the Census. Historical Statistics of the United States, Colonial Times to 1957. Washington, D.C.: U.S. Government Printing Office, 1960.

U.S. Department of Housing and Urban Development. Tomorrow's Transportation—New Systems for the Urban Future. Washington, D.C.: U.S. Government Printing Office, 1968.

U.S. Department of Labor, Bureau of Labor Statistics. "Employment Outlook—Driving Occupations." Bulletin 1650-94. Washington, D.C.: U.S. Government Printing Office, 1970.

_____. Handbook of Labor Statistics. Washington, D.C.: U.S. Government Printing Office. Published annually.

_____. _Tomorrow's Manpower Needs._ Vols. 1-4. Washington, D.C.: U.S. Government Printing Office, 1969.

_____. _Union Wages and Hours: Local-Transit Operating Employees._ Washington, D.C.: U.S. Government Printing Office, 1975.

_____. "Union Wages and Laws: Local-Transit Operating Employees." Bulletin 1667. Washington, D.C.: U.S. Government Printing Office, 1970.

_____. _Dictionary of Occupational Titles._ Washington, D.C.: U.S. Government Printing Office, 1965.

U.S. Department of Labor, Division of Labor Standards. _Bulletin No. 77, President's National Labor-Management Conference, 1945._ Washington, D.C.: U.S. Government Printing Office, 1945.

U.S. Department of Labor. News Release, USDL 71-217, pp. 2-3. Washington, D.C., April 16, 1971.

U.S. Department of Labor, Labor Management Services Administration. _Summary of State Policy Regulations for Public Sector Labor Relations: Statutes, Attorney Generals' Opinions and Selected Court Decisions._ Washington, D.C.: U.S. Government Printing Office, 1971.

U.S. Department of Labor, Labor Management Services Administration, Division of Public Employee Labor Relations. _State Profiles: Current Status of Public Sector Labor Relations._ Washington, D.C.: U.S. Government Printing Office, 1971.

_____. _Summary of State Policy Regulations for Public Sector Labor Relations._ Washington, D.C.: U.S. Government Printing Office, 1975.

U.S. Department of Transportation. "A Study of Urban Mass Transportation Needs and Financing." Report of the Secretary of Transportation to the U.S. Congress pursuant to Section 138(a), Public Law 93-87, Federal Highway Act of 1973. Washington, D.C.: U.S. Government Printing Office, 1974.

_____. "Feasibility of Federal Assistance for Urban Mass Transportation Operating Costs." Washington, D.C.: U.S. Government Printing Office, November 1971.

_____. National Planning Manual (1970-1990), Manual C. Urban Public Transportation. Washington, D.C.: U.S. Government Printing Office, 1971.

_____. 1974 National Transportation Report: Current Performance and Future Prospects. Washington, D.C.: U.S. Government Printing Office, 1975.

_____. Urban Mass Transportation Act of 1964 and Related Laws. Washington, D.C.: U.S. Government Printing Office, 1964.

_____. Urban Mass Transportation Act of 1974. Washington, D.C.: U.S. Government Printing Office, 1975.

_____. Excerpts from External Operating Manual. Washington, D.C.: U.S. Government Printing Office, 1972.

U.S. Department of Transportation, Urban Mass Transportation Administration. "Background Information of the Urban Mass Transportation Administration." Washington, D.C.: U.S. Government Printing Office, 1970.

U.S. National Capital Transportation Agency. Recommendations for Transportation in the National Capital Region. Washington, D.C.: U.S. Government Printing Office, 1962.

Wolff Packing Company v. Court of Industrial Relations. 262 U.S. 522 (1923); 267 U.S. 552 (1925).

OTHER

AFL-CIO. Adjusting to Automation. Washington, D.C.: AFL-CIO, 1969.

Altshuler, Alan, and T. Melone. "Site Selection for a Dial-A-Ride Demonstration." Report USL TR-70-16. Cambridge: Massachusetts Institute of Technology, Urban Systems Laboratory, 1971.

Altshuler, Alan, and Daniel Roos. "Dial-A-Bus." Mimeographed. Pittsburgh: Carnegie-Mellon University, Transportation Research Institute, Advanced Urban Transportation Systems, 1970.

Amalgamated Transit Union, AFL-CIO. Local Division Directory. 1975. Washington, D.C.: ATU.

American Public Transit Association. Passenger Transport. Washington, D.C. Published weekly.

American Transit Association. "Comparative Tabulation of the Features of Public Transit Authorities." Mimeographed. New York: American Transit Association, 1958.

_____. "Publicly Owned Transit Systems in the United States." Mimeographed. New York: American Transit Association, 1961.

_____. Special Report of Law Committee, Re Public Law 757, 84th Congress, and Related Matters. New York: American Transit Association, June 1, 1961.

_____. Transit Fact Book. New York: American Transit Association. Published annually.

_____. Wages, Overtime and Related Provisions, Bulletin No. 718. New York: American Transit Association, February 1947.

Associated Transit Guild. "Conclusions and Recommendations of Transportation Career Development Conference." Mimeographed. New York: Associated Transit Guild, 1968.

Bailey, John A. "A Survey of Transit Management Attitudes in Large Cities in the United States: Development Since 1962." Monograph. Evanston: Transportation Center at Northwestern University, 1970.

Bakr, M. M., Daniel Rober, and Thomas S. Miller. "Role and Effectiveness of Contract Management in the Transit Industry." Report prepared for the Urban Mass Transportation Administration of the U.S. Department of Transportation. Milwaukee: Marquette University, 1974.

Barnum, Darold T. "Collective Bargaining and Manpower in Urban Transit Systems." Ph.D. dissertation, University of Pennsylvania, 1972.

Barton-Aschman Associates. Guidelines for New Systems of Urban Transportation. Vol. 1, Urban Needs and Potentials. Report prepared for the United States Department of Housing and Urban Development, May 1968.

Bierwagon, W. "Labor's Response to Innovation in the Transit Indus-
try." In Proceedings of A Series of Conferences on Organized
Labor, Transportation Technology, and Urban Mass Transit
in the Chicago Metropolitan Area, edited by Stanley Rosen and
Scott Schiave, pp. 236-37. Chicago: University of Illinois at
Chicago Circle, 1973.

Bond, Langhorne M., and Richard J. Solomon. "The Promise and
Problems of High-Capacity Buses in Service in the United States."
Preliminary draft. Pittsburgh: National Transportation Center,
1971.

Burke, J. E. "Protective Agreements and Unified Mass Transit."
In Proceedings of a Series of Conferences on Organized Labor,
Transportation Technology, and Urban Mass Transit in the
Chicago Metropolitan Area, edited by Stanley Rosen and Scott
Schiave, pp. 121-28. Chicago: University of Illinois at Chicago
Circle, 1973.

Clark, R., Jr. "Legislated Interest Arbitration—A Management
Response." Industrial Relations Research Association Proceedings
of the Twenty-Seventh Annual Winter Meeting, edited by James
Stern and Barbara Dennis, pp. 319-23. Madison: Industrial
Relations Research Association, 1975.

Commonwealth of Massachusetts, Governor's Task Force on Transportation. Report to Governor Sargent, Part II. June 1970.

Crain, John L., and Sydwell D. Flynn. "1974 Strike Impact Study:
Southern California Rapid Transit District." Report prepared
for California Transit (CALTRANS) Division of Mass Transit,
1975.

Dana, Edward. "Can the Transit Industry Develop a Labor-Management
Policy?" In Proceedings of the American Transit Association,
pp. 153-56. New York: American Transit Association, 1946.

Derber, Milton, Peter Pashler, and Mary Beth Ryan. "Collective
Bargaining by State Governments in the 12 Midwestern States."
Mimeographed. Urbana: University of Illinois, Institute of
Labor and Industrial Relations, January 1974.

Freund, Peter. "Labor Relations in the New York City Rapid Transit
Industry, 1944-1960." Ph.D. dissertation, New York University,
1964.

Gambaccini, Louis J. "A Common Purpose: Labor and Management
    in the Future of Public Transportation." Speech delivered at
    the Conference on Unions, Management Rights, and the Public
    Interest in Mass Transit, Jacksonville, March 22, 1976.

Gerhart, Paul F. "The Scope of Bargaining in Local Government
    Labor Agreements." Ph.D. dissertation, University of Chicago,
    1973.

Graham, R. H. "Steps Necessary to Obtain an Agreement on a Labor
    Relations Program." In Proceedings Of the American Transit
    Association, pp. 164-66. New York: American Transit Associa-
    tion, 1946.

Hamermesh, Daniel S. "The Effect Of Government Ownership on Union
    Wages." Working Paper No. 42B. Princeton: Princeton Univer-
    sity, Industrial Relations Section, 1973.

Institute for Defense Management. Economic Characteristics of the
    Urban Transportation Industry. Washington, D.C.: Institute
    for Defense Management, 1972.

Institute of Labor and Industrial Relations Library. "Labor and
    Collective Bargaining in the Urban Transit Industry: A
    Bibliography." Mimeographed. Urbana: University of Illinois,
    1974.

Institute of Transportation and Traffic Engineering. "Selected
    References on Mass Transit." Mimeographed. Berkeley:
    University of California. Issued periodically.

In Transit. Washington, D.C.: Amalgamated Transit Union. Published
    monthly.

Jefferson Associates. "Administration of Section 13 (c) - Urban Mass
    Transportation Act." Report to the United States Department
    of Labor, January 1972.

Kulash, D. D. "Routing and Scheduling in Public Transportation
    Systems." Ph.D. dissertation, Massachusetts Institute of
    Technology, 1971.

Lisco, Thomas E. "The Value of Commuters' Travel Time: A Study
    in Urban Transportation." Ph.D. dissertation, University of
    Chicago, 1968.

Lurie, Melvin. "The Measurement of the Effect of Unionization on Wages in the Transit Industry." Ph.D. dissertation, University of Chicago, 1958.

McCarthy, John E. "Statement on Arbitration." In Proceedings of the American Transit Association, p. 95. New York: American Transit Association, 1947.

Mackin, John P. "Adjusting Public Employees' Retirement Benefits for Economic Changes." Ph.D. dissertation, University of Wisconsin, 1968.

Maroney, D. V. "Collective Bargaining in Mass Transit." Speech delivered at the Conference on Unions, Management Rights, and the Public Interest in Mass Transit, Jacksonville, March 22, 1976.

Metropolitan. Glenview, Ill.: Bobit. Published bimonthly.

Meyer, John R., John F. Kain, and Martin Wohl. "Technology and Urban Transportation—A Report Prepared for the White House Panel on Civilian Technology." Mimeographed. Cambridge, 1962.

Miller, David R. "Cost Functions in Urban Bus Transportation." Ph.D. dissertation, Northwestern University, 1967.

Morris, James O. Bibliography of Industrial Relations in the Railroad Industry. Ithaca: New York State School of Industrial and Labor Relations, Cornell University, 1975.

National Planning Association, Committee on the Causes of Industrial Peace under Collective Bargaining. Fundamentals of Labor Peace: A Final Report. Washington, D.C.: National Planning Association, 1953.

Nelson, Gary R. "An Econometric Model of Urban Bus Transit Operations." Paper P-863. Arlington, Va.: Institute for Defense Analyses, 1972.

Noortman, H. J. "The Effect of the Organisation of Transport Facilities." In Fourth International Symposium on Theory and Practice in Transport Economics. Paris: Conférence Européenne des Ministres des Transports, 1971.

Northrup, Herbert R. "Labor Relations in Urban Transit: Bleak Future for the 1970's." Speech delivered in a series on Frontiers of Urban Transit in the 1970s, University of Pennsylvania, Philadelphia, February 2, 1971.

Oi, Walter. "On the Federal Subsidization of the Transit Industry." Paper P-943. Arlington, Va: Institute for Defense Analyses, 1973.

Peterson, Charles Thomas. "An Economic Evaluation of the Southern California Rapid Transit District: Its Proposed Solution to the Transportation Problem in Los Angeles." Ph.D. dissertation, University of California at Los Angeles, 1970.

Robbins, R. Michael, Olaf Kekonius, and W. Howard Paterson. "Report of the Panel Appointed to Study the Safety of Train Operations on the Subway System of the New York City Transit Authority." New York: Metropolitan Transportation Authority, November 13, 1970.

Roberts, Thomas. "A History and Analysis of Labor-Management Relations in the Philadelphia Transit Authority." Ph.D. dissertation, University of Pennsylvania, 1959.

Rosen, Stanley. "Organized Labor, Technology and Innovation in Mass Transit." A speech at the Conference on Unions, Management Rights, and the Public Interest in Mass Transit, jointly sponsored by the Program of University Research of the United States Department of Transportation and the University of North Florida, Jacksonville, March 22, 1976.

Solomon, R. J., and Saltzman, A. "History of Transit and Innovative Systems." Report USL TR-70-20. Cambridge: Massachusetts Institute of Technology, Urban Systems Laboratory, 1971.

Tarpley, Jr., Fred Angus. "The Economics of Combined Utility and Transit Operations." Ph.D. dissertation, Tulane University, 1967.

Tomaginis, Anthony R., et al. "The Role of the State in Urban Mass Transit." Preliminary draft. Philadelphia: Transportation Studies Center of the Center for Urban Research and Experiment, University of Pennsylvania, 1971.

Transportation Act of 1940. 49 U.S.C. 5 (2) (f), 1971.

Transportation Center Library. A Reference Guide to Metropolitan
    Transportation: An Annotated Bibliography. Evanston: Transpor-
    tation Center Library, Northwestern University, 1964.

Transportation Research Board. Data Requirements for Metropolitan
    Transportation Planning. National Cooperative Highway Research
    Program Report, 120. Washington, D.C.: Transportation
    Research Board, 1971.

_____. Evaluation of Bus Transit Strategies—4 Reports.
    Record, 459. Washington, D.C.: Transportation Research
    Board, 1973.

_____. Federal, State, and Local Roles in Transit Planning—
    7 Reports. Record, 475. Washington, D.C.: Transportation
    Research Board, 1973.

_____. Issues in Public Transportation. Special Report, 144.
    Washington, D.C.: Transportation Research Board, 1974.

_____.. Public Transportation Research Needs. Special Report,
    137. Washington, D.C.: Transportation Research Board, 1973.

_____. Public Transportation for Small and Medium-Sized
    Cities—4 Reports. Record, 419. Washington, D.C.: Transpor-
    tation Research Board, 1973.

_____. Transportation Research News. Washington, D.C.:
    Transportation Research Board. Published quarterly.

Transportation Research Board, National Research Council, National
    Academy of Sciences. Transportation Research Abstracts.
    Washington, D.C.: Transportation Research Board. Published month

Transportation Research Board, Public Transportation Section.
    "Mass Transportation Management." Workshop Reports of the
    Conference on Mass Transportation Management, Tampa,
    August 12-15, 1975.

Tye, William B., III. "The Capital Grant as a Subsidy Device: The
    Case Study of Urban Mass Transportation." In The Economics
    of Federal Subsidy Programs—A Compendium of Papers Sub-
    mitted to the Subcommittee on Priorities and Economy in Govern-
    ment of the Joint Economic Committee. Part 6—Transportation
    Subsidies. Washington, D.C.: U.S. Government Printing Office,
    1973.

_____. "The Economic Costs of the Urban Mass Transportation Capital Grant Program." Ph.D. Dissertation, Harvard University, 1969.

Urban Mass Transportation Administration. "The Summary, Conclusions, and Recommendations of the Transit Industry Labor-Management Relations Research Conference and Symposium," November 20, 1975.

Urban Mass Transportation Act of 1964. SS 3(e), 49 U.S.C.A., SS 1609, 1971.

Vickrey, W. S. The Revision of the Rapid Transit Fare Structure of the City of New York. Technical Monograph No. 3, Finance Project. New York: Mayor's Committee on Management Survey of the City of New York, February 1952.

Wohl, Martin. "An Analysis and Evaluation of the Rapid Transit Extension to Cleveland's Airport." Working Paper 708-43. Washington, D.C.: Urban Institute, 1972.

Yud, Larry F. "Employee Protection." Speech delivered at the Conference on Unions, Management Rights, and the Public Interest in Mass Transit, Jacksonville, March 22, 1976.

Zagoria, Sam. "The U. S. Cities Tackle Impasses." In Industrial Relations Research Association Series: Proceedings of the 25th Anniversary Meeting, ed. Gerald G. Somers. Madison: Industrial Relations Research Association, 1973.

KENNETH M. JENNINGS, JR. is Associate Professor of Management and Industrial Relations at the University of North Florida. He has served in a variety of labor relations and personnel assignments with Union Carbide Corporation. He received his B.A. from Knox College, and M.A. and Ph.D. degrees from the University of Illinois. Professor Jennings has written several articles dealing with employee discipline, grievances and arbitration, personnel practices, and public sector bargaining.

JAY A. SMITH, JR. is Professor of Transportation and Logistics at the University of North Florida and Chairperson of the State University System Program of Distinction. He has served as Assistant Director of the Transportation Institute at Southern Illinois University. He has worked for the Interstate Commerce Commission and was employed as an operations analyst for the U.S. Steel Corporate Railroads. He received his B.S. from Louisiana State University, a M.S. from the University of Tennessee, and D.B.A from the University of Maryland. He is the Academic Vice-President of the Transportation Research Forum. Professor Smith has written of transportation policy, railroad cost information systems, computer-assisted decision making, and intermodal coordination. He is the author of several research monographs.

EARLE C. TRAYNHAM, JR. is Associate Professor of Economics at the University of North Florida. He received his B.S., M.B.A., and Ph.D. degrees from the University of South Carolina. Professor Traynham is the author of several articles and monographs on human migration, investment in human capital, labor relations and collective bargaining, and regional manpower policy.

ALTERING COLLECTIVE BARGAINING: Citizen
Participation in Educational Decision Making
Charles W. Cheng

MANAGEMENT OF TRANSPORTATION CARRIERS
Grant M. Davis
Martin T. Farris
Jack J. Holder, Jr.

MASS TRANSIT AND THE POLITICS OF TECHNOLOGY:
A Study of BART and the San Francisco Bay Area
Stephen Zwerling

RATE BUREAUS AND ANTITRUST CONFLICTS
IN TRANSPORTATION: Public Policy Issues
Grant M. Davis
Charles S. Sherwood

THE SCOPE OF BARGAINING IN PUBLIC
EMPLOYMENT
Joan Weitzman